Roy Frannie Ellie Jacob

Merry Chris.

May your bedtime be recous

by sharing these pages –

Love grampa &
grama

365 timeless devotions for families

My
DEVOTIONS

50th ANNIVERSARY

Edited by Deborah Henry

CONCORDIA PUBLISHING HOUSE • SAINT LOUIS

Foreword

This book is a celebration of fifty years of God's blessings to families through the daily devotions published in the *My Devotions* magazine. The devotions in this book are selected from the thousands printed since the magazine's first publication in 1958. God's children, of all ages, who used *My Devotions* may remember some of the devotions included.

Devotions for the seasons, special holidays, and other events are included. There are also a number of historical events and social/cultural references, which reflect the decade during which a particular devotion was first published. These will surely provide families across the generations with opportunities for discussion. You may want to ask your parents or grandparents about the events and discuss God's presence and activity throughout all history for us and for our salvation.

The original publication year of the devotion is indicated at the top of the page. In most cases, the text remains as it was originally written.

The designations at the bottom of each page indicate that the devotions are arranged according to the Church Year—from the festival half through the nonfestival half. Since certain events in the Church Year occur on different dates each calendar year, especially during the Lenten and Easter seasons, you may want to adjust your readings to accommodate the differences. Feel free to skip pages in order to read the devotion appropriate for the Church Year event.

The first author and editor of *My Devotions*, Allan Hart Jahsmann, encouraged children with these words:

"By choosing a certain time each day for some thoughts about God, a message from His Word, and a prayerful conversation with Him, children and youth as well as adults are more likely to live with God and grow in grace and in the knowledge of the Lord and Savior Jesus Christ." He suggested using *My Devotions* along with a Bible "for regular private worship before going to bed or the first thing in the morning," explaining the importance of developing this habit. Keep a copy of Luther's Small Catechism with this book and your Bible to help you learn more about God's love for you. God is with you through His Word every day to guide and bless you in your life.

It is my prayer that these devotions will help you learn about God's action in your life—loving you, forgiving you, and saving you. I hope you enjoy using this book for many years.

The Editor

A Cake for Christmas

Joel 2:12–13

You may know the song that begins "If I knew you were coming, I'd have baked a cake." When visitors come, we like to be ready for them. Baking a cake is one way of getting ready for company.

As the season of Advent (which means "coming") begins, we Christians begin "baking a cake." We're expecting a guest, and we'll celebrate because Jesus is coming. He came as a baby born in Bethlehem. Now our Lord reigns in heaven, and we await His return on the Last Day, when He will take all believers to be with Him. The cake we bake is whatever we do to prepare for the coming of our Savior.

What's the best way of getting ready for Christmas, the celebration of Jesus' first coming? Is it putting up a big Christmas tree or sending out a lot of cards? Is it decorating our home with lights and mistletoe? These things are fine, but they're not the best way to prepare for Jesus.

The color of Advent, purple, reminds us to repent of our sins. Only when we realize that we are sinners living in a sinful world can we see why Jesus came. He was born as a man so He could obey God's Law for us and take our sins on Himself.

God tells us through the prophet Joel, "Return to Me with all your heart" (2:12). He means for us to confess our sins and turn back to Him. "[God] is gracious and merciful, slow to anger, and abounding in steadfast love" (v. 13). He forgives our sins for Jesus' sake.

Christmas is still more than three weeks away. But we begin "baking our cake" now because we want to be truly ready to celebrate Christ's birth.

PRAYER

Lord Jesus, I am sorry for my many sins against You. But I believe that You came to carry them for me. In this Advent season, prepare my heart to receive You by faith. For Your own sake I ask it. Amen.

Alton Donsbach

ADVENT

Name above All Names

Isaiah 9:6–7

"Hey, Zip!" That's what I used to hear when I was growing up. I was a skinny kid. One day my brother told me that if I stood sideways and stuck out my tongue, someone would mistake me for a zipper. Unfortunately, some of my friends heard him say that, and I got a nickname.

A nickname usually tells something about a person. Sometimes it's a compliment, and sometimes it isn't.

Over the years things have changed, and the nickname Zip no longer applies. I guess you can say I've outgrown it.

The Bible gives many names for Jesus. These names *do* apply. The different names for Jesus tell us more about Him. Here are a few:

Wonderful Counselor. A counselor is someone who listens patiently and advises wisely.

Mighty God. The word *mighty* reminds us of power.

Everlasting Father. A father protects his children, provides for them, and cares deeply about them. *Everlasting* means this never ends.

Prince of Peace. A peaceful ruler brings contentment and well-being to his people.

Immanuel. This name means "God with us."

Son of God. This name tells us, without a doubt, who Jesus is. He came from heaven to make us His own and to win salvation for us.

These names for Jesus tell us that He is a powerful God who protects us, cares for us, and listens patiently to us. He is a peaceful ruler who is and always will be with us. And He is God's Son, our Savior.

PRAYER

Thank You, dear Jesus, that You are my Savior and Lord. Amen.

Valerie Schulz

ADVENT

Promises, Promises!

Genesis 3:15

How many times have you heard someone make a promise?

Four-year-old Julio promises never again to play with matches after Mom has just saved him from burning himself.

Fourth grader Lisa has just received a bad report card and promises Dad she will get much better grades next time.

It's midnight, and teenager Tom promises his worried mom and dad that he will try to come home earlier from now on.

God, too, makes promises. Long ago, after the devil tempted Eve to sin, God said, "I will put enmity between you and the woman, and between your offspring and her offspring; He shall bruise your head, and you shall bruise His heel."

What a strange promise! What did God mean? He wanted the devil to understand that he (Satan) was the enemy of God and people. This was really a promise that God would send a baby someday who would beat the devil and save all people.

This was the first promise in the Bible about the day Jesus would come. It was a threat to the devil and a promise to the first persons on earth. One day a future relative of Eve's would arrive to give the world a new start.

Because of God's promise, which was fulfilled when Jesus crushed our enemy, we now have freedom from sin, death, and the devil. We have hope for this life and the next.

PRAYER

Lord Jesus, God the Father promised Eve and the whole world that He would defeat the devil. We believe that promise and thank You for saving us from Satan and his evil desire for us to be in hell with him. When we feel we can do nothing right, as Eve must have thought after giving in to the devil's temptation, please help us remember that You always forgive us. Amen.

Edward Grube

ADVENT

Something to Sing About

Luke 1:39–56

Mother sat on the living-room couch with the extension phone on her lap. Dave and Lil sat beside her and watched her dial their grandparents' phone number. Father sat nearby, smiling at the excited faces of his family.

"Is it ringing now?" Lil asked.

"Yes. Now, shhh! Hi, Mom! Surprised?" Mother smiled as she listened to Grandma. "Yes, get Grandpa by the phone too. Every one of us wants to talk to both of you. This is a very special phone call."

Mother told Dave and Lil that Grandpa was coming to the phone. "Hi, Dad! How are you? . . . That's good. Are you ready for the big news? You two will have a brand-new grandchild in about six months! Isn't that wonderful?

". . . Yes, we're all pleased and happy and proud. I could sing for joy! Here are the children to tell you how they feel about it."

What a blessing the phone is! Within a few minutes, good news speeds to loved ones far away. Mary of Nazareth was also eager to share her good news of the coming Savior. But it was a long, tiring trip for her to visit her cousin Elizabeth, who lived about eighty miles away in Judea.

As soon as Mary arrived, Elizabeth was filled with the Holy Spirit. She knew without Mary's telling her that Mary was to be the mother of her Lord. Elizabeth's expression of faith touched Mary deeply. Mary then spoke one of the most beautiful "songs" in the Bible.

In the Magnificat, Mary rejoices that God has shown mercy to her and to the people of Israel. She also praises God for helping the generations following Abraham, which include all who believe in Christ the Savior.

In this Advent season, we Christians feel Mary's joy and thankfulness. Through the gift of His Son, God offers us new life and the sure hope of salvation. That's really something to sing about and to share with others.

PRAYER

Dear Jesus, help us look forward to the celebration of Your birth with more excitement, happiness, and thankfulness than we would the birth of a baby brother or sister. Amen.

C. Eileen Prole

ADVENT

The Man Who Ate Insects

Mark 1:1–8

John the Baptist was a man who ate insects! What do you think of that? St. Mark writes, "Now John was clothed with camel's hair and wore a leather belt around his waist and ate locusts and wild honey" (1:6).

For us, it's strange to think about a man eating insects and wearing camel's-hair clothing. We surely wouldn't want to eat grasshoppers!

God used John the Baptist for a very important job. It was John's duty to show people that they needed a Savior and that the Savior would soon appear.

God still uses John's words today. When we read the story of John the Baptist, we realize that we, too, are sinful and in need of God's forgiveness. All the writers of the Bible tell us about our sins. So do our pastors, Christian Day School teachers, and Sunday School teachers.

But these people also tell us more. John the Baptist said: "Behold, the Lamb of God, who takes away the sin of the world!" (John 1:29). Like John, our pastors, teachers, and parents show us that Jesus is our Savior. They explain that He died on the cross and rose again to make us God's children.

We may not join John in eating insects. But we do join him in our need for a Savior, Jesus!

PRAYER

Dear God, how thankful I am for the many people who tell me about my sins and about my Savior, Jesus. How glad I am that You have made it possible for me, through the Holy Spirit, to believe what these people have told me. For Jesus' sake, keep me strong in this faith. Amen.

Arne Kristo

ADVENT

Reason for Excitement

Luke 2:8–20

We hear a lot at Christmastime about a man named St. Nicholas. Legends tell about kind deeds he did for people in need. One story tells of some people who were starving because of a famine. When it seemed hopeless for them, St. Nicholas came with food and saved them.

In some parts of Europe, children still wait on this day for St. Nicholas to bring gifts of apples and nuts. This custom was brought to the New World by the Dutch settlers. Their name for St. Nicholas was *Sant Nikolaas*, which gradually became *Santa Claus*.

Although his name has been changed, young children are just as eager for his visit. As we grow older, of course, we no longer get excited about Santa Claus. However, we're still eager to find out what gifts we will receive.

Are we as excited about the coming of the Christ Child? We read in Luke's account of Jesus' birth: "And [the shepherds] *went with haste* and found Mary and Joseph, and the baby lying in a manger" (2:16). The shepherds were so anxious to find Jesus that they ran to Bethlehem. They couldn't wait to see for themselves what the angel had told them—that a Savior had been born who would bring joy to all people.

On Christmas Eve, many of us will sing praises to the Christ Child in our Christmas service. Let's ask God to fill us with the same desire to praise Jesus as the shepherds had.

The day after Christmas, Santa Claus is forgotten. All the impatient waiting seems unimportant. And, sadly, the day after Christmas, Jesus often is forgotten too, though He desires to remain the center of our lives. Only by His grace and the power of His Holy Spirit does our joy in praising Him stay with us. He is always eager to love us and to walk closely with us, for He is our Lord and Savior.

PRAYER

Lord God, give me a real desire to worship my Savior as I celebrate His birth. Don't let the earthly things of Christmas crowd Jesus out of my thoughts. Amen.

Lois Vogel

ADVENT

Rod of Jesse

Isaiah 11:1–5

Kris remembered the stump. Several years ago, he had gone with his uncle to cut a tree for Christmas and had left that stump behind. Kris thought the tree was dead, but now a new branch had sprouted from the old stump. If anything, it was taller than the original tree. Kris knew enough about plants to understand that this new branch was giving life to the old stump.

Isaiah spoke of Jesus, the promised Savior, as a branch, or rod, of Jesse's stump. Jesse was the father of King David and was an ancestor of Jesus. In Isaiah's day, it looked like the family of David might be cut off. They were defeated by foreigners and made slaves for a time. But from this stump of a family, Jesus was born, in keeping with God's promise.

Like His ancestor King David, Jesus is a King who saves His people from their enemies. But while David fought against temporary enemies like neighboring kingdoms and tribes, Jesus fought single-handedly against sin, death, and the devil. By His death on the cross, He overcame them all. It seemed at the time that Jesus Himself was cut off when He died on the tree. But three days later, He came to life again. He gives new life to His people, just as the branch Kris had seen gave life to the old stump.

PRAYER

O come, Thou Branch of Jesse's tree,
Free them from Satan's tyranny
That trust Thy mighty pow'r to save,
And give them vict'ry o'er the grave.
Rejoice! Rejoice!
Emmanuel Shall come to thee, O Israel Amen. (*LSB* 357:4)

Richard Zeile

ADVENT

Jesus Gives Real Peace

John 14:27

Peace. It's a word we hear often. On the nightly news, there is talk of war or peace between countries. Families argue on television talk shows while trying to come to some sort of peace. People wish for peace, especially around holidays.

But what is peace? Is it just the opposite of war? Is peace something we do or don't do? How do we find peace?

The peace Jesus speaks of in John 14:27 is not simply the ending of a war. He is not merely suggesting that enemies patch things up. He is referring to more than the peace of this world.

Notice that Jesus said He *gives* us peace. Real peace is a gift. We can't obtain it by ourselves. Jesus brings us the peace of the Garden of Eden. He gives us the original peace between human beings and their Lord.

We became enemies of God through our sin. We couldn't even approach God, let alone live with Him in heaven. But Christ intervened on our behalf. Because of His love for us, Jesus endured death on the cross. He paid for our sins and for our peace with God. Now, by faith in the Savior, we are made whole again. And someday we will enjoy perfect harmony with our Maker.

There will always be wars and fighting on earth. We live in a sinful world. But thanks to God, the peace that was lost in the garden has been found, through Christ, our Lord. He is the Prince of Peace.

PRAYER

Lord Jesus, the angels sang at Your birth. They proclaimed peace to people on earth. We praise You and thank You for such a gift. In Your name we pray. Amen.

Carla Fast

ADVENT

When Jesus Comes Again

John 14:1–6

During the Second World War, many children were tiny babies when their fathers went away to fight. Some of these children were four or five years old when their fathers returned home after the war.

Can you imagine how they must have felt when they heard that their fathers were coming home? They knew what fathers were—they saw their friends' fathers every day. But their own fathers were complete strangers to them.

As the day of his father's return came closer, a child might have all kinds of feelings. He would be happy. He would think, Now I'll have a father like everyone else! His dad would probably bring gifts with him. Still, the child might worry. Would his father like him? Would his father be kind and happy, or mean, like some fathers he knew? To a small child, it was a big experience.

Sometimes we may feel like a "war child" when we think of Jesus' promise to come to earth again. Thinking of His return may frighten us. Or we may just wonder what it will be like when Jesus comes back.

But our waiting for Jesus to come again is different from a child's waiting to see his father for the first time. Through the Bible we come to know Jesus now. We see that when Jesus was on earth, He was kind. He was ready to help people. He was ready to forgive them for their sins. He blessed children and comforted the sick.

That's why we know that we don't need to worry about Jesus' return. All we need to do is remember what the angel told Jesus' disciples on the day He ascended into heaven: "This Jesus . . . will come in the same way as you saw Him go into heaven" (Acts 1:11).

PRAYER

Dear Jesus, make me ready to meet You when You come back for Your people. Wash away my sins each day. Amen.

Richard Schultz

ADVENT

The Christmas Wreath

Hebrews 13:5–8

Do you know what the Christmas wreath tells us? The Christmas wreath is in the form of a circle. Since a circle never begins and never ends, it reminds us of God. God is eternal. He has no beginning and no end.

Christians believe in a triune God who is eternal. He always was, and He always will be. Jesus Christ, born on Christmas, helps us to know more about this triune God whom we worship. The Bible says that "Jesus Christ is the same yesterday and today and forever" (Hebrews 13:8).

The world around us may change. Once, man traveled by ox cart; in the near future, he will travel in spaceships! It is good to remember that God does not change, that He is eternal, that the Jesus who was cradled in a manger and was crucified on a cross also rose from the dead and is forever our Lord and our Savior.

What happened to the gifts you received last Christmas? They probably made you happy for a short time, but most of those gifts are already worn out. And now you are thinking of new things you may receive this Christmas. It is good to remember that the many gifts wrapped in pretty packages are not nearly as valuable and lasting as God's Christmas gift. They will soon be forgotten or worn out.

Isn't it wonderful that the oldest Christmas gift, Jesus Christ, is always the newest and the best? He is a gift who is always exciting though always the same! He gives lasting life and joy with God. That's why St. Paul wrote, "Thanks be to God for His inexpressible gift!" (2 Corinthians 9:15).

PRAYER

Thank You, God, for the Christmas gift that never loses its beauty and value and that always serves our needs. Bless our preparations for Jesus' coming this Advent time. In Jesus' name. Amen.

Henry F. Ressmeyer

ADVENT

Did Alice Steal?

Ephesians 4:32

Alice was earning money to buy Christmas presents. Every Saturday she did odd jobs for the neighbors. Last Saturday she spent the whole day helping Mrs. Jones clean house. Alice worked very hard washing windows and cleaning cabinets, polishing furniture and vacuuming rugs. At the end of the day, she went home proud and happy. She knew she had done a good job and was happy to have her pay.

That night, Alice's mother received a phone call from Mrs. Jones. She sounded very upset. She said she had put ten dollars in a drawer and now it was gone. Mrs. Jones hated to accuse Alice, but no one else had been in the house. And Alice had been left alone in that room to clean. "I thought Alice was trustworthy," she said. "I never thought she would steal."

When Alice's mother hung up, she called Alice. "I've just talked to Mrs. Jones. She is missing some money from a drawer and wonders if you might have seen it."

"I didn't clean any of her drawers, Mother. I didn't even open them."

"Mrs. Jones thinks you may have taken the money. So I must ask you: did you take the money?"

"No, I didn't. The only money I have is what she paid me for working."

Alice's mother called Mrs. Jones. "I've talked to Alice," she said. "Alice says that she did not take the money. She has always been honest, and I believe her this time too. I truly feel that she did not take the money."

How can Alice respond to Mrs. Jones? Reread Ephesians 4:32. Because of Christ's forgiveness, we can forgive others.

PRAYER

Lord Jesus, help me to be trustworthy. Help me not to be angry when I am judged wrongly. Help me to share with others the forgiveness I have from You. Amen.

Joan Cole

ADVENT

Judy's Gifts

Ephesians 2:8–9

"Mother, I need a large piece of paper and a pencil."

"What do you need a large piece of paper for?"

"Well," Judy answered, "Christmas is only twelve more shopping days away, and I haven't even made a gift list yet."

Mother gave Judy the paper and pencil and went to finish the dishes. And Judy started writing. As her list grew, her smile widened. She kept writing for forty-five minutes. After reading her list over, she showed it to her mother.

Mother started reading: "Barbie doll, Barbie clothes, slacks, blouses, wristwatch, toy typewriter . . ." The list seemed endless.

"Which gift did you have in mind for Dad? Which is for Ricky, or for your friend Denise?" Mother asked.

Judy looked surprised. "I didn't make a list of things to give, Mother. I sort of thought I'd wait and see what I might be getting from others."

Mother thought for a minute and then asked, "Why do you give gifts, Judy, or why do others give them to you?"

"Well," Judy hemmed, "I guess the answer is love."

"Yes, it is; but I hope you mean it. Our giving of gifts at Christmas is a reminder of the greatest gift of all, Jesus Christ." Mother put her arm around Judy and continued gently. "God didn't wait to see what value we were before He gave His gift. He gave His Son out of love. We did nothing to deserve it. And that's why we give our gifts."

Judy looked happy again and asked, "Could I have another piece of paper, Mother?"

PRAYER

Dear Father, as we get closer to Christmas, help us keep the gift of Your Son and our salvation through Him first in our minds. Amen.

Duane E. Hingst

ADVENT

Silly Excuses

Matthew 24:42–44

Have you ever wondered why fire trucks are red? Someone once gave the following explanation:

Fire trucks have four wheels and eight people.
Four and eight make twelve.
There are twelve inches in a foot, and a foot is a ruler.
Queen Elizabeth is a ruler and one of the largest ships on the sea.
The sea has fish, and fish have fins.
The Finns fought the Russians once, and Russians are red.*
Fire trucks are always rushin', and therefore fire trucks are red.

Isn't that a silly answer? We all know fire trucks aren't red for that reason. However, this explanation is no more far-fetched than some of the excuses people give for not coming to church or not believing in Jesus. Even sillier will be some of the excuses Jesus will hear when He comes back to judge all people.

Jesus is going to come again someday. He's coming when we least expect Him. The Bible tells us so.

However, we who are God's children don't have to be afraid. We are ready. Jesus has made us ready through His death and resurrection. We belong to Him because He bought us with His precious blood, His very life. We became His children through Holy Baptism.

No, we don't have to be afraid or think up silly excuses when Jesus comes again. Like St. Paul we say: "Rejoice in the Lord always; again I will say, Rejoice. . . . The Lord is at hand" (Philippians 4:4–5).

PRAYER

Heavenly Father, thank You for making me Your child through Jesus Christ, my Lord. Help me look forward to His return with great joy, because it will be the start of an eternity of happiness with You. Amen.

Roger Sonnenberg

ADVENT

*During the Cold War years, when Russia was part of the Union of Soviet Socialist Republics and a Communist country, Russians were sometimes referred to as "reds"; thus the use of the word *red* in this devotion.—Ed.

The Heart of Christmas

Titus 2:11–14

It just won't seem like Christmas if . . . we don't have any snow.
It just won't seem like Christmas if . . . the whole family isn't together.
It just won't seem like Christmas if . . . we don't have a Christmas tree.
It just won't seem like Christmas if . . . we don't make any cookies.
It just won't seem like Christmas if . . .

You finish the sentence. Are there certain holiday customs that are an important part of your Christmas? Many people associate Christmas with things like trees, decorations, cookies, snow, Christmas cards, and gifts under the tree.

Some of these things do help us celebrate Jesus' birth, but sometimes we become wrapped up in them and stop thinking about our Savior. It can become easy for us to look for the gift wrapped in bright paper instead of the babe wrapped in swaddling cloths.

Christmas is celebrating Christ's birth and what that birth means for us. Even without the gifts, decorations, and parties, our hearts would still have much to be happy about. We would have that "blessed hope, the appearing of the glory of our great God and Savior Jesus Christ, who gave Himself for us to redeem us" (Titus 2:13–14).

Even if, at Christmas, we didn't have a tree,
Our hearts would glow with joyfulness at the birth of Thee.
Even if, at Christmas, colored bulbs gave off no light,
Our hearts would still be shining with God's love warm and bright.
Even if, at Christmas, we had no gifts to give,
We could share the gift of Jesus that God gave so all might live.

PRAYER

Dear Father, help us not only to see the gifts, parties, and decorations at Christmas, but also help us to use them in celebrating our Savior's holy birth. Amen.

Jacqueline Pickar

ADVENT

More Than Candy

Galatians 4:4–5

By this time in December, you've probably eaten at least a few candy canes. Maybe you've eaten so many that you're beginning to feel like one giant peppermint! The candy cane has been a popular treat during the Christmas season for many years. You may be surprised to learn that the candy cane was originally created for another purpose.

A number of years ago, a candy maker in Indiana wanted to make a candy that would demonstrate his faith in Jesus Christ as his Savior. He started with a stick of white hard candy. He used white to symbolize that Jesus was without sin. Its hardness reminds us that God's promises are firm.

The candy maker formed the candy in the shape of a J to represent Jesus' name. The cane is also a reminder of the shepherd's staff and of Jesus, our Good Shepherd.

Finally, the candy maker added three red stripes to the candy to represent the blood shed by Christ on the cross so that we may have eternal life. The three stripes also remind us that Jesus is part of the triune God.

As you eat candy canes during the next few weeks, remember why the candy maker originally made them. Share a candy cane and its story with a friend. It will be a wonderful Christmas witness!

PRAYER

Dear Jesus, thank You for being my Good Shepherd. And thank You for shedding Your blood for me. Help me be a witness of Your love in all that I do. Amen.

Lisa Ellwein

ADVENT

A Word to Remember

Hebrews 2:14–18

Do you know what a mnemonic (ni-MON-ik) device is? It's a code word or sentence to help you remember something. If you want to remember how to spell *principal*, you can learn this code: He's my *pal*. To keep *stationery* straight from *stationary*, remember that station*ery* is pap*er*.

The word *Immanuel* is something like a mnemonic device. We hear it in Matthew's account of Jesus' birth. There he quotes the prophet Isaiah: "'Behold, the virgin shall conceive and bear a son, and they shall call His name Immanuel' (which means [in Hebrew], God with us)" (Matthew 1:23).

There's a true story about a man who used this word to help his friend. Both were missionaries in China when it was first taken over by the Communists. On their way home from preaching one Christmas Eve, they were captured. Their Bibles and other possessions were taken away, and the two men were put into a small room with a guard watching them. They weren't allowed to talk, nor were they told what would happen next.

When one missionary woke up on Christmas morning, he felt very sad. He thought about the many happy Christmases he had spent with his family and how different this one was. Then he looked at his friend who'd been sick during the night. He must feel even worse, the missionary thought. I wish there were some way I could cheer him up. Suddenly he had an idea. While the guard was idly looking out the window, the missionary pulled pieces of straw from his bed mattress and spelled out a word for his friend to see: *Immanuel*.

The sick man's face lit up. *Immanuel* . . . "God is with us." Of course! What a difference this made in their day!

Isn't *Immanuel* what Christmas is all about? It's a good word to help us remember. Although you won't find the word itself in today's Bible reading, you will find much about the meaning behind the code. After reading Hebrews 2:14–18, how would you explain *Immanuel*?

PRAYER

Dear Lord, thank You for Your Son Jesus, the Immanuel, who became like me so that I could be like Him. Amen.

Donna Schlimpert

ADVENT

Three Trees

Genesis 2:15–17; Romans 5:15–17

It's the first Christmas for our new baby. Although he is only ten months old, he enjoys the beautiful decorations around the house. His favorite place is the area around the Christmas tree.

A Christmas tree can be a fascinating thing to a baby, but it can also be deadly. The glittering ornaments that hang so nicely on the branches might cause choking. The lights and cords could create an electrical shock. One too many tugs on the tree could cause it to fall over.

Isn't it incredible that something as lovely as a Christmas tree could be so dangerous? Do you remember another tree that attracted people but was also deadly? Read Genesis 2:15–17.

God warned Adam and Eve about the tree. He told them that if they ate the fruit of it, they would die. Yet they were fascinated by this tree and its fruit. Like our baby, they reached for the glittering "ornaments" on the tree. Because they ate the fruit, they brought sin and death into the world. But our loving Father did not abandon His children.

Read Romans 5:15–17. We receive the sin passed on to us from Adam and Eve. Yet we're like infants, completely unable to save ourselves. But God loved us so much that He had already planned Jesus' victory over Satan and us. He planned this victory before the world was even created. He saved us from our sinful selves.

That *first tree* in the Garden of Eden reminds us of our sinfulness. Christ came into the world to remove the choking pain of sin and death from us. We celebrate His birth with the *Christmas tree*. But we don't stop there. We look to the *final tree*, the cross, where Christ died before He rose again to complete our salvation. Thanks be to God!

PRAYER

Heavenly Father, thank You for the gift of life. We praise You for creating us and for saving us from our sins through the death and resurrection of Your Son. In Jesus' name we pray. Amen.

Carla Fast

ADVENT

An Original Present

Matthew 20:25–28

Jeff had a problem. Christmas was almost here, and he didn't have money for presents. He thought of presents to make, and everything he thought of needed money.

All of a sudden, Jeff got an idea. He took paper and cut it into squares. He printed something on each square. Working with colored pencils, he decorated some envelopes.

On Christmas morning, Jeff waited for his parents to open the envelopes. He hoped they wouldn't laugh at him.

Father opened his envelope first and pulled out ten papers that read, "This ticket good for one shoe shine," "This ticket good for one car wash," ". . . one snow shoveling," " . . . one lawn raking," ". . . one lawn trimming," and so on. Father smiled and thanked Jeff.

Mother opened her envelope and looked just as pleased as Father.

Jeff confided, "I was worried that no one would like my present. I thought you would think it was a gyp."

Mother hugged Jeff as she said, "Jeff, you gave the best gifts of all. You gave yourself."

Mother looked through her tickets, selected one, and handed it to Jeff. "I'd like to collect on this one right now."

Jeff read, "Clean the living room." He looked at all the wrapping paper, ribbon, and empty boxes lying around. Jeff grinned and started to work.

In our Bible reading, Jesus tells us He came to earth to serve, not to be served. He came to give His life as payment for our salvation. What better present can we have from Jesus than the gift of Himself! What better way to respond to His love than by serving others!

Pʀᴀʏᴇʀ

Lord Jesus, You told us the secret of being great is to serve others. Make us willing and happy to serve people in Your name. Amen.

Carol M. Barton

A D V E N T

Happy Re-Birthday

Titus 3:4–7

Today is Ken's Baptism birthday. He and his family will celebrate it at suppertime. They'll light his baptismal candle in remembrance of his Baptism ten years ago.

Ken was barely a month old when it happened, so he can't remember any of the details. But his mom told him what she could recall:

"It was a cold and snowy Sunday morning. Underneath several warm blankets, you wore the long white christening gown your great-grand-mother made for her children.

"During the worship service, Pastor Bucher called us forward. Your dad and I went up front along with your sponsors, Dave and Aunt Shirley.

"'I baptize you in the name of the Father and of the Son and of the Holy Spirit,' Pastor Bucher said as he poured some water on your head. That's when you were reborn in Jesus."

"It sounds so strange to me," said Ken, "being reborn when I was just a month old."

Ken's mother tried to explain: "At your Baptism, the Holy Spirit came into your life and gave you faith in Jesus. In Baptism, God called you His child. You inherited all His blessings."

"Just like I inherited Great-Grandma's christening gown—right, Mom?" Ken chuckled.

Martin Luther encouraged us to remember the promises of Baptism every day. Today's Bible reading suggests some thoughts to help you. I've rewritten it here to use as your closing prayer.

PRAYER

Thanks to You, God, I'm saved! It's not because of anything I've done, but simply because of Your kindness and mercy. Thank You for sending the Holy Spirit to give me faith at my Baptism. Through Jesus, I am made right with You. All my sins are forgiven. All Your blessings of forgiveness, life, and salvation are mine, now and forever. Amen.

Donna Rathert

ADVENT

Say It with Song

1 Timothy 4:12

Mr. Herman was the grumpiest old man William and Janice Grant had ever met. The Grants had tried to be friendly to their neighbor, but Mr. Herman constantly complained. He kept the children's ball if it rolled into his yard. He yelled if they stepped on his grass or made too much noise.

When Janice asked where they would carol this year, Dad replied, "We have a few names of shut-ins from church, but I think we will begin in our own neighborhood."

"Great!" said William. "That nice Mrs. Swanson across the street will love having us sing for her. She'll probably even have some treats for us."

"Mrs. Swanson isn't our only neighbor," Dad continued. "We're going to carol for Mr. Herman too."

"You're kidding, Dad. He'll never even open the door!"

"Still, we must try. Jesus didn't preach only to His friends. He loved *all* people. Let's carry the joyous news of His birth to Mr. Herman too."

The Sunday before Christmas, the Grants and their friends set out to carol. Mrs. Swanson welcomed them warmly. She even sang along with a few carols. Janice and William felt good. But their feet dragged as they approached Mr. Herman's front door. To their great surprise, Mr. Herman invited them inside. He sat in his big chair as the group sang out. Then, in a shaky voice, he asked, "Can you sing 'Silent Night' in German?"

"We just learned it in school!" the children replied excitedly. "*Stille Nacht, heilige Nacht . . .* ," their voices sweetly sang.

Tears came to Mr. Herman's eyes. As they were leaving, he clasped everyone's hands and said, "This is the first time anyone ever came to sing to me. I haven't celebrated Christmas since my wife died. You've reminded me how important Jesus is in my life. Thank you, thank you, and . . . uh . . . Merry Christmas!"

PRAYER

Father, help me have courage to spread cheer and Your love, even to those I don't like very much. Amen.

Jewel L. Laabs

ADVENT

The Lamb of Christmas

John 10:11; Psalm 23

Christmas was coming—it was only four days away. The tree was in its stand; the lights were strung. Now came the best part. It was time for the girls to put on the ornaments and see who would find it this year.

The ground rules were simple: no digging through the boxes to find it, and whoever found it could hang it on the tree. The "it" was a small ornament, a wax lamb with a painted red bow around its neck. The three sisters loved that lamb.

Happily they decorated the tree, each secretly hoping to be the one to call out, "I found it! I found Lamb!" When the announcement was made by Lori, everything stopped. Then Lori hung Lamb in its place of honor on the Christmas tree—top, front and center.

Think back to when the announcement was made that the true Christmas Lamb, the Lamb of God, had been born. Look at the reactions God's people had to this good news. Mary praised God, Joseph obeyed God, and Simeon and Anna believed God. Do you think the shepherds shouted "We found Him! We found Him!" as they left the stable?

Jesus later said, "I am the good shepherd. The good shepherd lays down His life for the sheep" (John 10:11). David, too, thinks of Jesus as a shepherd in Psalm 23: "The LORD is my shepherd; I shall not want" (v. 1).

In these Bible readings, *we* are the sheep of the Shepherd, Jesus. As a wolf sneaks up on sheep, the devil would like to sneak up on us and devour our faith. But Jesus fought and defeated the devil and all the evils of sin. Jesus even laid down His life to save us. By His resurrection, He opened up the way to heaven and eternal life.

Whether we call Jesus the Lamb of God, the Lamb of Christmas, or the Good Shepherd, one thing always is the same. Jesus loves us so much that He came to earth for our sake many Christmases ago.

PRAYER

Heavenly Father, thank You for sending Your Son, Jesus, as the Lamb of Christmas. Help us give all the honor and glory due Him. Let our lives be sacrifices of love and service. Amen.

Jeanette Dall

ADVENT

Looking for Angels

2 Kings 6:15–17

Have you noticed how busy the angels were in the Christmas story? Gabriel told Zechariah and his wife they would have a special son named John who would prepare people for Jesus' coming. Gabriel visited Mary and told her that she, too, would have a son. She should name Him *Jesus*. An angel told Joseph not to be afraid to take Mary for his wife.

An angel told the shepherds where to find baby Jesus, and then a sky full of angels praised God for the victory and peace our salvation in Jesus would win us. But the angels' work wasn't over yet. After the Wise Men visited young Jesus, an angel warned them not to go back to King Herod. An angel told Joseph to hide Jesus in Egypt so that Herod's soldiers could not kill Him.

Wouldn't it be great if angels could let us know everything that would happen to us and just what we ought to do in every situation? Life would be pretty easy with all that angel help. Maybe our eyes just aren't used to seeing angels.

In the Old Testament, long before Jesus' birth, Elisha's servant worried when he saw that the city where they were staying was surrounded by enemy horses and chariots. Elisha asked God to open his servant's eyes. Then the servant could see hills full of horses and chariots of fire surrounding the enemy soldiers. God's angels were ready to go to work.

Many years after Zechariah, King Herod, and Elisha, God's angels are still working. God's angels are still busy. They are circled around you right now, ready to serve God!

PRAYER

Father, thank You for keeping Your angels working overtime to watch over me. Thank You for the salvation You give to me. In Jesus' name. Amen.

Ruth Geisler

ADVENT

Love's Pure Light

1 John 4:7–10

Tomorrow is the anniversary (in 2008, it will be the 190th anniversary) of one of our best-loved Christmas carols. The carol? "Silent Night" (*LSB* 363).

On Christmas Eve, 1818, the church organ in the Austrian village of Oberndorf was out of order. The Christmas music planned for the service just couldn't be sung without the organ. Joseph Mohr, the assistant pastor, sat down and wrote the words for a new Christmas song.

Once he had completed the words, he gave them to the substitute organist, Franz Gruber. He asked him to compose a melody to go with the words, a melody that could be accompanied by a guitar. That night at worship, Christians in Oberndorf heard "Silent Night" for the first time. Two solo voices and a chorus sang the carol.

In the third stanza of the carol, Pastor Mohr expressed very simply the whole meaning of Christ's birth: "Son of God, *love's pure light* . . . beams from Thy holy face."

That's what Christmas means for us. In the face of Jesus Christ, we best see God's love for us sinners. We see the baby of Bethlehem grow up to love, accept, and forgive even a thief like Zacchaeus. We see Jesus forgive the wrongs of a sinful woman rather than join her cruel accusers in punishing her. We know God accepts and forgives us. We see Jesus make Peter one of His witnesses and workers, though Peter denied Him three times. So we know God can use even us.

Our Bible reading tells us "God is love" (1 John 4:8). This we believe because, as Pastor Mohr's carol reminds us, we've seen love's pure light beam radiantly from the face of Jesus, God's own Son.

PRAYER

Lord Jesus, I praise You on the holy day of Your birth. For You were born into my world to show me God's love. I will praise You always for Your kindness. Amen.

Richard Hinz

ADVENT

The Greatest Story of All

Luke 2:1–7

A king once called his advisers together and chose three of the very wisest ones. The king then told them, "I want you to go to your rooms and think. Bring back to me the most amazing and exciting story you can imagine. I want to tell this story to my people during the coming holidays."

The three advisers went away and spent many days alone. Then they returned to tell their stories. The first wise man told about a great hero who sailed across the sea and discovered a new world filled with gold and jewels.

The second wise man told a story of a poor peasant who saved the life of the king's son and was given a kingdom of his own.

The third wise man told of a city in the sky that men could reach on winged horses and where they could live forever.

The king looked at his wise men and shook his head. "I can tell a greater story than any of you," he said. "And it's more than a story—it's true."

Then he opened the Bible and read, "While they were there, the time came for her to give birth. And she gave birth to her firstborn son and wrapped Him in swaddling cloths and laid Him in a manger" (Luke 2:6–7).

The wise men bowed their heads to the king. They knew that this was a greater story than any man could imagine.

The birth of Jesus is wonderful because Jesus came to earth for our sake. He was born to save us from sin. The baby who lay in the manger is the same person who later died on the cross to win eternal happiness for us. O come, let us adore Him!

PRAYER

Babe of Bethlehem, I worship You as my Redeemer and Savior. How wonderful it is that You came to earth as a little child to live and die for me! Dear Lord, I give You my heart, for it belongs to You. Amen.

Robert Randoy

CHRISTMAS
Christmas Eve

The Sun Rose on Christmas

John 1:12–14

Christmas was coming to an end. The presents, all unwrapped, still lay under the Christmas tree. Susan had just finished burning all the paper wrappings. As she walked back to the house, she noticed that it was getting dark already.

After she took off her coat, Susan stretched out on the couch and thought about all the fun they'd had over the holidays. She thought about the Christmas service at church. Then, as she remembered the singing and the pageant, her mind wandered back to the first Christmas Day. She wondered what that day had been like.

Suddenly the thought came to her: There weren't any celebrations or holidays or gifts or trees at all on the first Christmas! There wouldn't be because most people didn't even know what was going on. How strange that when such an important thing happened—the birth of the Savior—so few people realized what was happening! So few people knew that God had come to live as a man and to take away the world's sin.

It was just as if the sun had come up on a dark, cold world when Jesus was born. In fact, long before Jesus' birth, God called Jesus a "sun" in the Bible. He said, "But for you who fear My name, the sun of righteousness shall rise with healing in its wings" (Malachi 4:2). All the darkness of sin was taken away by the Savior who was to come into the world. The forgiveness Jesus earned heals us of the disease of sin.

In a few hours, Christmas celebrations will be over. Everybody will have opened his or her gifts. Soon the decorations will come down. But Christmas is never really over. It stays with us all the time, because the "Sun" has come up, and we need no longer live in the darkness of sin. Now every day can be as joyful as Christmas for the believer in Jesus.

PRAYER

Thank You, God, for sending Jesus, the Sun of Righteousness, to overcome the darkness of sin for me and all people. Forgive my sins. In Jesus' name I pray. Amen.

Norman Utech

CHRISTMAS
Christmas Day

An After-Christmas Argument

2 Corinthians 9:15

"I got the best present. My doll is so pretty," bragged Susan as she cuddled her doll.

"My electric race car is better," countered Harold. "It cost more than your doll."

Don couldn't resist getting into the argument. "My BB gun is the best. And I'm the only one old enough to have a gun," he taunted.

Mr. Bates interrupted. "What is this? Haven't you three got anything better to do than quarrel about your gifts?"

Mrs. Bates asked, "What's the best Christmas gift? Or maybe I should ask, *who* is the best gift?"

Don thought for a moment and then said, "I know—Jesus!"

Mr. Bates said, "Now you've got it. Jesus was sent to earth to save us from our sins. That's surely the best gift."

Mrs. Bates added, "Our other gifts break, or sometimes we just outgrow them. We never outgrow Jesus or our need for Him. Jesus is our 'forever' gift."

PRAYER

Jesus, You are my greatest gift because through You, I have forgiveness and eternal life. Thank You for loving me and being with me forever. Amen.

Carol M. Barton

St. John the Divine

Revelation 21:1–5

On December 27, many Christians around the world give thanks to God for St. John the Divine, the man God the Holy Spirit inspired to write the Book of Revelation.

There were many men named John during and after Jesus' life. Many scholars think this John was a close disciple of Jesus. Others are not sure, because no records exist to make it clear.

Whether he was the same person or another man, we are sure of one thing: John was inspired by God to write about the vision of what he called "a new heaven and a new earth."

In those days, people were required to worship the Roman emperor. Whoever refused was punished. John had been banished to the island of Patmos because he would not give up believing in Jesus Christ. God had him write the book to encourage other Christians and to declare that no power on earth will ever conquer the kingship of the true Messiah. The message of Revelation is that we should not be fooled. It may look like the evil ones of the world are winning the struggle, but they will fail in the end.

Instead, everyone who believes in Jesus and is baptized is "more than [a] conqueror" and has the assurance of God's promises to love, forgive, save, and deliver us. We will live forever with God.

PRAYER

Praise to You, dear God, for inspiring John with Your vision in the Book of Revelation. Help us to trust Your promise of salvation, through Jesus. Amen.

Dot Nuechterlein

CHRISTMAS
St. John, Apostle and Evangelist

We Are the Lord's

Matthew 2:13–23

The babies in your neighborhood all cry. Everyone expects babies to cry. But it would be a great surprise if one day the *mothers* in your neighborhood all began to cry! You would know that something had upset them.

This did happen once. Many years ago in Bethlehem, all the mothers—and fathers too, no doubt—began to cry. They cried because soldiers had come through the town and killed all the baby boys two years old and younger.

The soldiers were carrying out the orders of King Herod, who had heard of Jesus' birth. Herod tried to kill Jesus because he was afraid the child would grow up and take over his kingdom.

But God protected Jesus. He told Joseph to take Mary and their son to Egypt. He couldn't let Jesus be killed then, because the Savior was to grow up and die on the cross.

God is trying to teach us something by telling us about the murder of the innocent children. He wants us to see what great dangers Jesus faced to save us. His life wasn't hard just on the cross. No, it was difficult for Him to be our Savior from the beginning.

God tells us something else too. He shows us that no matter what happens to us, He will be with us. Young people are sometimes frightened by world events and evil rulers. In Jesus' day there was Herod. Today there are the communists and others who try to keep God's will from happening. We hear our parents talking about many things that alarm us.

But we Christians can trust that, whatever happens, even if we die, we will be with Him. While we live, He will protect us and care for us. The Bible assures us, "Whether we live or whether we die, we are the Lord's" (Romans 14:8).

PRAYER

Dear God, sometimes I become frightened. But when I hear about how You took care of Your Son, Jesus, I know that I don't have to be afraid. Be with me always and help me in every trouble, for I belong to You. Amen.

Arne Kristo

CHRISTMAS
The Holy Innocents, Martyrs

Patient Simeon

Luke 2:25–32

Do you know the Bible story about Simeon? Simeon was a man who spent his life serving God. God promised Simeon that he would not die before seeing the Savior. God kept that promise as He keeps every promise.

When Jesus was only forty days old, Joseph and Mary brought Him to the temple. Simeon was also at the temple that day. When Simeon saw the baby, he rejoiced. He knew in his heart that this child was the Savior of the world.

Then Simeon took Jesus in his arms and prayed. He thanked God for letting him see the One who would bring light to a world dark with sin. Simeon finally saw the promised Savior, who would redeem His people from sin. He told God he was now ready to die peacefully.

As He gave Simeon, God also gives us a faith that trusts in Him to keep His promises. We are at peace with God because Jesus came into the world.

Also like Simeon, we may have to wait a long time to see how God will work something out. There are things about God that we can't understand. We don't know why certain things happen. Sin gets in the way too. We may not have the answers to all our questions until we live with God in heaven.

Simeon looked forward to the Savior's coming. We look forward to His second coming. This time, Jesus will come not as a baby, but as the glorious Son of God.

Below is the prayer Simeon prayed when he held the Christ Child. It's often sung in the Divine Service in another translation. Say this version as your prayer today. Remember that you, with eyes of faith, have seen in Jesus the salvation God prepared for all people.

PRAYER

"Lord, now You are letting Your servant depart in peace, according to Your word; for my eyes have seen Your salvation that You have prepared in the presence of all peoples, a light for revelation to the Gentiles, and for glory to Your people Israel" (Luke 2:29–32).

Dawn Napier

CHRISTMAS

Fading Christmas

1 Peter 1:3–5

Walking past the Christmas tree, Tina heard the tinkling sound of needles falling off the tree. Was Christmas fading?

Then she set a bag of Christmas garbage on the curb and noticed that some of the bulbs wrapped around the Christmas garland on the porch had burned out. Was Christmas fading?

Later, she saw her dog chewing on the leftover bone from the Christmas ham. "It seems that everywhere I look, Christmas is over. Even the short candles don't seem to burn brightly. Everything seems sad now."

"It does seem sad when the needles fall, the lights burn out, and the festive dinners are over. But Christmas isn't over, Tina," said her mother. "The shiny decorations, the family gatherings, the pretty cards, even the gifts we exchange—things we do to help us celebrate Christmas—fade away. But the real meaning of Christmas will never fade.

"In Baptism, we receive the living hope that God provided through the sacrifice of His Son. Hope in Him won't die like those needles. Hope in Him won't burn out like those lights. Hope in Him won't get used up like our Christmas ham."

For Tina, for her mom, and for us, Jesus won His fight against sin, death, and Satan. God's Christmas gift came to us at Easter. On the Good Friday cross, He won a crown of glory for each of us, and that crown is "imperishable, undefiled, and unfading" (1 Peter 1:4).

PRAYER

Dear Jesus, thank You for the living hope we have been given through Your death and resurrection. Amen.

Cheryl Honoree

The Salvation Parade

Hebrews 12:1–2

"Oh, boy, tomorrow we get to watch the New Year's Day parades," said Julie.

"Good," said Jared. "They're the best parades of the whole year. I hope I can be in one someday."

Have you ever thought of the characters in the Bible as being in a parade? All the people and events of Scripture make a fascinating parade, showing God's mercy and salvation through many years.

Imagine the head of the parade. There's Jesus! "He was in the beginning with God" (John 1:2). Right behind Him come Adam and Eve, carrying flowers and fruit from the Garden of Eden. And here comes Noah with his family. They're all leading animals. That man over there must be Abraham with his sheep. There's Isaac and his son Jacob. That beautiful woman must be Rebekah, and near her is Rachel.

This parade could stretch for miles and miles. From Adam to the apostles, thousands of Israelites and Gentiles from Scripture fill the streets of history, all of them believers in the Lord of creation, all of them sinners in need of salvation through Christ, just like you.

Look. There's a gap in the parade, a space right behind the apostle Paul. That space is yours. As God's baptized child, you are also in God's line of grace. Jesus has redeemed you. He leads you through this life to everlasting life in heaven. By His grace, He gives you this gift, this honor.

So if you see any parades tomorrow, be reminded of God's salvation parade. It is the most spectacular one of all time. And, just think, by God's grace, you're in it!

PRAYER

Heavenly Father, thank You for making me Your child through Baptism and the Holy Spirit. Keep me in Your grace through the parade of this life and into eternity. In Jesus' name I pray. Amen.

Kristine Moulds

A New Year's Hymn

Psalm 90

Isaac Watts was always a head shorter than everyone else, and he hated it. He had eight brothers and sisters, another reason he was usually overlooked. But Isaac could do something that made others pay attention to him. He was very good at making up verses.

One morning while his father was reading the Bible at the breakfast table, Isaac burst out laughing. "Why did you laugh in the middle of devotions?" his father asked sternly.

"Sir," said Isaac, "I saw a mouse on the bell rope, and I thought of a verse:

> There was a mouse for lack of stairs,
> Ran up the rope to say his prayers."

Isaac's father reached for the willow stick. Isaac fell to his knees, pleading:

> "O Father, Father, pity take,
> And I will never verses make."

But Isaac Watts did make verses. When he grew up, he was so successful that he became known as "the Father of English Hymn Writing." He wrote such well-loved hymns as "Jesus Shall Reign Where'er the Sun," "Joy to the World," and "When I Survey the Wondrous Cross."

Today, on New Year's Day, we especially remember another famous hymn by Isaac Watts, "O God, Our Help in Ages Past." Based on Psalm 90, this hymn praises God for keeping us through past years and for being our hope in years to come. Our life on earth is very short, but God is "from everlasting to everlasting" (v. 2). He will keep us safely in His arms and bring us to our eternal home for Jesus' sake.

PRAYER

O God, our help in ages past,
Our hope for years to come,
Be Thou our guard while troubles last
And our eternal home! Amen. (*LSB* 733:6)

Theodore J. Kleinhans

CHRISTMAS
New Year's Day/Circumcision and Name of Jesus

What a Name!

Hebrews 1:3–6

W. T. Monds III was once a minor-league outfielder with the Atlanta Braves organization. His father, W. T. Monds Jr. was a Nebraska Cornhusker defensive back from 1973 to 1975. But more interesting than those facts is the name these two men share.

You see, "W. T." stands for "Wonder Terrific." After eleven girls, W. T.'s great-grandmother finally had a son. "Wonderful! Terrific!" Great-Grandpa exclaimed when he heard the news. In his joy, he gave the baby those happy words for a name. Thus began three generations of Wonder Terrifics.

Jesus had some special names too. On January 1, the Church celebrates the giving of His name *Jesus*. One of those is spoken about in today's reading. That name for Jesus has only three letters, but it's a big name. The name is *Son*. The writer of Hebrews tells us that the name *Son* (with a capital S) is reserved only for Jesus. No angel may use it. No other human fits it.

What's so important about being called the Son of God? Whoever bears that name is fully God, just like God the Father. He is perfect and all-knowing. He can forgive sins and heal lives.

Jesus fits the description of the Son of God. Only God's Son could die for our sins. Only God's Son could send the Holy Spirit to us. Only God's Son could prepare a home in heaven for us.

Wonder Terrific is a great name. But only one person was ever called the Son of God. We know Him as Jesus, our Savior. Jesus has other names too. Read Isaiah 9:6.

PRAYER

Dear Jesus, Son of God, what a beautiful, powerful name You have! Thank You for using Your power as the Son of God to save me from eternal death. In Your name I pray. Amen.

Carol Albrecht

CHRISTMAS

A Happy Year

Psalm 98

Have you ever gone to a funeral? If so, you may have noticed many people crying. But still, what do Christians do at some funerals? They sing!

Singing is a sign of joy. Believers in Jesus can sing at funerals because underneath their sadness they are sure that Jesus will take His people to heaven.

In his Small Catechism, Martin Luther suggests that we go joyfully to our work every morning, singing a hymn ("Daily Prayers," Morning Prayer). It is good to memorize many hymns, so that we can sing them at any time or place.

Of course, there are many times when we don't feel like singing. When we have to do our homework instead of watching television, we grumble. When we don't get our way, we grow stubborn and sulky. That's why we need to remember the words "Rejoice in the Lord always" (Philippians 4:4). It's a sure way to have a happy new year.

Why can we always rejoice or be happy? We belong to Christ. We have His love, no matter what may happen to us. St. Paul said: "I am sure that neither death nor life . . . nor things present nor things to come . . . nor anything else in all creation, will be able to separate us from the love of God in Christ Jesus our Lord" (Romans 8:38–39).

PRAYER

God, I am so happy that You made me Your child. Please forgive me for not always remembering Your love. Give me joy in knowing that the Holy Spirit has given me faith to believe in Jesus, my Savior. In Jesus' name I pray.

Donald Hoeferkamp

God at the Controls

Psalm 27

A boy was traveling by himself on a jet airliner. The big plane shot across the country at a speed almost as fast as the speed of sound. Once or twice it hit rough weather and started to bounce and jerk.

When the jet reached its destination and came in for the landing, an elderly woman sitting near the boy watched him to see if he would be afraid. But even when they touched the ground with a thud and the great jet engines roared to a stop, the boy hardly blinked. He seemed as calm as if he were in his living room, watching television.

Finally the lady asked him, "How can you sit there so calm and confident? Aren't you a little afraid?"

"Why should I be afraid?" replied the boy. "My father is the pilot."

We are beginning our "flight" through a new year. We don't know everything that lies ahead in the new year. There may be some bumpy moments and rough spots and unexpected obstacles to cross. But God is at the controls of our lives. Because He is our pilot, we needn't be afraid of the future. We may say as David did, "The LORD is my light and my salvation; whom shall I fear?" (Psalm 27:1).

Through faith in Jesus, we are God's sons and daughters. In our Baptism, God took us into His family and made us His own. He will take care of us throughout this year and throughout our lives. So we trust in Him and ask for His keeping.

PRAYER

Dear Lord, thank You for the year that is past, and keep me safely through the coming year. When the going gets rough, help me remember that You are controlling my life and that there is nothing to fear. Amen.

John Ellwanger

Our Priceless Gift

1 Peter 1:18–21

It began as a silly mistake. You see, the Willis family traditionally celebrated all twelve days of Christmas—from Christmas Day to Epiphany—by exchanging small, inexpensive gifts each night after supper. In this way they extended the excitement of celebrating the birth of Jesus.

As one of the children opened her gift, she discovered that the price tag on her pocket mirror had not been removed. "Twenty-five cents! The gift I gave cost more than this!" she exclaimed.

Picking up on the lighthearted comment, someone else responded, "You can't prove it. There are no price tags on our presents."

From then on, every gift had a price tag announcing an exaggerated price, with each giver trying to outgive the others. A box of crayons was marked $15.95. A bag of balloons carried a $19.29 price tag, and a bottle of bubble bath bore a sticker with a price of $23.84. The prices grew. On the last of the twelve days, a pencil-and-eraser "set," held together with cellophane tape, proudly displayed the value of $165!

As we think about the gift of our salvation, one thing is certain: God cannot be outdone as the ultimate gift giver. God gave us the very best He had—His only Son. God's Word reminds us of salvation's cost: the very blood of Christ. Its value can't be exaggerated. More precious than gold or silver, this gift made us free of the sins that trouble and condemn us. What a tremendous gift is ours!

PRAYER

Dear Lord, thank You for the gift of salvation won for me through the suffering and death of Jesus. May I treasure it always as my prized possession. Amen.

Rodney Rathmann

The Journey's End

Matthew 2:1–12

When was the last journey you took? Maybe it was during the Christmas season, or maybe it was a long time ago. Perhaps a journey to you means a trip across a city. Possibly it means a trip out of your state or province or even out of your country. No matter the length of the journeys, they have something in common. The purpose of a journey is to get to a new place.

Anticipation about the end of our journeys is what makes us willing to deal with cramped cars and vans. The desire to "go somewhere" is the reason we sacrifice time and expense for travel. We're willing to put up with a lot just to get where we want to go—whether it be to visit relatives or to shop at a mall.

The journey taken by the Wise Men had a far greater purpose. They wanted to worship their Savior in person and bring their gifts to the King of the Jews.

When you think about it, our life here on earth is a journey. The end is heaven. We, like the Wise Men, are traveling in order to see our Savior face-to-face.

Along the way, we follow, by God's grace and strength, the path He lays out for us. Then, because of Christ's sacrifice for our sins, we reach our final destination. The journey's end is heaven. Praise God that our future is certain!

PRAYER

Dear Lord, give us faith like the Wise Men had so that we will follow where You lead all our lives. Thank You for sending Jesus to save us and for promising that our journey's end will be heaven. Amen.

Susan Watermann Voss

EPIPHANY
The Epiphany of Our Lord

You're a Star

Philippians 2:14–16

It's the Epiphany season, a time to see Jesus revealed as God's Son. The Wise Men followed a bright star to Jesus. As Christians, sometimes we picture ourselves as lights in a dark world—like stars in a dark night sky.

Here are some fascinating facts about stars:

1. There are five different colors of stars.

2. Reactions in the core of a star are what cause it to glow.

3. Half of the stars we see are actually two or more stars orbiting each other.

Here are some more fascinating facts about Christians!

1. There are endless different ways they are called to serve one another in God's kingdom. Whether talkative, quiet, athletic, or musical, all have special ways to share the love of Christ.

2. Christians do good things because of what is new inside of them—God's grace! It is only because of the Holy Spirit that Christians can shine at all!

3. Sometimes Christians shine especially bright when God joins them together to work for Him. This gift of fellowship can really shine brightly in others.

So, are we a bit like the stars shining in this dark world? Absolutely! Jesus has overcome our sin so that we can live for Him. Unlike stars that will one day fade and fall, we will shine forever. Even on days when we are not feeling very "shiny," reading God's Word will strengthen our faith and remind us of His promises, especially the promises He gives us in Baptism. Enjoy being a star today!

PRAYER

Thank You, God, for rescuing me from the darkness of my sin. Help me to be a bright witness today. In Jesus' name I pray. Amen.

Lisa Hahn

EPIPHANY

The Morning Star

2 Peter 1:19

Think how dark it must have been at night during Bible times. There were no streetlights, neon lights, headlights, flashlights, night-lights, or light switches. If a person was sick or afraid or lost, he had to depend on the light from a small oil lamp, if he had any light at all. People waiting for the dark night to end were excited when they saw a light in the sky, which they called the "morning star."

Now we know that the morning star that people in biblical times looked for was the planet Venus. Except for the moon, Venus is the brightest body in the nighttime sky. People could see Venus in the eastern sky as long as three hours before the sun rose. The sight of the morning star gave people hope—the night was almost over.

We call Jesus our morning star. He gave His life to pay for the darkness of our sin. He came to conquer the shadow of death and the powers of the devil. Peter explains in today's verse that God's Word is like a light that leads us to Jesus. He says it will help us as "a lamp shining in a dark place, until the day dawns and the morning star rises in your hearts."

God's Word of forgiveness shines when siblings squabble or friends feud. God's Word of peace shines when family troubles lead to frustration. God's Word of hope shines when loved ones are sick or die. God's Word shines each morning—even when we can't see the stars.

PRAYER

Jesus, thank You for being the author and giver of the only light I'll ever need. In Your name I pray. Amen.

Ruth Geisler

Christmas Meets Easter

Galatians 4:4–7

There is one Christmas I will always remember. It was during World War II. My Uncle Arthur was in the army. He had been sent to India. He was supposed to come home on leave for Christmas. Everyone in the family was happy. We hadn't seen him for a long time. We all missed him very much.

Christmas came, but there was no Uncle Arthur. For some reason, his leave was delayed. My mother wanted to keep our Christmas tree up till he came home. The end of January arrived, and our Christmas tree was still in the living room. Needles were lying on the floor in piles under the bare tree. But my mother insisted, "We'll keep the tree up till Easter if we have to."

There's an important thought connected with keeping your Christmas tree around till Easter. Some churches save part of their Christmas tree trunk. They make a cross out of it for the Lenten season. Maybe your church does this.

This custom reminds us that Jesus was born so that He could die. God's Son was born a baby in Bethlehem. When the baby grew up, He died for our sins on Calvary's cross. Then came Easter Sunday and Jesus' resurrection.

So, you see, Christmas and Easter do go together. The birth and resurrection of Jesus are side by side in God's plan to save us.

PRAYER

O Lord, Advent helped us remember why Your Son, Jesus, came to earth. Because of our sins, Jesus gave His life on the cross to save us. Knowing that He rose again sealed the victory over sin, death, and the devil. Because of Your love, O Lord, we can say "Merry Christmas" and "Happy Easter." Amen.

Eleanor R. Schlegl

EPIPHANY

I Can Do It

Philippians 4:10–13

"Got it!" Emily yelled as she crashed to her knees, trying to get to the volleyball. Her bump went astray, and the point was lost.

I can't do it, Emily chided herself.

This doesn't make sense, Matt said to himself as he struggled with his math test. What good did it do to study all that time if I don't get it anyway? I just can't do this.

Aaron watched from his window as some children played outside his new home. He wanted to join them, but what if they didn't like him? What if they didn't think his jokes were funny? What if they made fun of his hearing aids? "I can't go out there," Aaron murmured.

St. Paul experienced God's "can do." God helped Paul in good times and in bad, in abundance and in need. St. Paul says in the Bible, "I can do all things through Him who strengthens me" (Philippians 4:13). What did he mean?

Jesus had a "can do" attitude when He suffered and died for your sins. In His Word and in Baptism, God is present to strengthen you. Through His Spirit, God continues to know about your good times and your bad times.

This doesn't mean you will score every point in volleyball. It doesn't mean you will get 100 percent on every math test. It doesn't even mean everyone will like you. It does mean that God will be with you. It does mean that you won't go at these tasks alone. Now you "can do" your best for Him!

PRAYER

Dear Lord, thank You for the life You have given me—full of Your love and grace. Thank You for the promise of eternal life. Amen.

Valerie Schulz

Numbers

Romans 8:31–34

Today is January 11. Big deal, you say. Well, it *is* a big deal if you're a numerologist. A numerologist is a person who studies numbers and finds special meaning in them. For instance, when today's date is written in shorthand numbers (1/11), it reads the same forward and backward.

Numerologists also figure out special days for certain people. For example, if you were born on January 11 and you were eleven years old today, this would be your special day because you would be eleven on 1/11.

Some people call these "magic" numbers. They say the Bible has "magic" numbers too, like three, seven, and ten. We have a three-in-one God who created the world in seven days (counting the Sabbath) and gave us Ten Commandments. All of this is interesting, but we need to be careful with it.

Some people get carried away with adding special meanings to things. They start looking to these signs for guidance in their lives. Some of the methods they use are Ouija boards, astrology, fortune-telling, palm reading, and handwriting analysis.

God gave us His Word to guide us in our lives. He sent His Spirit to lead us day by day. We Christians don't need magic or witchcraft to help us along.

So don't let games become your guide. God guides us without guesswork or parlor tricks. His plan for each of us is a good one.

The Bible assures us, "If God is for us, who can be against us? He who did not spare His own Son but gave Him up for us all, how will He not also with Him graciously give us all things?" (Romans 8:31–32).

PRAYER

Dear Lord, help us follow You and Your plan for our lives. Protect us, watch over us, and guide us so that we may inherit heaven. In Jesus' name. Amen.

Douglas A. Noel

EPIPHANY

Independence

Titus 3:4–8

On this day in 1737, John Hancock was born. He was a leading figure in the fight to win independence from England.

Hancock served as president of the Continental Congress from 1775 to 1777. It was during this time that the Declaration of Independence was signed. John Hancock was the first signer of this important document. He is usually remembered because of the boldness and size of his signature. You might want to find out more about this famous American from an encyclopedia or history book.

Many years before John Hancock, there was another declaration of independence. This, however, was not a declaration for Americans only. This declaration was not signed by pen in ink as Hancock's signature was. It was signed in blood.

Let me clue you in to the identity of this signer. He was not man only, but also God.

Yes. More than nineteen hundred years ago, Jesus Christ signed a declaration of independence for all people. Humankind had become slaves of Satan because of sin. In order to declare us independent of the powers of the devil, Christ freely gave Himself as an offering for us.

Let's celebrate God's great freedom earned by Jesus: our freedom from sin, death, and Satan's power.

PRAYER

Dear Jesus, thank You for the freedoms gained by the men more than two hundred years ago. Thank You also for the much greater freedom You won for us on the cross. Help us to share freedom from sin and guilt with our friends and relatives. Amen.

Norman Schake

A Lifetime Guarantee

Hebrews 13:8

Christmas is now a couple of weeks past. Maybe it's time for us to take a second look at all the gifts we received.

Some of them have probably ended up on a shelf or in a closet. They may not be very much fun, or maybe we're just not interested in them anymore. Sometimes they're fun to play with or use right after we open them. But then, in a few weeks, the gifts aren't new anymore, and we just put them aside. Even worse, some of them may be broken already. Even though they come with little warranty cards, this doesn't guarantee that we will like them or that the gifts will last forever.

But there's one gift we all received at Christmas that is absolutely perfect. We will never outgrow it. It will always be special to us—and best of all, it will never break. As a matter of fact, this gift has a lifetime guarantee.

In case you haven't guessed, this special gift of Christmas is Jesus Christ. He is exactly right for us all the time. He is what we need and will never become old-fashioned. And the guarantee is in today's Bible verse. It promises us that Jesus will always be around, offering the things only He can give us—forgiveness, life, and salvation. What a wonderful gift for Christmas with a guarantee for a lifetime!

PRAYER

Thank You, God, that Your Son is the gift that will last forever. Amen.

Cathy Krueger

Blind Faith

John 20:26–29

Art always enjoyed visiting Grandpa, but especially in the wintertime. Somehow the lake in the backyard looked like a fairyland with the frozen water and frosty snow. And today Art and Grandpa would be part of it all. Grandpa was going to show him what it was like to go ice fishing.

So they took their fishing poles and bait and walked out onto the lake. As Grandpa was cutting a hole in the ice, Art began to wonder about something. "Grandpa," Art asked, "how will we be able to catch the fish if we can't see them? Maybe there aren't any fish here at all!"

"Well, Art," said Grandpa, "every once in a while I get a glimpse of the fish moving around under the ice or tugging at my line. And even if I can't use my senses to make sure there are fish under the ice, I still believe they are there."

"Now I know what they mean by 'blind faith,'" said Art. "We can't see, but we believe."

"You know, that's what Jesus meant when He talked to His disciples after His resurrection," explained Grandpa. "He wanted them to know that even when they weren't seeing Him or feeling His presence, they could still believe in Him as their Lord and Savior."

Art threw his line into the icy water. "I guess it's easier to believe when I can see for myself," he admitted. Just then he felt a tug on his line.

Art laughed and squealed at the same time. "And I couldn't even see it!" he said as he pulled in the fish.

PRAYER

Lord Jesus, I get scared when I'm not sure You are with me. Help me be aware of the signs You give that show You're watching over me. And send Your Holy Spirit to increase my faith when I cannot see. Amen.

Cathy Krueger

EPIPHANY

The Birds of Winter

Matthew 6:25–33

As you read today's Bible text, what time of year did you think of? No doubt it was summer. As Jesus points out the lilies of the field, you can see the green grass in which they grow. You can feel the warm sun and the gentle breezes. That's a welcome thought in January.

But in the middle of winter, the grass has turned brown, the leaves have fallen, and some of the birds have flown south. What happens to the birds that stay through the long winter? How do they survive?

Jesus' answer in Matthew 6:26 is not just for summer. Our heavenly Father cares for the birds in winter as well as in summer. Birds probably need more care in the winter than in the summer, but God still does it.

Then Jesus asks, "Are you not of more value than they?" (v. 26). When He asked that, He knew the answer. We are worth much, much more. We're worth the life of Jesus Himself, laid down for us more than two thousand years ago.

God cares also for *us* in summer and winter. It's easy to remember that God is near when everything goes well. We may have gotten what we wanted for Christmas. Teachers and students at school may like us. Mom and Dad proudly show our pictures to relatives and friends. These are the signs of God's care in a summer of blessings.

But when winter comes, does God still care? When the cold, icy grip of sickness holds us; when family members separate; when our friends are no longer our friends; when death takes someone near and dear to us— who cares then?

Remember what Jesus said about the birds, even the birds of winter: "Your heavenly Father feeds them" (v. 26). And you are worth more to Him than birds—winter, summer, spring, and fall.

PRAYER

O Lord, You created us and You care for us. Thank You for all the people who care for me day after day in my life. Thank You for Jesus, my Savior, who died for me. In Jesus' name I pray. Amen.

James Klawitter

EPIPHANY

A Miracle!

John 4:46–54

During Epiphany, we hear Bible readings in church that tell us that Jesus is God. He showed this by the many miracles He performed. But is Jesus still showing He is true God today? Yes! Recently, a boy named Scott was riding horseback near his grandparents' cabin. Suddenly he was thrown from the horse, and the horse stepped on him. The family rushed him to a nearby hospital, where they were told the injury was much too serious for them to treat. Scott was sped by ambulance sixty miles to a large hospital. There the doctors learned that Scott's liver had been severely damaged.

The following two months were long for Scott and his family. Scott was finally released to get well at home. The family learned from the doctors that the process used to repair Scott's liver had been in use for only a year. If the accident had happened before that time, Scott probably wouldn't have lived.

In the Bible reading, John records the story of another boy who was very ill. The boy became alive and well because of a miracle Jesus performed.

But what Jesus has done for us is even more miraculous. He took our wrongdoings as His own. He suffered the punishment for them, which was death. But Jesus even beat death; He rose again. His suffering, death, and resurrection became ours through faith—faith given to us at our Baptism. Now we're alive and well spiritually because of what Jesus has done for us.

Yes, Jesus shows He is true God today.

PRAYER

Thank You, Jesus, for performing a miracle on me. I was a sinner; now I am saved by You. Praise the Lord! Amen.

Judy Williams

It Never Melts

Romans 6:20–23

Katie lived in one of the Southern states, so there was seldom snow. Yet she woke up one morning with two strong feelings: she was late for school, and the light was too bright.

Then she opened her eyes and saw the snow.

"Mom! Mom!" she shouted as she ran to the kitchen. "It's snowing!"

"Yes, it is," Mom agreed. Sausage links sizzled on the stove.

"Where's Dad? Is he here too?"

"No, he drove his truck to work."

"Oh," Katie said, disappointed. "Did you stay here to take me to school?"

"No, it's too risky to drive a car. Under this snow is a thick layer of ice."

"How will I get to school? Are the buses running?"

"No school today," Mom said, smiling. "It's been canceled."

Katie let out a whoop of excitement. "Wow! Can I play in the snow? Can Alice come over to play too? Can we have cocoa for breakfast?"

"Whoa! One thing at a time," Mom said.

A snow day for some seems like real cause for celebration. Yet we have a much better reason to rejoice every moment of every day. The Good News that Jesus died for our sins will never melt away like snow. It will never become trampled and worn. Now and always, it will be as beautiful as when we first heard it. Because we are God's forgiven people, we can rejoice all the time.

PRAYER

Dear Lord, thank You for many joys in life—like extra days off from school. Because You died for me, I give You thanks. In Jesus' name I pray. Amen.

Glenda Schrock

Cold and Flu Season

Psalm 103:1–4

It's cold and flu season again! Commercials on television remind us constantly of the awful condition of aches, pains, fever, stuffy head, and the like. Actually, we wouldn't need the reminders. The memories of last year's aches and pains are enough to make us keep a ready supply of medicine in the cabinet.

You know all the remedies—pain killers, decongestants, and cough medicine. Then throw in the old standards—chicken soup, orange juice, and heating pads. Often the doctor is consulted and, if necessary, stronger medication is given.

The cold or flu eventually does go away. Gradually we start to feel normal again, and life goes on. So what happened that made the illness go away? Oh, we can tell others about the fantastic new purple pills Dad bought at the drugstore or tell how much the doctor's bill was. We can brag about Aunt Marie's chicken soup recipe or give a long explanation of the human immune system. However, those answers by themselves do not tell the whole story.

It is God who heals us. He is the one who gives us medical knowledge. He alone is responsible for the creation of our wonderful bodies, which can renew and replace injured cells. The Lord makes us well.

Out of God's great love for us, He heals our souls as well as our bodies. When we are sick in sin, He forgives us and grants healing to our injured heart and spirit. Through Jesus' victory over every evil, He gives us a joyful hope and a glorious future. One day there will be no crying or pain or death anymore.

PRAYER

Dear Lord, thank You for Your great work of healing. Please help us remember that You are our constant source of health—both physical and spiritual. Amen.

Susan Watermann Voss

EPIPHANY

Winners

1 Timothy 1:15–16

Jason and Nick arrived at the basketball game early to warm up. Their team, the Dukes, was undefeated.

"We'll crush 'em!" Jason yelled to Nick, grinning.

"No, we're gonna destroy 'em!" Nick hollered back, with a bounce pass to his friend. Jason dribbled up the court and laid one in. This game would be no problem.

No problem at all! The Dukes not only beat their opponents, but they left some kids on the other team with tears in their eyes.

As Nick was putting on his jacket, he overheard Sam, from the other team, talking to his mom. "That was embarrassing," Sam said. "I'll never play basketball again."

Jason ran over to Nick. "That was awesome!" he said.

Nick hesitated. "The guys on the other team seem pretty beat up about it."

Jason smirked. "Well, they are first and foremost losers, with a capital L."

"But one kid said he never wanted to play basketball again," Nick countered.

"That leaves more wins for us, dude," Jason said as he ran ahead.

Nick walked home alone. He was definitely excited to win. It felt great to make five baskets for his team, but he felt bad for the other kids.

He remembered a Bible verse he'd heard the week before at church, and then he caught up with Sam from the other team. "You guys played hard," Nick told Sam. "Bet you'll catch us next season. In the meantime, remember that you are a winner with Jesus. He has been merciful to sinful losers." Sam suddenly broke into a smile.

And Nick did too.

PRAYER

Lord Jesus, You have given me everything. I need Your love and forgiveness. Help me to remember that You mercifully saved me and made me a winner. In Your name I pray. Amen.

Julie Stiegemeyer

EPIPHANY

Friends Are Great

Ecclesiastes 4:9–12

There was an embarrassing hesitation as Ashley slid out of her chair and walked to Mrs. Kingston's desk. Ashley grabbed the packet, not even hearing what Mrs. Kingston said, and walked quickly back to her seat. She didn't even want to take a look as she placed the envelope deep in the pages of her science book. Ashley didn't want anyone to see her school pictures. They never turned out anyway. Her hair was always sticking out on one side, and her braces were shining back at the camera.

After school, Ashley and her friend Kristi sat by each other on the bus. "We got our pictures today," said Kristi. "I'll show you mine if you show me yours."

"Yours turned out great!" said Ashley. "My pictures are awful again this year. I always look so dumb."

"Come on, Ashley, you know I like you for who you are, not for what your school pictures look like," explained Kristi. "You're such a great friend. You listen when I'm grumpy. You help me with my homework, and I help you with yours. What I like best about you, Ashley, is that you cheer me up when I feel down. And when we get in an argument, we forgive each other."

Good friends are a special blessing God gives us. Think of how your friends help you. Think about ways you show you're a friend to others. Think of ways you can show your thankfulness for friends. Think of something special a friend has done for you recently.

Thank God for the loving gift of friends. Thank Him especially for Jesus, the friend of sinners, who laid down His life to give us life and salvation.

PRAYER

Thank You, dear Jesus, for the loving gift of friends. Help me be a friend by reaching out to others. Thank You for befriending me and saving me from my sins and eternal death by dying on the cross. In Your name I pray. Amen.

Linda Mueller Gillam

EPIPHANY

Whiter than Snow

Psalm 51:7–9

"Hey, everybody! Get up!" Andy yelled at his family.

"Is everything okay?" Mother asked as she rubbed her eyes and tied her robe.

"Look at the snow!" exclaimed Andy as he stood at the front window. "It's so bright that it almost hurts my eyes."

All the commotion woke up the whole family. "What's going on?" Father asked. "Is something wrong?"

"I'd say that something is right, not wrong," Mother explained. "Look at the new snowfall."

During the night a blanket of snow had covered the neighborhood. The tracks in the old snow and the mud from the cars had disappeared. Everything looked clean and fresh.

Snow can make a messy scene look new. The Bible tells us that when Jesus washes away our sins, we become whiter than snow (Psalm 51:7). In our Baptism, Jesus' sacrifice washes away our messy sin and grants us the newness of forgiveness and life eternal.

When cars start driving in the snow and people start walking in it, the landscape becomes dirty again. When we daily sin, we can remember our Baptism and its blessings. We can daily and richly receive God's forgiveness. We can daily wake up with joy. We are made whiter than snow, clean and fresh.

PRAYER

Dear Jesus, please forgive me when I sin against my family, friends, and neighbors. Help me to forgive them when they sin against me. In Your name I pray. Amen.

Darla Rosendahl

How We're like Manatees

Isaiah 53:3–5

Have you ever heard of a manatee? A manatee, or sea cow, is a large mammal that lives in water. It can be observed in the Gulf of Mexico, off the coast of Florida, and in the West Indies.

Manatees are thick-skinned. They grow to be 1,200–1,500 pounds and ten feet long. They have no back legs, but they use their broad tails to swim. Manatees are slow, harmless, and defenseless. In many areas, they are protected by law.

People who protect manatees have a unique way to keep track of them. They identify each manatee by the size and number of scars on its back. Being defenseless and slow, these creatures are often wounded by the propellers of motorized boats.

People have scars too. Often we think we're so strong that we can't be hurt. But careless words or unkind actions hurt us. Sometimes we wound others by what we say or do. Sin causes the wounds of this world.

Jesus is our protector and defender. He came to earth and suffered hatred and death on the cross in our place. He forgives the wounds we have caused. He also heals us. Jesus knows the pain we are going through. The scars on His hands, feet, and side prove His great love for us.

Because God loves us, we can reflect His love to others. We can identify with persons who have the same scars or problems that we have. The Holy Spirit gives us God's Word to help people whose wounds are hurting.

PRAYER

Dear Lord, by Your wounds I am healed. Thank You for loving me and caring about me. Amen.

Carol Delph

EPIPHANY

The Best Phone Service

Jeremiah 33:1–3

More minutes. Cheaper rates. An extra phone. Telephone companies spend millions of dollars on television commercials. They want to catch our attention and convince us to switch to them. The choices can be confusing. Each company insists that the product they have is best. How do we know whose words to believe and trust?

Have you heard of God's long-distance plan? It's called prayer. There isn't an 800 number to call. You won't be put on hold or have to use voice-mail. "Call waiting" is never used, and you won't hear a busy signal. God is always at home, ready to receive your call. The Bible is filled with His advertisements. Jeremiah 33:3 is one such notice: "Call to Me and I will answer you."

We often forget to use God's prayer line. We get sidetracked with other concerns and forget the wonderful power of God. That's why the Bible is filled with His prayer reminders. God invites and invites. We can trust Him and His promises.

Throughout the Bible, we see God's gift of prayer used. Moses asked for food in the wilderness, and God provided. Hannah asked God for a child. God blessed her with a boy named Samuel. Solomon prayed to the Lord when the temple was finished and requested God's blessings.

Today's telephone companies may offer great plans, but God's plan can't be beat. He gives us an open line of communication, twenty-four hours a day. We can come to Him at any time because Jesus opened the way for us with His sacrificial death and His glorious resurrection.

PRAYER

Dear God, help me remember Your gift of prayer at all times. In the name of Jesus, through whom I can freely approach You, I pray. Amen.

Julie Dietrich

EPIPHANY

Tell It like It Is

1 Kings 22:6–8

James sneaked through the door, put his books on the table, and tip-toed to his room. He was trying to delay talking to Mom as long as possible. James knew Mom would want to know how he'd done on his big test. How could he tell her he'd really bombed?

James couldn't blame anyone or anything but himself—he had played video games instead of studying. That was not what Mom wanted to hear! Sometimes it's really tough to "tell it like it is." We'd rather "tell it like we *wish* it was." Or maybe "tell it like someone wants to hear it."

Israel's King Ahab wasn't obedient to God. He used false prophets to predict the outcomes of his battles. Many of these prophets, to please Ahab, simply said what he wanted to hear.

One time, Ahab and the king of Judah, who obeyed God, were joining forces in a battle. The king of Judah wanted to call in a prophet of God. So Micaiah was called, even though Ahab hated him because "he never prophesies good concerning me, but evil" (1 Kings 22:8).

Micaiah told it like it was even though it displeased Ahab. Micaiah prophesied Ahab's defeat if he went to battle. Disregarding Micaiah's words, Ahab fought—and was killed.

We can't always tell if people are being completely honest. But we never need to worry about God. He always "tells it like it is." God tells us we're sinners and deserve to be punished. But He also tells us that He "so loved the world, that He gave His only Son, that whoever believes in Him should not perish but have eternal life" (John 3:16).

PRAYER

Dear God, thanks for always being completely honest and for sparing me from Your just punishment. Help me "tell it like it is" and be honest in all I say and do. Amen.

Jeanette A. Dahl

EPIPHANY

A Prayer for Patience

Romans 15:1–6

Peter overheard his mother praying, "And give me patience, Lord. I know You have been patient with me."

Peter had never really thought about God being patient. But when he heard his mother's words, he knew it must be true. Peter's mother was asking for help to be patient with Peter and his brothers and sisters. And the reason she prayed for this gift was that God had been patient with her.

God has always been patient with people. Adam and Even returned God's love for them by disobeying Him. But instead of destroying Adam and Eve as they deserved, God promised them a Savior.

God was patient with the people of Israel too. When they were in the wilderness, they often complained. They worried about their needs, even though God miraculously provided for them again and again. The children of Israel even worshiped false gods. Still God looked after them, and one day He sent His Son, Jesus, to die for them and the whole world.

When St. Paul was a young man, he persecuted the Church by putting Christians in jail. But God was patient with Paul. And by His grace, Paul became the greatest missionary who ever lived.

God is patient with us too. He does not punish us for our many sins against Him but forgives us again and again for Jesus' sake. The Bible says, "The Lord . . . [is] patient toward you, not wishing that any should perish, but that all should reach repentance" (2 Peter 3:9).

God also wants us to be patient with others. That's why the Bible tells us, "The fruit of the Spirit . . . [is] patience" (Galatians 5:22).

Peter was glad to hear his mother asking God for patience. Before he went to sleep, he thanked God for His love and for giving him patient parents. Then Peter, too, prayed, "And give me patience, Lord."

PRAYER

You, O Lord, are a God of patience. Thank You. Forgive me for my sins of impatience, and help me to be patient with others. In Jesus' name I pray. Amen.

Victor Constien

EPIPHANY

World Famous

Exodus 9:13–16

Few people are so famous that their names are recognized all over the world. Can you name any world-famous people? You may think of Prince Charles, Pope John Paul II, or Billy Graham. What makes these people so famous? Is it only their names?

Years ago, six-year-old Diane Disney rushed home from school bubbling with excitement. Eagerly she ran to her daddy, asking, "Are you Walt Disney?"

Laughing, her daddy reminded her that she knew his name.

"But *the* Walt Disney?" Diane persisted.

Diane's friends had been discussing Walt Disney movies. She loved those movies too, but had never connected them with her father. To her he was "Daddy." Now recognizing him for what he did, Diane surprised her father by asking for his autograph.

The Bible overflows with stories about God's loving actions for His people. We see His power shown again and again as He saves His people from disasters and enemies. Can you tell about some of those rescues? Have you ever recognized this hero God as *your heavenly Father?*

God has rescued the whole world from sin and eternal death. That's why He wants His name to be "proclaimed in all the earth" (Exodus 9:16). All that a person *is* and *does* is wrapped up in his or her name. Think of the power of Jesus' name! Acts 4:12 says, "There is no other name under heaven given among men by which we must be saved." Let's spread that holy name!

PRAYER

Heavenly Father, sometimes I forget You are my Father. Thanks for making me Your child and sending Your Son, Jesus, to rescue me from sin and death. Help me spread Your name and the name of Jesus so that others may have salvation. Amen.

Barbara A. Martin

EPIPHANY

Never Too Old for Milk

1 Peter 2:1–3

"I think I'm getting too old for Sunday School," Barry announced one Saturday night. The day before, he had celebrated his twelfth birthday. "Sunday School is okay for little kids," Barry said. "But I'm no baby anymore. I'll just stay home tomorrow morning."

Barry's dad sat down on the couch where his son was sprawled out. "You really *are* a baby, you know," he said.

Barry sat straight up. "What do you mean, a baby? I'm twelve years old!"

"Sure," said his father, "but in God's eyes, you and Pat and Mom and I are still babies."

During devotions that evening, Barry learned what his dad meant. This was the Bible verse they read: "Like newborn infants, long for the pure spiritual milk, that by it you may grow up to salvation" (1 Peter 2:2).

"That's why Dad and I go to Bible class on Sundays," said Barry's mother. "We're thirsty for God's Word, just as baby Timmy is thirsty for his milk."

Barry looked over at Timmy in his mother's arms, eagerly sucking his bottle. He could see now what God meant by "longing for the pure spiritual milk."

The next morning, Barry was ready for Sunday School earlier than usual. He was looking forward to the church service too. He wanted to be a growing Christian "baby."

We're never too old for the milk God gives us. We are His children through our second birth in Holy Baptism. And by the milk of His Word, God feeds our faith in Jesus. Let's take our milk gladly, so we may "grow up to salvation."

PRAYER

Dear Father, thank You for my new birth in Baptism. Help me to long for the milk You give me through my parents, teachers, and pastor, that I may be a growing Christian. For my Savior's sake I ask it. Amen.

Kenneth Kausch

Do You Understand?

Acts 8:26–35

Draw a capital O on top of the curve of a lower case *h*. Then place a small capital M on top of the capital O. Finish with a small sideways *s* in the center of the capital O. What do you have?

"A big mess!" Shelly crumpled the paper and tossed it into the trash can.

"What's wrong, dear?" her mother asked.

"Oh, it's this puzzle. I just can't do it. I need someone to explain it to me."

Her mother walked over to Shelley's desk, picked up the wad of paper, and smoothed it out. "Let's see what we have here. Hmmm. Look, Shelley, here's how it works." Mother showed her that the puzzle was a cat sitting on a chair.

Do you sometimes read something but have no idea what it means? You're not alone.

The Ethiopian man in today's Bible reading couldn't understand the Bible. But what did God do? He sent Philip to help the Ethiopian. Philip sat with him and explained the Scriptures. He told him how Jesus was sent to suffer, die, and live again for all people. That includes each of us.

God gives us His Spirit to help us understand His Word. But does God give us people to help us when we have trouble understanding Scripture? Yes, all the time. He gives us parents, pastors, and teachers. They share the Gospel with us and lead us to a better understanding of His Word. God blesses us through them in the same way that He blessed the Ethiopian through Philip.

PRAYER

Heavenly Father, thank You for sending Your Son to be our Savior. Thank You also for the gift of parents, pastors, and teachers who nurture us in the Christian faith. In Jesus' name. Amen.

Carla Fast

EPIPHANY

The Lost Hamster

Luke 15:3–7

Dawn was allowed to take the fifth grade's pet hamster out of his cage and play with him on the floor. She stroked Edward's soft fur with her fingers.

Dawn looked up to watch Mr. Bode explain a math problem. She gasped as she turned back and saw Edward disappear under a cabinet. Dawn crawled to the cabinet and found a small, round hole where the wood met the floor. Edward was gone.

Dawn's face was white when she told Mr. Bode what had happened. Lindsey jumped up to close the door. Daryl suggested that everyone pray. He prayed, "Dear God, please bring Edward back to us." For the first time in history, the fifth grade voted to skip recess. If Edward came out while they were outside, they might miss him.

Manuel suggested that they put food from their lunches around the hole. Edward might smell it and come out. Grant broke a banana into pieces. Blair crumbled up pieces of cheese. Brenda brought potato chips, and Jonah spread his fruit roll in a flat circle in front of the hole. The class gathered around the hole and waited.

Five minutes went by. Then Edward's whiskers quivered as he peeked out. The class froze while Mr. Bode grabbed him and put him into his cage. Then they broke into loud cheers: "Edward's back!" Grant taped a piece of cardboard over the hole, and Blair scooped all the crumbs into Edward's cage so he could have a picnic. Mr. Bode declared an extra recess to celebrate, with Edward coming along in his cage.

When we sin, we run away from God. We get lost just like that foolish hamster. Then God works in us to make us feel sorry for the sin. He tells us that His Son came to seek and save the lost. When we repent, God and His angels cheer more loudly than Dawn's class.

Confess the sins that you have done today. Ask God to forgive you.

PRAYER

Dear God, thank You so much for sending Jesus to die for my sins. Please forgive me and help me live as Your child. In Jesus' name. Amen.

Ruth Geisler

EPIPHANY

Invisible Protection

Psalm 34:7–10

The prophet Elisha was in trouble. The king of Syria was very angry with him. When the king found out that Elisha was in the city of Dothan, he sent horses, chariots, and soldiers to capture him. Elisha wasn't worried, but his young servant was. When Elisha's servant saw the king's soldiers surround the city, he hurried to Elisha. "What can we do?" he pleaded.

Elisha answered, "Do not be afraid, for those who are with us are more than those who are with them" (2 Kings 6:16).

This must have seemed odd to the servant, for he saw no one around. He was still afraid.

Elisha asked God to open the eyes of this young man so that he could see the protection God had placed around them. God did just as Elisha had prayed. What a thrill it must have been for the young servant! He looked around and saw the mountain full of horses and chariots of fire. Now the servant knew that he and Elisha were safe (v. 17).

We can be sure of God's protection too. The Bible promises, "The angel of the LORD encamps around those who fear Him, and delivers them" (Psalm 34:7).

In his Morning and Evening prayers, Martin Luther prayed, "Let Your holy angel be with me, that the evil foe may have no power over me." We can say this prayer too, knowing that God will hear us. He will send His angels to take care of us who love Him and trust Him.

PRAYER

I thank You, my heavenly Father, through Jesus Christ, Your dear Son, that You have graciously kept me this day; and I pray that You would forgive me all my sins where I have done wrong, and graciously keep me this night. For into Your hands I commend myself, my body and soul, and all things. Let Your holy angel be with me, that the evil foe may have no power over me. Amen. (Luther's Evening Prayer)

Martin Wessler

Not Dead, Just Sleeping

1 Thessalonians 4:13–18

Have you ever looked closely at the bare trees, the empty bushes, and the brown grass in wintertime? They look dead, don't they?

But you know they are really only sleeping. Spring will change things. When God sends His rain and His warm weather, these dead-looking fields and trees will come to life. Bare branches will sprout new leaves. Empty bushes will burst forth with beautiful blossoms. The brown grass will turn green.

And so it is when people die. We look at a body in the coffin, and we wonder how life could ever come back to it. It seems dead for good.

But the Bible says that death is just like falling asleep. Someday God will come again and bring back life to our dead-looking bodies. And we who trust in Jesus Christ and have His forgiveness and love will live with Him forever.

How can we be sure of this? We can be absolutely sure of it because Jesus rose from the dead on the third day after He was crucified. Because Jesus, our Savior, rose from the dead, we shall rise too. This is what Paul says in his First Letter to the Thessalonian Christians:

"For since we believe that Jesus died and rose again, even so, through Jesus, God will bring with Him those who have fallen asleep" (1 Thessalonians 4:14).

What a promise! This is really something to look forward to!

PRAYER

Lord God, we praise You for raising Jesus from the dead. Now we know that we also shall someday rise from the dead. Help us not to be afraid of death. Through faith, help us to look forward to our life with You forever. In the name of our risen Savior we ask it. Amen.

Joseph Ellwanger

EPIPHANY

Who's In Charge?

John 19:10–11

Perhaps you've learned this old saying:
Thirty days hath September,
April, June, and November;
All the rest have thirty-one,
Excepting February alone,
Which hath but twenty-eight in fine,
Till leap year gives it twenty-nine.

But do you know that February used to have thirty days? Julius Caesar, a famous Roman emperor, took one day from February and added it to the month named for him, July. Augustus Caesar, another Roman emperor, took a second day from February and added it to the month named for him, August. Julius and Augustus Caesar were important and powerful men.

There are other persons in history who felt powerful and important. The pharaoh of Egypt believed he had control over God's people. But it was really God who was in charge. God used the pharaoh to save His people in a time of famine. God showed how powerful He was when He decided it was time for His people to return to the land He had promised them. The Lord sent ten plagues upon the Egyptians to force them to set His people free.

God also showed He was in charge when His Son, Jesus, was on trial before Pilate. Jesus' enemies were pressuring Pilate to sentence Him to death. Pilate told Jesus, "Remember, I have authority to release You and authority to crucify You." But Jesus told Pilate that His Father was really in charge.

God used Pilate to complete His plan to save the world from sin, death, and eternal punishment. It was necessary that Jesus suffer and die for the sins of the world. It was necessary for our salvation. God planned for His Son's death so we could live with Him.

PRAYER

Thank You, God, for times when You have shown You are in charge in my life. Help me always to trust in You. In Jesus' name. Amen.

Judy Williams

EPIPHANY

The Wolf and the Lamb

Isaiah 11:1–9

Since it was Groundhog Day, Ms. Krause had explained about groundhogs, shadows, and the coming of spring. When she asked if anyone had ever seen a groundhog, Sophie told all about her trip to the zoo. Then Ethan raised his hand and started talking about his new puppy. Ethan always talked about his puppy. And Juliet always got tears in her eyes.

The class enjoyed their religion class, but they couldn't wait until "Q-Time." Ms. Krause let them write their questions, and one was answered every afternoon before the end of school.

At "Q-Time" Ms. Krause took the top slip out of the box. She read out loud, "Do pets go to heaven?" Everybody thought it was Juliet's question, because three weeks ago, her dog had died from cancer.

Ms. Krause thought for a minute. Then she said, "We don't know exactly what our next life will be like. God did create animals and said, 'It is good.' Sin ruined life for everything, even pets. The Bible says that 'all creation groans' when it talks about how we want Jesus to come back. Pets may not have souls, but Isaiah says that in the place where Jesus rules, the wolf and the lamb and the leopard and the goat and the calf and the lion and the child will all live peacefully together. It is possible that animals will be in our next life. Whether they are or not, God will wipe away all of our tears, and we will never, ever be sad. That's the gift God gives through faith in Jesus, our Savior!"

PRAYER

Dear God, thanks for giving us pets to love and enjoy. Help us to take good care of them. In Jesus' name. Amen.

James Gimbel

EPIPHANY
The Presentation of Our Lord

Nothing to Fear

Luke 2:25–32

We don't know how often Simeon thought about his death. But whenever he did, he remembered the promise from the Holy Spirit that he wouldn't die until he had seen the Savior. Having seen Jesus, Simeon was ready to die. He asked God to take him peacefully to heaven.

Unless Jesus comes first to bring an end to the world, we, too, will die. Like most of us, a boy named Paul Adams never thought much about death. But when he was in fifth grade, something happened that made death seem real to him. Paul was in a cemetery helping his grandmother clean around his grandfather's grave. A tombstone nearby caught Paul's attention. He was stunned to see his own name written as follows:

ASLEEP IN JESUS

PAUL ADAMS

1882–1893

Paul's grandmother explained that the boy buried there was a cousin of his grandfather's who had died when he was about Paul's age. The fact that they had the same name was by chance. Paul has never forgotten the tombstone with his name on it. It reminds him that he, like the first Paul Adams, will die. But the thought of dying doesn't make him afraid, because he is a Christian.

Death holds nothing for a child of God to fear. Like Simeon of old, Christians who think about death are comforted by a promise from God. Jesus' words in John 14:1–3 are meant for us too: "Let not your hearts be troubled. Believe in God; believe also in Me. In My Father's house are many rooms. If it were not so, would I have told you that I go to prepare a place for you? And if I go and prepare a place for you, I will come again and will take you to Myself, that where I am you may be also."

Like Simeon, someday we will see our Savior face-to-face. And we will live with Him in heaven forever!

PRAYER

Dear Jesus, thank You for winning over death through Your resurrection from the dead. Help us not to be afraid to die but to remember that You are always with us. Amen.

Rodney Rathmann

EPIPHANY

Thanks and Laughter

1 Peter 1:3–9

Mazie was 85 years old when we met her. Her health was failing. She didn't get out much. Her tiny home was falling apart. Her husband had been dead for twenty years, and she had even lived long enough to see several of her children die. By most standards, she had a lot to complain about.

Despite what some may view as hardship, Mazie was known for her laughter. In fact, Mazie's joyful spirit was so infectious that wherever she went, she was the center of attention. No one could laugh like Mazie. She shook herself and the rafters with her laughter. When something struck her as funny, Mazie would begin to laugh. Then the children would laugh. Soon the adults would join in, and the room would shake with gales of laughter.

"How do you do it, Mazie?" I asked her. "How do you find it in yourself to laugh all the time?"

She smiled and laughed a little. "Easy," she said. "I have a choice each morning. Either I can keep the day to myself and worry my way through, or I can give it away through laughter. Since God has given me the day, I don't have to solve all the world's problems. I just want to celebrate. 'Thank You, God,' I say. And then I laugh."

Our journey to the cross can seem quite sorrowful at times. Jesus' death reminds us that God takes our sins very seriously. But the journey to the cross ends at the empty tomb, and we celebrate the joyful news of the resurrection. God's greatest gift is salvation, and we have great joy in that. Even as we look toward the season of Lent, we can say, "Thank You, God"—and laugh.

PRAYER

Lord, remind me of the gift of joy You have for me in Jesus, my Redeemer and Savior, so that I can share that joy through my laughter. Amen.

Ted Schroeder

EPIPHANY

On Top of the World

Mark 9:2–5

Can you remember a time when you felt so good about something that you wished it would never end? Perhaps you felt on top of the world when you brought home a good report card from school. Or maybe you were very popular with your friends and had a lot of fun together. Or perhaps it was the time your team won first place.

I'm sure Peter felt that way when he saw Jesus show His heavenly brightness for a few moments. Peter was so amazed that right then and there, he wanted to build three tents. Peter wished this event could last forever, but this mountaintop experience had to end. Peter and the rest of the disciples had to come down from the mountain.

So it is with us. Our personal mountaintop experiences will come to an end. Perhaps you've heard the phrase "When you are number one, there is no other way to go except down." When we feel on top of the world, we know the feeling won't last. We have to return to our normal life, which may include sadness, discouragement, and even tears.

But even though we do have our ups and downs, we have a final victory in Christ. The mountain of the transfiguration ultimately led Jesus Christ to another mountain called Calvary. There He made it possible for all of us to have the greatest mountaintop experience of them all, life with God now and forever.

PRAYER

Lord, thank You for permitting us to have times in our lives when we feel on top of the world. When things seem to turn for the worse, help us remember that we always have our greatest joy in living with You. Amen.

Carl Kramer

EPIPHANY
Transfiguration

Meet Zacchaeus

Luke 19:1–10

Zacchaeus–you either love him or hate him. He may be like someone in your class. In Jesus' day, most people hated him, and he gave them plenty of reasons.

Zacchaeus collected taxes for the government. In itself, that wasn't a bad job; somebody had to do it. The problem came when Zacchaeus collected more taxes than what people owed. He kept the extra for himself. He probably had several other bad habits too. In your case, he might be like the worst-behaved kid in your class.

Lots of important people were in a crowd waiting to see Jesus. Zacchaeus was too short to see over the crowd, so he climbed a tree. Many people in the crowd thought they were good. They fooled themselves into thinking that they obeyed all of God's laws. Many people thought they were better than Zacchaeus. They thought that Jesus should pay attention to them.

Jesus surprised them. He looked up and saw Zacchaeus in the tree. He told Zacchaeus to come down. They were going to have lunch together! The crowd was angry. They didn't think Jesus should eat with a cheating tax collector!

The great thing about Jesus is that He came to save sinners. Jesus wanted to know sinners like Zacchaeus. He wanted sinners to know Him.

Jesus wants to be with you too. You might not be as sinful as Zacchaeus, or you might be worse! It doesn't matter. Jesus wants to be with you. In His Word and in Baptism, He promises to be with you and forgive you. He died to take away your sins. He listens when you say you're sorry for your sins and gives you power to resist sin.

PRAYER

Lord Jesus, thank You for coming to save sinners. Thank You for coming to save me. Help me learn more about You as I read the Bible. Amen.

Edward Grube

God Loves Me

1 John 3:1–3

Curtis was scanning the night sky with his telescope. He tried counting the stars, but there were too many. There must be millions of enormous and very bright stars in the universe, he thought.

Curtis had read that the sun is actually a star, so large that it can hold more than a million earths.

Then Curtis remembered the Bible section from his family's evening devotions. "When I look at Your heavens, the work of Your fingers, the moon and the stars, which You have set in place, what is man that You are mindful of him . . . ? Yet You have made him a little lower than the heavenly beings and crowned him with glory and honor" (Psalm 8:3–5).

And Curtis thought, God made the stars shine so brightly, giving each star its own place in the sky. He made the sun to give us light and heat for a long time. And He made the earth just right for us to live on. Curtis thought about how big the universe is and how small he was compared to it. He said, "We don't get much taller than seven feet, and most of us don't last 1,000 years, and we sin a lot. But God loves us anyway. He loved us enough to send His Son to die on the cross. I bet His love fills the whole universe!"

Curtis went to bed happy. He knew his Father in heaven had made a beautiful world and that he was God's child. He also knew that God saw him, no matter how small he was. Best of all, he knew that God loved him.

PRAYER

Dear God, thank You for a beautiful universe to look at. Thank You for sending Your Son into the world to make me Your child. Help me remember how much You love me. Amen.

Robin J. Williams

Power for Presidents

Philippians 4:13

Some time ago, a seventh grader came home with some good news: she was elected president of her class. Later on, her sixth-grade brother brought home a similar report: he, too, was elected president of his class.

Being a class president is not as important as being a national president. But to those children, their elections were just as exciting. Besides, they had new, challenging responsibilities to carry out.

Whether we become president of a class or a country, or a friend simply looks to us for leadership and guidance, we have an important responsibility. Even if we are followers rather than leaders, our lives still influence those around us. And that is a responsibility.

When we think about responsible work, we may be afraid of making mistakes. We might even think that if we avoid the work, we can also avoid the mistakes. But we don't have to be afraid of making mistakes. God has assured us that He will not hold our mistakes against us. Jesus is with us to give us courage, to guide us, and to help us. And with St. Paul we can confidently say, "I can do all things through Him who strengthens me."

PRAYER

Lord, because You have the responsibility for being my Savior and Lord, grant me the strength to carry out my responsibilities in Your name. Amen.

Edward Melchior

No Longer Guilty

Psalm 103:8–12

Long ago in American history, two young men had a fight over a girl they both loved. The fight ended when one man received a blow that sent him falling to the ground with a thud. Simon Kenton, the youth who delivered the final punch, listened frantically for his opponent's breath and heartbeat. He felt for a pulse, but the fallen man lay still on the ground, having no signs of life. In panic and despair, Simon Kenton fled to the frontier and changed his name. He tried to forget what he had done, but couldn't.

Through the years, Simon traveled continuously, fearing that someone would recognize him and turn him in to the authorities to pay for his crime. Yet, during this time, Simon taught pioneers how to survive in the wilderness so they could tame the land and build new homes. Serving as Indian scout, guide, and woodsman, he helped prepare the way for others.

After nine years, Simon met some settlers who came from his hometown. Eager for news of his family, he asked about the Kentons and inquired whether or not the lawmen were still looking for Simon Kenton, the murderer. To his amazement, Simon learned that the man with whom he had fought was still alive. He had merely been knocked unconscious. For Simon Kenton, nine years of living in constant fear and guilt were suddenly over.

Do you know how guilt feels—a tight sensation in your stomach and throat? Like Simon Kenton, all of us are sinners. All of us know the guilt and desperate feelings that result from sin.

But because of Jesus, we can feel the same relief and joy that Simon must have felt when he learned of his innocence. The suffering and death of Jesus have won innocence for us. The Savior has made us free of guilt, shame, and despair. John 8:36 proclaims, "If the Son sets you free, you will be free indeed." Jesus has paid for all of our sins. When we ask to be forgiven, our sins need trouble us no more. In the eyes of God, we are completely innocent. It is as though these sins never happened!

PRAYER

Heavenly Father, forgive my sins for Jesus' sake. Amen.

Rodney Rathmann

EPIPHANY

Shaping an Elephant

Job 10:8–12

One of my favorite pieces of furniture from Ghana is an elephant chair. It began as one big log. A craftsman saw the wood with his creative eyes. His hands began to work with tools. He chiseled the big log. Chip by chip, a form emerged. When the master craftsman was done, the log had become a unique elephant chair. With my eyes, I saw only a log. Through his master artist's eyes, he saw an elephant.

Today God is molding and shaping you. Perhaps He is teaching you lessons in patience. Maybe He is pushing you to study His Word and learn more about Him. He may be encouraging you to play an instrument or to write devotions. He may be shaping you to share the Good News of His love and salvation with people you will meet each day.

There is nothing in a log that turns it into an elephant. There is nothing in us that makes us beautiful or valuable. God alone declares us worthy through the death and resurrection of Jesus. He fashions us into a new shape, a new creation, clothed in His forgiveness and strengthened with His power.

Today is a good day to ask God to continue the shaping and molding that began in Baptism. Ask Him to make you a willing servant ready to do the vocation He has in mind for you. Thank Him for the blessings you receive as His dear child.

PRAYER

Dear Jesus, thank You for making me Your own. Please continue to mold and shape me so that I can be a good servant in Your kingdom. Amen.

Jeanette Groth

EPIPHANY

Love Others

John 13:34–35

Nicholas says, "I can't love David. He's a ball hog. He doesn't know the plays, and he never makes layups. And every time he gets the ball, he heads straight for the basket!"

Derek says, "I can't love Ryan. No matter how many times I try to explain what happened at recess, he refuses to listen."

Leah says, "I can't love Emma. I spent hours finishing my mosaic. Emma plopped her water bottle right on top of my artwork, and now it's ruined."

Nicholas, David, Derek, Ryan, Leah, and Emma are all in the same sixth grade. They are all Christians. In their classroom, there are problems. In their classroom, there are opportunities. In their classroom, God is helping them grow in friendship and understanding. They are growing with the help of God's Spirit to make problems into opportunities to love one another as Jesus loves.

It isn't easy to love those who hurt us. That's why Jesus showed us how to do it. He was selfless, understanding, and forgiving. He even became the perfect sacrifice for sinners.

We can't be perfect like Jesus was, but with God's help, we, the imperfect people, can love other imperfect people. And by this kind of love, others will know that we must be part of God's family.

PRAYER

Dear Jesus, You showed all people what love looks like. Help me to share Your kind of love. Amen.

Christine Ross

EPIPHANY

Do You Like to Read?

2 Timothy 3:14–17

Many stories are told about Abraham Lincoln. While some are true, some have been stretched over the years. A popular (and probably true) story about Lincoln concerns his schooling. Young Abe wanted an education, but he couldn't get to school regularly. He made up for this by doing a lot of reading at home. And to get the books to read, he often walked miles through the forests. It is said that his father even punished him for reading so much at night by the flickering light of a fireplace.

Do you like to read as much as Lincoln did? Perhaps you are thinking, Well, he had to do something to pass the time. There wasn't much excitement in those days—no TV, radio, stereo records, ball games. So what else could he do but read?

In our Bible reading, Paul wrote to Timothy, whose mother and grandmother taught him to love the Bible. Possibly your mother and father led you into the Bible too. I hope you love it as much as Paul and Timothy did. It's the best book ever, because through it, God brings us to faith in Christ Jesus, our Savior. And God's Spirit continues to work through it to keep us His, now and forever.

PRAYER

Dear Lord, You have given me the ability to get Your message from Your Word, the Bible. May Your Spirit always help me believe it and live it. Amen.

E. W. Lichtsinn

Hearts and Valentines

John 17:9–10, 20–23

As Karen was reading her valentines to her mother, she asked, "Why do all the valentines have hearts on them?"

"A heart is a symbol of love," her mother replied. "It's a pretty good symbol, because we couldn't live without a heart, and we wouldn't want to live without love. Everyone needs love just as much as they need a heart."

Karen hadn't thought of that. "Sometimes when I disobey you, I start worrying that you'll stop loving me, that you might not want me anymore. Mother, when you punish me, do you ever stop loving me?"

"No, Karen. You are mine, and I am yours."

"That almost sounds like a valentine greeting, Mother—'You are mine, and I am yours.'"

What Karen discovered about her mother's love is even truer of God's love. He says to us, "You are Mine." Even though we disobey Him often and deserve His punishment, He keeps on loving us, forgiving us, and claiming us for His own.

He also tells us, "I am yours." It sounds too good to be true that God gives Himself to us like that. But He does. He sent His Son to give His life to save ours. God has already sent us a far better valentine than we'll get on Valentine's Day. This valentine is cross-shaped, and we get the message:

"Be Mine, for I am yours."
With love,
God

PRAYER

Father, help me love You as You love me. And help me share Your valentine of love with everyone. Amen.

Joan Cole

EPIPHANY

No Longer Outcasts

Mark 1:40–42

Sheila felt as if she were about to cry. She had given valentines to the two most popular kids in the class. She wanted them to like her and be friends with her, but they hadn't given her a valentine. They hadn't even thanked her. They just ignored her. Sheila felt like an outcast. Just then, her friend Kim gave her a beautiful homemade valentine. Kim had written on it, "I'm so glad you're my friend!" This made Sheila feel much better. She knew she had a friend who cared about her. She realized that she wasn't an outcast after all.

The man in our Bible reading truly was an outcast. He had a skin disease, and the law said that he had to live apart from other people. No one would have dared to come near him for fear of catching his disease. He must have felt lonely and very unlovable. But Jesus showed His love for this man. He was willing to get close to him, talk to him, and even touch him. Best of all, Jesus healed him. Now this man could rejoin his family and his community. He was no longer an outcast.

Because of our sin, we are all outcasts from our heavenly Father. But Jesus is willing to get close to us and touch us. He healed us of our sinfulness by dying on the cross for us. Because of Jesus, we are no longer outcasts. Because of Jesus, we are the children of God, and He loves us very much and is glad to have us in His family.

PRAYER

Dear Jesus, thank You for being willing to come to me and heal me. Please keep me close to You and help me bring others to You. Amen.

Eunice Graham

Stormy Times

Luke 8:22–25

Let me tell you about the worst storm our family ever experienced.

Last summer, we went on a camping trip in the Land of Lincoln—Illinois. We spent the mornings seeing the sights and the afternoons swimming in the pool. One afternoon the skies turned black, so the camp closed the pool. The rain drove our family inside our camper trailer. The camper felt safe; we'd been rained on before. We zipped the windows shut and turned on the light.

My little brother and I played games. It rained harder, and we started counting seconds between the lightning and the thunder. Soon there was *no* time between them! The wind was blowing and howling.

We stopped playing and huddled close together when we weren't mopping up the water that was blowing into our camper. The wind got so strong that our camper began rocking and the canvas walls billowed like sails. Even Mom and Grandma were scared.

Mom said, "This trailer is rocking like a boat. Remember when Jesus and His disciples were on a boat in a storm? The disciples woke Him up because they were afraid, just like we are. Let's talk to Jesus."

We prayed and sang songs for a long time. When the storm had moved on, we looked out. The tents were flat on the ground. Broken tree limbs were everywhere. We were safe. Jesus stilled our storm and protected us, just as He did for His disciples.

There are other kinds of storms in life. There can be arguments, hard times, illnesses, and accidents. God promises to be with us and protect us at those stormy times.

PRAYER

Dear Jesus, thank You for all the times You have protected us. Please be with all people who are having stormy weather. Protect me from storms and from all kinds of harm and danger. Be with me when I'm afraid and wherever I go. Amen.

Elaine Dautenhahn Richter

EPIPHANY

Too Many Rocks

Isaiah 53:4–6

Dixon collected rocks. He had rocks in boxes, in his closet, and in the basement. He put his collection in shoe boxes, Christmas boxes, and even a cereal box.

His mom came in to clean his room. She smacked her toe on a pillow-case full of rocks. "Dixon!" she yelled. "Get rid of these rocks, now! Find a new home for all of them."

Dixon loaded his wagon with his boxes. He slung the pillowcase full of rocks over his shoulder. He tried to give his rocks to his best friend, Tim, but Tim had his own collection of bottle caps.

Dixon pulled the heavy wagon down the road. Soon he came to a small pond with a sign on the bank: "ROCKS WANTED." He guided his wagon through the weeds and over the bumpy ground until he came to the shore. There he saw a small pile of rocks that someone else had left. Dixon removed the lid from a shoe box and dumped the rocks on the bank. He continued until the rocks were gone. He noticed that pulling the wagon home was easier now that it was empty. Happily, he ran home with the wagon banging behind him.

Have you ever felt weighed down by the guilt of your sins? Sometimes we carry around our guilt, and it gets heavy. We don't know what to do with it. No one wants our guilt. Wait! There is someone who has taken away all our sins and guilt! Because of Jesus, we don't have to carry our load around. Jesus took all our sins on Himself when He died on the cross. We can rejoice because our wagon is empty too.

PRAYER

Father, thank You for the lightness we feel from having our load of guilt taken away. Amen.

Diana Lesire Brandmeyer

A Vast Future

2 Corinthians 4:16–18

The United States celebrates Presidents' Day, honoring especially Abraham Lincoln and George Washington. Washington led troops in the Revolutionary War and became the first U.S. president. Lincoln held the country together during the Civil War.

Both men struggled through hard times, trying to do what was best for the country and making difficult decisions without giving up. They knew they were working for a cause greater than themselves. Lincoln said, "The struggle of today is not altogether for today—it is for a vast future also."

The apostle Paul knew he was working for an even greater future. He endured prison, shipwreck, illness, and persecution, but he did not despair. He knew that God was with him. No matter how bad things got, Paul kept preaching. He told about Jesus' death on a cross to save humankind from its sin. He told about Jesus' victorious resurrection over death.

Paul knew that everything earthly is temporary, but everything godly is everlasting. He kept his focus on the big picture—eternal life in Christ.

Hard work and struggles come to everyone. What are your struggles today? Do you have problems at school or home? Do you have trouble with friends or enemies? Today's problems are temporary. God is with you to help you through them. As a believer in Jesus as Savior, you, too, can look forward to eternal life in Christ. You can survive today's struggles for a vast future.

PRAYER

Dear God, help me through my struggles as You helped Paul. Keep my focus on You and eternal life with Jesus. Amen.

Jane Heitman

EPIPHANY

The Trouble with Grumbling

Numbers 21:4–9

Do any of these complaints sound familiar to you? "I don't see why he had to give us such a long assignment." "Are we having hamburger again tonight?" "Why can't I stay up a little longer?"

Most of us are pretty good at grumbling. It may be such a habit with us that we do it without thinking. We may not even consider grumbling a sin. Yet it displeases God to hear us complain.

When the Israelites were traveling on their way to the Promised Land, God fed them every morning and evening with manna. At first, they were very thankful for this miraculous food. But after forty years of eating nothing but manna, the Israelites began to complain. But this grumbling of the Israelites and lack of trust in Him made God so unhappy that He sent fiery serpents among them, biting them, and causing many to die.

God doesn't send snakes to bite us every time we grumble about studying or having to go to bed or not getting to watch our TV program. Yet, when we grumble, we do suffer. We make ourselves even unhappier and more irritable than we were before. Worst of all, we forget for a moment how good God is and how most of these things we grumble about are His gifts, which He wants us to enjoy and be thankful for.

God gave the Israelites a way to be saved. He told Moses to place a bronze serpent on a pole in the middle of the camp. Whenever anyone was bitten by a serpent, he could look at the bronze serpent and live.

Jesus said that He Himself was like this bronze serpent of Moses. By being lifted up on the pole of the cross, Jesus took away the sin of grumbling and all our other sins and saved us from eternal death. This gives us a happiness that can outlast the annoyances and disappointments of daily life.

PRAYER

Lord Jesus, keep me from the sin of grumbling. Help me better appreciate all Your good gifts, especially the forgiveness of sins. Amen.

John Ellwanger

EPIPHANY

A Time to Help

Ecclesiastes 3:1–8

Jason stared out the window at the big snowflakes coming down. "It's not fair!" he said. "It's snowing again. I can't ride my bike or play ball. It's cold outside. There's nothing to do."

Jason's father came up behind him, giving him a big hug. "I know how you feel," he said. "It seems like many of the activities we enjoy during warmer months come to a standstill during the winter. I often feel like God made winter months to slow us down. Winter can be a time for us to slow down and think about others."

After thinking about this for a moment, Jason looked up at his father and asked, "Can you help me make a list of things to do?"

Just then they saw some squirrels scamper across the snowy lawn. Jason ran to get bread crusts to feed them. Before the afternoon was over, Jason and his father had made cocoa for their mail carrier, delivered groceries to their older neighbor, Mr. Grabowski, and chopped wood for another neighbor. They also took time to write a letter to Jason's grandparents and plant some seeds for an indoor garden.

At the end of the day, Jason's dad came into his bedroom to pray with him before he fell asleep. Together they thanked God for the snowy day and the time to do things together for others. As Jason's eyes closed, he was busily thinking about things to do the next day. He fell asleep with a smile on his face.

Christians enjoy helping others because we know how much God has done for us. Jesus loved us so much that He gave His life as a payment for our sins. We can serve Him by serving others.

PRAYER

Dear Lord, thank You for making winter a time for us to slow down. Help us think of others and share Your love with them. We ask this in Jesus' name. Amen.

Beth Firnhaber

EPIPHANY

Our Shepherd's Voice

John 10:1–5

When your mother calls you, you know who it is without seeing her. How? By her voice. And when your father calls, even in the dark, you answer, "Yes, Dad." You know it's your father by the sound of his voice.

When Jesus said "Mary!" on Easter, Mary knew Him right away. She knew it was the voice of her Friend and Savior.

Jesus knows us better than anyone else knows us. And we're not lost among the millions of people in the world, like a boy or girl getting lost in a crowd. The Bible says that Jesus, the Good Shepherd, "calls His own sheep by name" (John 10:3). He knows us, and He loves us even though we are sinful.

But do we listen gladly to His loving voice when He calls us? Jesus also said, "The sheep [of the Good Shepherd] hear His voice. . . . When He has brought out all His own, He goes before them, and the sheep follow Him, for they know His voice" (vv. 3–4). May the Holy Spirit help us follow our Shepherd and obey His voice every day!

I am Jesus' little lamb, Ever glad at heart I am;
For my Shepherd gently guides me,
Knows my need and well provides me,
Loves me ev'ry day the same, Even calls me by name. (*LSB* 740:1)

PRAYER

My Good Shepherd, please help me listen to Your voice as I study Your Word. Give me also the power to follow You and obey You. I ask this because I belong to You and I know You love me. Amen.

William Beck

Saying Good-bye

Matthew 20:17–19

"It's not fair," Lisa moaned. "Why does Toni have to move away? She's my best friend. She can't move away! I won't let her!"

Mrs. Li leaned against the kitchen counter. "I understand, Lisa. You're angry and frustrated. I know you're hurt. But you and I both know Toni and her parents have to move because of her dad's job."

"But, Mom!" Lisa cried. "She's the best friend I have in the world. What am I going to do?"

"Well," Mom said soothingly, "I know it will be hard. You two have lived next to each other since you were toddlers, gone to school together, played in Little League, spent nights together—everything. But Toni *has* to move. And you have to let her go."

Did you ever lose a best friend? It hurts when you know you may never see your buddy again. All you have are memories of the terrific times you've had together.

I think Jesus' friends felt that way too. He had told them two or three times, "I *must* go to Jerusalem to die." But they never really understood until it happened. And then Jesus was gone—dead. They were sad, angry, hurt, and confused, thinking they had nothing left but memories.

How surprised they must have been to discover that Jesus was alive again! The Friend they thought was gone forever was back again. Only then could He really help them understand. Jesus *had* to go to Jerusalem and die because that's what His Father wanted. That's how He would take all our sin and get rid of it forever. But that wasn't the end of Him. He became alive again so that He would live forever.

As our living Lord and Friend, He's said to each of us, "I am with you always" (Matthew 28:20). That's good news. We know we're forgiven, and our best Friend is always right here with us.

PRAYER

Jesus, how hard it must have been for You to go to the cross! As our loving Friend, heal our sadness when we lose someone we love. Remind us that You'll always be with us. Amen.

Richard A. Davenport

EPIPHANY

Crowned with Honor

Philippians 2:5–11

Today is the birthday of George Washington. He was America's first president and the commander of the colonial army during the Revolutionary War. Most of us have learned about Washington's bravery and his leadership during the severe winter campout at Valley Forge. The men went for months on very little food, worn-out boots, and a lack of proper clothing and shelter. Many soldiers became sick and died.

What many people do *not* know is that while the soldiers were huddling together for warmth in small, open huts, General Washington was living comfortably in a nearby farmhouse with plenty of food and warm clothing. His life during that winter was far from equal to that of his men. He was treated like a king.

Our Bible reading says that when Jesus came to earth, He left glory behind. He humbled Himself to become one of us. He was born into a poor family. He never owned a house or a donkey. His life ended in a cruel death. Yet the Bible tells us that the risen Jesus was received back into heaven with all glory and honor. All creatures in heaven and on earth will someday bow to Him.

Because we are part of God's family, we, too, will share in His glory in heaven. It makes no difference how famous or infamous, how loved or unloved we are on earth. Because of Jesus' redemption, we who believe in Him will become heirs of His kingdom. Isn't that an exciting thought?

PRAYER

Glory be to Jesus,
Who in bitter pains
Poured for me the lifeblood
From His sacred veins! Amen. (*LSB* 433:1)

Beth Firnhaber

EPIPHANY

Shelter from Storms

Isaiah 41:10

Mom checked the weather outside. The sky was filled with dark clouds. The announcer on the radio said, "The winter storm appearing from the northwest is developing faster than expected. We have a severe-weather warning. School buses have left early. All parents are asked to be on the alert and watch for their children."

Mom kept watching for the bus, but it was nowhere in sight. She thought of her three children—Jake and John, the twins, and little Susan. "Please, dear God," she prayed, "take care of them and help them get home safely." The winds and snow grew steadily worse. The radio blurted out the same message over and over. Mom paced the floor and kept praying.

It seemed hours before she noticed the faint outline of the bus moving slowly through the blowing snow. But sure enough, there it was. She grabbed her coat and went out to help the children. They put their arms around one another, and together they made it to the door of the house. As they were stomping the snow off their feet, Jake looked up at his mother and said, "Boy, is it great to have a nice warm house to come home to!"

In our lives, sudden and severe storms often arrive unexpectedly. We feel worried and frightened. Isn't it wonderful that we have a God who shelters and protects us with His love? "Fear not," He tells us, "for I am with you; be not dismayed, for I am your God."

PRAYER

Heavenly Father, thank You for being with me every day. Thanks especially for being close in times of trouble. Help me look to Jesus, my Savior, for rescue from all evil. Amen.

Dorothy J. Haggstrom

EPIPHANY

George's Way?

Isaiah 43:25

How many Curious George books have you read? Many children enjoy his adventures. The stories follow the same basic steps: George finds himself in a new situation; George becomes curious; George does something he isn't supposed to do. Then, just as he is about to get into big trouble, he manages to do something good. Suddenly he becomes a hero. People forget the trouble he caused.

Have you ever followed the "George plan"? When you think you may get into trouble, do you try to do some extra nice things? Do you hope that doing something good can make up for your sin?

This may work for Curious George, but it doesn't work for God and us. No matter how many good things we do, we can never do enough to make up for our sins. Doing something wonderful never makes God forget that we sin.

In fact, there is only one thing that makes God forget and forgive the wrong we have done. Do you know what it is? It is Jesus' death and resurrection. Because of Jesus, God forgives and forgets every one of our sins. Jesus *did* do enough to make up for our sins. He lived a perfect life and died to take our punishment. He rose from the dead and lives forever.

Next time you feel like trying Curious George's way of getting out of trouble, don't! Instead, remember that Jesus is the way. He is our hero. In Baptism and through God's Word, His forgiveness and new life are ours.

PRAYER

Dear Jesus, thank You for taking the punishment for my sins. Thank You for not keeping track of all the wrong things I do. Help me to forgive others freely. Thank You for the promise of the gift of eternal life. Amen.

Lisa Hahn

Break-fast

Jonah 3:3–10

To *fast* means "not to eat." Every morning, we break the fast of our sleeping hours. We eat breakfast. Nutritionists tell us not to skip breakfast. Some call it the most important meal of the day.

The Old Testament people of God fasted and prayed in times of trouble. God sent Jonah to tell the people of Nineveh to repent. Their city would be destroyed in forty days because of their sin. The Ninevites believed God. The king of Nineveh ordered the people not to eat or drink and to wear sackcloth as a sign of repentance.

The Ninevites knew they deserved God's wrath. They prayed for God's mercy. God saw their repentant hearts and heard their prayers. He had compassion on them and spared them and their city.

God's Holy Word convinces us we have sinned. He calls us to repentance. Christ paid for our sin on Calvary's cross. He rose to tell us about His victory over sin, death, and the grave. He gives us His Word of forgiveness in Holy Baptism.

Instead of God's wrath, we have been shown God's great mercy. We rejoice in God's compassion, goodness, and love given to us for Christ's sake.

PRAYER

Lord, convince me of the sins I commit but cannot see. Help me to repent and live as Your forgiven child for Jesus' sake. Amen.

Carol Delph

Life Goes On

John 11:17–27

I knew something was the matter when Dad came home, looking upset. He said that a friend named Pat had to have an operation. The doctor said he had a growth on one of his kidneys and that it was probably cancer. I was surprised. I liked to ride my bike over to Pat's house to see him and his family. He hadn't seemed sick the last time I saw him.

After the operation, the doctor said he couldn't get all the cancer. Pat had only six months to live. I felt sad; Pat's wife and two little boys would really miss him. I wondered what Pat would do before he died. After I thought about it for a while, I decided he would thank God he would go to heaven when he died.

I told this to Mom. She and I both felt bad about Pat. Mom told me that Jesus had a friend named Lazarus who became sick and died. We read the story in the Bible together. After Lazarus died, Jesus told his sister Martha that Lazarus would rise again. Martha knew that Lazarus would come to life on the Last Day. Jesus promised that people who believe in Him will never die. He also made Lazarus come alive that very day.

I'm sure Pat will be with Jesus in heaven. I guess that's why when Christians get sick and die, we are happy and sad at the same time. We're sad because we miss them, but we're happy because we know they're with our Savior in heaven.

PRAYER

Dear Jesus, thank You for coming to bring us life forever. Give us a happy heart whenever we think about being with You always. Amen.

Judy Williams

All Will Be Different!

Revelation 21:1–5

Michael's team had just finished their warm-ups, and the big baseball game was about to start. Michael took off his glasses and laid them on the bench while he wiped the sweat off his forehead.

Whomp! Someone threw a heavy bag of bats on the bench, smashing his glasses into little pieces. "No!" Michael yelled as he rescued the pieces from under the bag. Tears ran down his face as he realized he couldn't even *see* the ball without his glasses, much less hit it.

Everyone has sad times like this—and even worse ones. Grandparents die, parents divorce, bikes are stolen, and people get hurt. Life will not always be this way. Jesus Christ has changed everything. There will be no more crying or pain when Jesus comes again. All these "old" things will be gone forever.

In heaven, there will not be glasses or braces. There won't be fights or divorces. Funerals will be a thing of the past. Everything will be different because Jesus died on the cross to take away sin and give us eternal life. He rose from the dead to proclaim victory over sin, death, and the power of the devil. We can feel God's comfort even when sad things happen, knowing that Christ helps us and will soon end all pain and problems.

PRAYER

Heavenly Father, thank You for sending Jesus, who gives me hope in the middle of problems and who promises to come again to take away all pain and problems. In His name. Amen.

John Juedes

EPIPHANY

Spelling Bee

Matthew 5:48

"Christine, it's your turn to spell. Your word is *excellent*," announced the teacher.

Christine stood and pronounced, "Excellent, e-x-c-e-l-e-n-t, excellent."

"I'm sorry. You are incorrect," said Mrs. Martin.

It was clear from Christine's tears that misspelling the word upset her. She had hoped to be the champion. Christine really wanted to spell all the words perfectly.

Sometimes I feel just like Christine. No matter how hard I try to be perfect, I fail. Our Bible reading tells us, "Be perfect, as your heavenly Father is perfect." How can I be perfect? I often fail to keep God's commands. I think of myself and forget about God and others.

Then I remember the spelling word my Sunday School teacher once gave me. "How do you spell *salvation*?" But before I could answer, he said, "The only way to spell salvation is J-e-s-u-s C-h-r-i-s-t."

When I said "Huh?" my teacher asked me to look up John 14:6. There Jesus says, "I am the way, and the truth, and the life. No one comes to the Father except through Me."

It's true—the only way to spell salvation is J-e-s-u-s C-h-r-i-s-t. Because He took away our sins by His suffering and death, God says we are now holy and righteous (forgiven). Through faith in Jesus, we're winners eternally.

PRAYER

Dear Jesus, thank You for giving me Your perfection so that I am saved from my sins. Help me trust only in You as the way to heaven. Amen.

Philip Lang

EPIPHANY

Everything Changes

Hebrews 13:7–8

Ann drives a Honda, votes, and works as a teacher. But she's only celebrated six birthdays! She must be a pretty smart kid, right? Actually, Ann is twenty-four years old. She was born on February 29 during a leap year.

Most years, the month of February has only twenty-eight days. But once every four years is a leap year, and then February has twenty-nine days. Of course, Ann celebrates the other years too—on March 1. Wouldn't it be strange to have a birthday that changes?

Lots of things change. You may change schools, or your family may move. As you grow older, your body changes a lot. Sometimes change is fun, and sometimes it can be scary. But one thing is for certain—life is always changing.

There is someone who never changes. God is the same. He promises to love and protect us always. God shows that love by sending His Son to rescue us from our sins and gain eternal joy for us. He also gave us His written Word, the Bible, so that we will always know His will for us.

Try this—take your Bible and open it to Hebrews 13:8. Read what it says. Now close the Bible, and put it away. In a few minutes, open your Bible again to the same verse. It didn't change, did it?

Just as God's Word stays the same, so does Jesus. Isn't it wonderful to know that no matter what else changes in life, our Savior will never change? He is always ready to forgive us, and His love is never-ending.

PRAYER

Heavenly Father, thank You for Your constant love and protection. Help me remember that no matter what may change in my life, You are always the same, and Your promises are eternal. Amen.

Jennifer AlLee

EPIPHANY

March Madness

Mark 15:6–15

Do you know anyone who has March Madness disease? If they have it, they will watch more than sixty college basketball games in one month. In fact, the disease is attacking fans now!

Is March Madness a real disease? No. It's actually the name of college basketball's championship tournament. Sports fans will do some crazy things to support their teams. They will paint their faces, wear funny hats, and wave banners. Fans will jump up and down and yell and scream like . . . well, like crazy!

Sometimes people do crazy things because the rest of the crowd is doing them. When you're cheering for your team, that can be fun. But sometimes what the crowd is doing is not what Jesus wants us to do. Some crowds have burned cars and destroyed property just because their team lost! Really crazy!

Crowds in Jesus' time made wrong choices too. When Pilate wanted to release Jesus, the people wanted a murderer freed instead. They were upset because they wanted Jesus to be an earthly king, not a heavenly one. The crowd was so angry that they told Pilate to crucify their Lord.

But Jesus knew the people were confused. He still loved them, even though they crucified Him. Jesus loved them so much that He asked God to forgive them.

Jesus knows that we can be confused too. Sometimes we follow the crowd instead of Him. But Jesus still loves us, and He wants to forgive us. That's why Jesus died on the cross and rose again. Jesus' victory over sin, death, and the power of the devil is the greatest championship of all time! Three cheers for Jesus, our champion!

PRAYER

Dear Jesus, forgive me when I follow the crowd instead of You. Thank You for loving me. Amen.

Nicole Dreyer

EPIPHANY

Why Ashes?

Genesis 18:27; Job 42:6; Isaiah 61:3; Matthew 11:21

"What's that stuff on your face?" asked Jothan. He and Greg went to different schools but often walked home together.

"It's from chapel," said Greg. "We could have ashes put on our foreheads if we wanted to."

"I guess it's a cross, huh?" said Jothan.

"Yeah," Greg agreed. "It's an old custom for Ash Wednesday. Lent starts today."

Ashes had special meanings long before Jesus' death, long before Lent existed. Already in Genesis 18:27, Abraham spoke of ashes to show humility. In the Lord's presence, Abraham felt as lowly as what's left after something burns up.

People in the Bible also used ashes to indicate deep sorrow, usually as a result of sin. Ashes showed repentance when people felt sorry about sinning and looked to God for forgiveness and help in changing their ways. Check today's readings from Job, Isaiah, and Matthew.

Now that we understand what ashes on one's forehead mean, we might think that a gloomy time starts on Ash Wednesday, the beginning of the Lenten season. That's not the whole story. Yes, we are sad about our sins. Because of them, we deserve to die. But Jesus has taken away our guilt. He was punished in our place. He died on the cross to save us. During Lent, which lasts forty days (not counting Sundays), we remember that with thankfulness.

Lent leads to our celebration of Easter. We rejoice because Jesus lives again, and He has given us eternal life. The greatest joy is known by people who have gone through great sorrow. We were condemned as sinners, but—praise God—our sins are forgiven. Our gladness has no end.

PRAYER

O God, we are like ashes before You, our Maker and Redeemer. When we see our sins in all their ugliness, lead us to confess them and change our ways. Thank You, Jesus, for humbling Yourself to earn forgiveness for us. By Your Spirit, give us the great joy of Your salvation. Amen.

Mary Krallmann

L E N T

Ash Wednesday

People of Christ's Passion

Mark 15:37–39

Normally there isn't homework for Sunday School, so the students groaned when Ms. Thompson first told her fifth and sixth graders that they would be doing a special assignment during Lent. With her warm smile and excited voice, she explained more so that the class mood changed from moans to curiosity.

"Hey," Thad whispered, "she could sell ice cubes to Eskimos."

Drew laughed and rolled his eyes, but then raised his hand and said aloud, "I want to do the soldier."

That had been three weeks ago. Now, during the announcement time just before the Ash Wednesday service, Drew was supposed to read his report in front of the whole congregation. He was nervous. Pastor Cawthorn had prayed with him, though, and that helped a lot. Drew did not look up at all. The congregation listened quietly.

"A Roman officer in charge of one hundred soldiers helped crucify Jesus. We don't know his name or where he was from. On Good Friday, he was doing his duty, close to Jesus' cross.

"After watching Jesus be tortured, mocked, and forced to carry His cross to the execution site, the soldier may have helped nail Jesus to the cross. The soldier probably heard the crowd make fun of Jesus and the crying from Jesus' followers. He probably heard the seven sayings of Jesus from the cross.

"Nobody knows if this solder ever met Jesus before Good Friday. He probably hadn't started the day either on Jesus' side or against Him. God helped the soldier see and hear the truth that day: Jesus is the Son of God, the Savior of the world.

"Jesus died on the cross to forgive sins, so even though our bodies will return to ashes and dust, we will live forever with Him."

PRAYER

God, help others who hear the story of Jesus' suffering and death to know and believe that Jesus is the Son of God, their Savior. In His name I pray. Amen.

James Gimbel

LENT

Wonderful Whispers

1 Kings 19:9–13

Shhh! Whisper something to yourself quietly. Does anybody else know what you said? Whispers are for special messages.

Shhh! Whisper something to someone else. Now two of you share a secret. Whispers are for friends.

Shhh! It's bedtime. Maybe someone will whisper to you. Maybe she will say "Good night" or "I love you." Whispers are for people who care for each other.

Most of the time, whispers are gentle signs of a close relationship. If you've ever spent a day being yelled at or surrounded by loud noises, you might really look forward to a gentle whisper from someone you love.

Elijah needed to hear a kind word from God. He had had a lot of bad days. People were about to kill him. And yet, God had so much power; God was so big. Who would expect God to come and talk in a whisper? But He did so because He knew what Elijah needed.

When Jesus rose from the dead, He came to see His disciples. He said, "Peace be with you." It was His way of telling them that now everything was okay. He was alive, and He loved them.

In good times and bad, God whispers to us too, because He loves us. He doesn't shout down angry words from the sky that would frighten us. But He comes to speak to us when our parents, pastors, teachers, or others share the whispers of God's Word.

PRAYER

Keep whispering to me, Jesus, as I read and listen to Your Word. Help me to hear clearly how much You love me. In Your name I pray. Amen.

Steven Graebner

LENT

Impossible Odds

1 Peter 5:8–11

Sometimes two groups fighting each other can be so mismatched that it's impossible for one side to win. That side may fight valiantly, all the time knowing they are almost sure to lose.

This is how it was at the Alamo in San Antonio. The Alamo was the site of a famous battle when Texans were fighting for their independence from Mexico. Only 187 men were defending the Alamo against 5,000 soldiers. Even worse, there was no way for these few people to get supplies and ammunition.

The Texans held off their opponents for 13 days. Finally, when the ammunition ran out, the other side was able to storm the fort. All the Texans lost their lives defending the Alamo.

The odds were impossible, but the Texans didn't stop fighting. They never gave up hope for some miracle to happen.

We, too, have impossible odds to fight. Our Bible reading says that our enemy is the devil. He is always looking for a chance to trap or catch us. If the devil can get us to follow him or turn away from God, then he has won the battle.

By ourselves we don't have the strength to withstand temptation or defeat the devil. But for us, a miracle *has* happened. God has joined our side. St. Peter says that Christ will strengthen us. With His power, we are no longer fighting impossible odds.

Jesus defeats the devil for us and wins the battle. The victory He gives us is life with God forever. As Peter says, "After you have suffered a little while, the God of all grace, who has called you to His eternal glory in Christ, will Himself restore, confirm, strengthen, and establish you" (1 Peter 5:10).

Prayer

O Lord, help us remember that Satan's power can pull us away from You. Give us Your power to resist him and remain firm in our faith. In Jesus' name we pray. Amen.

Paul W. Wangerin

Icicles

2 Corinthians 11:14

For Northerners who love winter, this cold time of the year can be one of extreme beauty. When the sun hits an icicle in the right way, it becomes an object of beauty. Icicles can transform an old gray house into an icy castle. They add to the brilliance of a cold, snow-covered morning.

This beauty created by nature can also be an object of extreme danger. Once I was walking down the streets when an icicle fell from a tall building. It narrowly missed me. Had I been walking a few steps faster, I might not be telling you of this experience now! Yes, an icicle can be an object of beauty *and* danger.

Satan, like an icicle, can be beautiful and dangerous. An icicle is neither morally good nor bad, but Satan is always evil. He may appear to be beautiful, but all the time, he is plotting to turn us away from God and keep us from Him. Satan may mislead us by telling us to cheat on a test at school. "An A on your report card would be beautiful." Or he may say, "How beautiful it would be if we could have that toy we've been looking at in the store! Why not just steal it?" And if he is successful in turning our heads, he tries to keep us by showing us how "beautiful" it is to live without God.

Jesus was tempted three times. The devil presented some beautiful promises to Him too. All three times, Jesus overcame the temptations. He completely defeated Satan on the cross. Because of Christ's victory, we need not believe or follow the so-called beautiful promises of Satan. Only with God's help can we resist Satan's powerful temptations. And when we do sin, we know we have forgiveness.

PRAYER

Almighty God, give me the wisdom to see the devil as one who is always a spiritual danger. Thank You for saving me from him through Jesus, my Savior. Amen.

Carl Kramer

LENT

The Color Purple

Genesis 17:3–8

What color do these things remind you of?

Basketball? Sunset? Canary? Canaan?

In Acts 16:14, we meet Lydia, a woman who sold rare purple cloth. Kings and rich people wore clothing dyed in costly purple. Shellfish used in making purple dye swarmed in the nearby Mediterranean Sea. It took ten thousand murex shellfish to produce a single gram of purple dye.

God promised the Holy Land to Abraham. God Almighty also told Abraham that kings would come from him and he would be the father of many nations. Abraham believed God.

Later, Abraham purchased ground to bury his wife, Sarah. Abraham believed in God's promise. But Abraham himself could not save his wife or his people from eternal death. He looked forward to the promised Savior, the Messiah, who would deliver all people from their sin.

Jesus was not born in the land of purple, but in a lowly stable. While on earth, this King of kings fulfilled all of God's promises in the Promised Land. Soldiers robed Jesus in purple on the day of His death. They crowned Him king of the Jews and nailed Him to the cross.

During this Lenten season, your church may have purple cloths on the altar. This royal color reminds us of Jesus and His death. In God-given faith, we look forward to our Lord's promise to take us to live with Him in His kingdom forever.

PRAYER

Dearest Jesus, I praise You for the robe of righteousness You won for me on Calvary. Amen.

Carol Delph

LENT

The Pelican and Her Young

John 10:7–11

An ancient legend tells how the mother pelican provides food for her young in times of famine. With her sharp, pointed beak, this bird pierces her own breast, causing drops of blood to seep out. The young pelicans then drink the mother's lifeblood so they won't die of starvation.

Christians have adopted the picture of the mother pelican and her young as a symbol for the season of Lent. This symbol reminds us that Jesus gave His blood to save all people from eternal death and, in His Supper, feeds us His own body and blood.

Without Jesus, there would be nothing but sin and evil in the world. No one would love God or be able to go to God's home in heaven. But the blood of Jesus has washed away sin and given us new life. We depend as completely on our Savior as young pelicans depend on their mother for life.

During Lent, the prayer for this devotion will help us remember and give thanks for the great sacrifice Jesus made that we "may have life and have it abundantly" (John 10:10).

PRAYER

Glory be to Jesus,
Who in bitter pains
Poured for me the lifeblood
From His sacred veins!

Grace and life eternal
In that blood I find;
Blest be His compassion,
Infinitely kind! Amen. (*LSB* 433:1–2)

Carol Granger

Are We Worth It?

1 Peter 1:18–21

Every ship going through the Panama Canal pays an average toll of $5,000. Some large vessels pay as much as $30,000.*

Is it worth it? We might not think so. Not just to sail a ship through a waterway less than fifty miles long. But the shipowners who pay the big fees know differently.

The canal can save a ship going from New York to San Francisco almost 8,000 miles and twenty days of traveling time. Also, the ship doesn't have to pass through the dangerous waters at the southern tip of South America. By using the Panama Canal, shipowners save many times the amount of the tolls. It's worth it!

In Lent, we are reminded of the tremendous price God paid for our salvation. Peter tells us we were redeemed not with silver and gold, "but with the precious blood of Christ" (1 Peter 1:19). How dearly God paid! It cost Him more than all the money in the world. It cost Him the death of His own Son.

Is it worth that much that we should be saved? Not when we think of how sinful and unloving we are. With all our hate and disobedience, we don't deserve God's goodness. We deserve to have Him abandon us forever to the judgment we have coming to us. Are we worth the cost of being rescued? Never!

Amazingly, God thought differently. He gladly paid the price. He willingly allowed our guilt to fall on Jesus. He did it because He loves us and wants us to live with Him forever.

This side of heaven, we'll never understand how our salvation could be worth that much to God. We simply are glad that it is so. And we thank and praise Him.

PRAYER

Lord Jesus, thank You for paying such a high price to save me. In everything I do, help me show my love for You. Amen.

Carl Bretscher

LENT

*According to the Panama Canal Authority, the average toll in 2007 was $80,263, and the most expensive toll that has been charged was $274,590. According to Wikipedia, the least expensive toll was $0.36 for a man who swam the canal in 1928.—Ed.

God Erases Guilt

Psalm 103:8–13

Tina felt very sad when her father died of cancer. After a while, however, she began to wonder why her father had to get sick. Maybe, thought Tina, I did something to make God mad. Tina remembered that she had talked back to her father. She had complained about going to Sunday School, and once she had even lied about breaking her mother's vase. If I hadn't been so bad, Tina reasoned, God would not have punished me by making my dad die.

From then on, Tina tried to be perfect. She did her homework. She obeyed her mother. She stopped teasing her friends. But no matter how hard she tried, she could not stop being jealous of her sister. No matter how hard Tina tried, she could not be perfect.

Psalm 103 brings words of comfort and peace to Tina. It says that God is full of love for us. Ever since Adam and Eve first sinned, God has been busy providing a plan to make us perfect. He sent Jesus, His Son, to die on the cross so that all our sins are forgiven. God does not hold our sin against us anymore.

Tina's father did not die because God was mad at Tina. In fact, because of Jesus, Tina's father will live forever with Him. Tina could never be good enough to earn forgiveness or eternal life. They are completely God's gifts. God also gives Tina power to love Him in return.

When you feel guilty because of something you have done wrong, ask God to forgive you. Trust that He does forgive you completely. He will be with you in all your troubles as your Comforter and Friend.

PRAYER

Dear heavenly Father, thank You for loving me and taking my sins away. Help me for Jesus' sake. Amen.

Carolyn Sims

LENT

It's Possible with God

Matthew 19:23–26

Here's a fun addition problem. If you add up the numbers of all the hairs on a frog, the onions in a banana cream pie, the wings on an elephant, and the things that are impossible to do through God's grace, what number do you come up with?

You come up with zero, nothing. There are no hairs on frogs, no onions in banana cream pies, no wings on elephants, and there's nothing that's impossible with God's grace.

That's an amazing promise. And it is possible only through God's amazing power. He created the world from nothing. He brings each life into being. He gave His only Son to die on the cross for the sins of all people, and to give to all who believe in Christ everlasting life.

Nothing is impossible with God's grace. And through His gifts to you of faith, forgiveness, life, and salvation in His Word and Baptism, His grace is always with you.

PRAYER

Dear Lord, remind me always of Your great power and love. Help me remember that by Your grace, all things are possible. In Jesus' name. Amen.

Bert Minkin

Deep Roots

Psalm 1:1–3

Brandon and his dad were hiking along Pickle Creek Trail. All weekend they had been camping by themselves in their tent at Hahn Park. It was a special time for Brandon and his dad to be alone.

As they walked along, they stopped to look at a young oak tree growing from the side of the cliff next to the path. Many of its roots were exposed.

"Dad," said Brandon, "look how long these roots are! How can this tree live with so many roots outside the ground? How does it hang onto the bare rock?"

His dad replied, "You know, we usually see only half of a tree. Most of it is underground. You can be sure that this tree has more roots deep in the earth than the few that are showing here."

Trees and Christians have a lot in common. A tree sends roots deep and wide into the soil for many reasons. Through its roots, it finds food and water to live each day. In its roots, it has a way to protect its precious, life-giving sap deep in the earth during the winter. Because of its roots, it can stand tall, straight, and steady during storms.

Christians are rooted deep in the love of Jesus Christ. The Holy Spirit gives us faith at our Baptism. He strengthens us as we gather together at church. He teaches us as we study the Ten Commandments. He builds us up at our confirmation. He forgives us and strengthens our faith as we take part in the Lord's Supper. He feeds us as we read the Bible.

Through all these things, the Lord gives us grace and strength to grow tall in His love. He protects us and keeps us steady in difficult times. When we are deeply rooted in Him, we're like a tree planted by streams of water. We bear fruit. Our leaves don't wither. God blesses whatever we do for Him.

PRAYER

Jesus, keep me closely rooted in You. Feed me with Your Word. Protect me from temptation and the difficult times that will come my way. Don't let the devil uproot me from Your love. Help me grow strong in my faith by the power of the Holy Spirit. Amen.

Dino F. Pacilli

LENT

Remember His Love!

1 Peter 3:15–18

"What did you give up for Lent?" Matt asked his new friend David.

"Lint? You mean lint like in the washing machine?"

Matt laughed. "No, *Lent*, like the weeks before Easter. It's what we call the time when we remember Christ's suffering and death. And it's when we get ready to celebrate His resurrection."

David seemed embarrassed. "Oh. Well, I didn't know I was supposed to give anything up."

"You don't have to," Matt said. "But some people do. It's usually something they like a lot. I gave up eating candy—and, man, do I miss Twisty Taffy!"

"What's the point?" David asked. "Why quit eating what you want just because Easter is coming?"

"Because every time I think about giving up taffy, I remember what Jesus gave up for us. He gave His life on the cross to pay the punishment for our sins. Giving up candy doesn't make me extra good or anything," Matt said. "It doesn't make Jesus love me any more than He already does. It's just a way to remind myself of what Jesus did for me."

Lent is a season in the Church Year. The Church Year is built on events that are important in a Christian's life. During Advent, we remember how people longed for the promised Savior, and we prepare for His coming at Christmas. During Lent, we remember why Jesus died on the cross.

Jesus took the place of all sinners! He paid for our sins. And then He rose again, overcoming death itself for us. He did all this because He loves us.

PRAYER

Dear Jesus, thank You for loving me. Thank You for dying for me. I am so glad that I am Yours! Amen.

Glenda Schrock

LENT

Cascarones

Matthew 28:7–8

I went home with my new friend Jorge after school. I had not been to his home before. In his kitchen, I noticed a tall stack of egg crates with eggs in them.

"What are you going to do with all those eggs?" I asked Jorge.

"Those are just the shells," he said, walking over and picking one up to show me. "We already ate the eggs."

"But why are you saving the shells?" I questioned.

"To make *cascarones* for Easter," he stated matter-of-factly. He saw my puzzled look. "You've never heard of *cascarones?*" he smiled.

"No, I haven't. We have hard-boiled eggs at Easter," I told him.

"Where we came from in Mexico, everyone has *cascarones*," Jorge explained. "For weeks before Easter, we empty the eggs as we use them to cook, but we save the shells. Then, before Easter, our whole family works to fill each egg with confetti. We glue tissue paper over the opening. We decorate the eggs and save them for our celebration at Easter. The empty egg is like Jesus' empty tomb. And the confetti shows our joy because He has risen."

"But what do you do with the eggs on Easter?" I asked.

"We crack them over one another's heads, of course," he said, laughing.

I couldn't wait to tell my family about the *cascarones*—another way to celebrate Jesus, who died on the cross for us all and rose again on Easter.

PRAYER

Dear Father, be with us as we prepare to celebrate with great joy the resurrection of Your Son, Jesus Christ, with Christians from all parts of the world. Bless all believers in Christ, and unite us in heaven someday. Amen.

Cathy Spieler

Safe with Jesus

Mark 10:13–16

Linda's mother and dad had told her that very soon, God would give her a baby brother or sister. Everyone in the house was excited. Mrs. Simmons was busy getting ready for her baby, and Linda could hardly wait for the day to arrive.

One morning, Linda's grandmother came to stay with her while her parents went to the hospital. About suppertime, Mr. Simmons phoned home. "Guess what?" he told Linda. "You have a baby brother!" Linda was so happy she could hardly sleep that night.

Early the next morning, the telephone rang. Mr. Simmons answered it, and Linda noticed that right away, he became very serious. He told Linda and her grandmother that something was wrong with the baby and that he was going to the hospital. Just before lunch, he came home. Quietly he told Linda, "Jesus has taken our little baby to heaven. He died this morning."

Linda looked at her dad for a long time. Then she asked, "How do you know Jesus took him to heaven?"

"I asked our pastor to come to the hospital," said her father. "The pastor baptized the baby before he died. You remember what Jesus promised to all who believe in Him and are baptized?"

"He promised they would be saved," Linda answered, feeling a bit better now. She had learned in Sunday School that Jesus loves everyone, including little children, and that He wants everyone to belong to Him through Baptism.

Linda was glad that her baby brother was safe with Jesus. And that night, she said a little prayer thanking God that she, too, was baptized.

PRAYER

Dear God, thank You for making me Your child and giving me eternal life through Jesus, my Savior. Help me every day to remember my Baptism and to live as Your child. Amen.

Walter Holzheimer

Potatoes and People

John 13:34–35

You probably know that St. Patrick's Day in the United States is a celebration of the Irish people and the contributions they have made. But do you know the reason that thousands of Irish people left their homeland to come to America? It was because of a shortage of potatoes!

In the early 1800s, most of Ireland's population depended on the potato for food. When a plant disease caused a failure of the potato crop in the 1840s, hunger forced many people to leave their homeland. Many of those came to the United States, where they and their descendants added much good to their new homeland.

The potato has always fascinated me. As a child, I dug potatoes in the garden. They were like buried treasure. I couldn't wait to turn over the next shovelful of dirt to see how many potatoes it contained.

Later, while I washed them, I would look for potatoes with unusual shapes and imagine them to be animals or people.

Then I would watch as my mother peeled off the potato skin, revealing the white, fleshy portion beneath. No matter how different on the outside, the potatoes always looked the same on the inside.

Potatoes are a lot like people. Our heavenly Father has made us in a variety of sizes, shapes, and colors. Yet, underneath, each of us is the same. We all have a soul, and we all need God.

God cared so much about us that He sent His Son to "dig" us out of the darkness of sin. Through Baptism, He washed us clean of all the dirt and grime that was the result of our sinful nature.

Through the working of the Holy Spirit, we can come to love and appreciate different types of people and their customs and traditions. Whether we are of Chinese, German, African, or Irish heritage, we have much in common—Jesus took on sin and death for us.

PRAYER

Lord, help me regard all other people as my brothers and sisters, loved and redeemed by You. Amen.

Rodney Rathmann

LENT
St. Patrick's Day

I Could Eat . . .

Psalm 34:8–10

The campers started their hike down the mountain at eight in the morning. By ten o'clock, no one was talking about squirrels or pinecones anymore. "I could eat a mountain of ice cream," Matthew sighed.

"What's your favorite pizza?" yelled Jody.

"Pepperoni!" someone shouted.

"Sausage!"

"I'd like to drink a barrel of Coke," Barb said.

"I'd like to jump into a barrel of Coke!" laughed Brandon.

But at noon, everyone yelled, "There's my favorite food!" when they saw hot dogs cooking on the fire by the lake.

"Try them and see," said their counselor. All the campers agreed. The hot dogs were the best thing they had ever tasted.

One time King David talked about God as if he were talking about food. He said, "Taste and see that the LORD is good!" (Psalm 34:8). That's a great thing to say about God, isn't it?

Pretend you're on a hike with the campers. You feel super hungry. Now think of your favorite food. Think how good the first bite will taste.

Now think about God. Think how empty you would feel without Him. Think of just one thing God has done for you. You might think about how God sent His Son to die for you, or about the family God has given you, or about a time God has helped you. How does a "taste" of God's love feel?

Sometimes you might get so hungry that you could eat a whole pizza or a carton of ice cream. With God's love, you never have to stop with one little taste. His love and goodness fill you up.

PRAYER

Thanks, Lord, for pizza and hot dogs and ice cream, for hikes and camp-outs, for friends and family. Thank You most for Your love in Jesus, which truly satisfies us. Amen.

Ruth Geisler

An Unusual Will

Matthew 13:44–46

In his will, the famous American patriot Patrick Henry gave all his possessions to his family. But he added, "There is one thing more I wish I could give them, and that is the Christian religion. If they had that and I had not given them one cent, they would be rich. If they had not that, and I had given them the world, they would be poor."

What Patrick Henry wrote agrees with what Jesus meant in His parable about the pearl of great price. Jesus told of a merchant who bought and sold pearls. One day he found one that was so valuable that he went out and sold everything he had so he could buy it.

Christ is like that pearl. He's worth giving up everything else to have. What are your most prized possessions? An autograph of a famous ballplayer or TV star? A report card with high marks? A medal you won in a swim meet? A bankbook showing a good sum of money that you've saved? All these valuable possessions will someday be gone—used up, lost, torn, or burned.

Jesus brings us possessions that no one can take away. He gives us life that lasts forever in His heavenly kingdom because we have been given faith to believe in Him. You can see why Patrick Henry wished he could give this faith to his family and why he thought they would be rich if they had it.

PRAYER

Heavenly Father, I am rich because I trust You and believe in Jesus as my Savior. Strengthen my faith in Jesus, my priceless treasure. Amen.

Lois Vogel

God Counts Them All

Matthew 10:28–31

Are you a blonde, brunette, or redhead? Did you know that blondes have more hair than those with darker colors? Someone has estimated that redheads have about 90,000 hairs; black-haired people have more than 100,000; brunettes, 109,000; and blondes, probably more than 140,000.

You could probably never count them—but God knows. "Even the hairs of your head are all numbered" (Matthew 10:30).

This is one of God's ways to tell us that He really knows us and cares for us. In another verse, Jesus tells us that His Father even cares for sparrows—and we usually call them worthless. Now, if God is concerned about worthless things like sparrows and the number of your hairs, you know He is concerned about the really important things in life: people.

Our God, who has counted our hair, also knows all our sins. But God took care of this problem through the offering of His Son. His Word assures us, "The blood of Jesus His Son cleanses us from all sin" (1 John 1:7). Isn't this a good reason to sing for joy?

> Jesus loves me! This I know,
> For the Bible tells me so.
> Little ones to Him belong;
> They are weak, but He is strong.
> Yes, Jesus loves me! Yes, Jesus loves me!
> Yes, Jesus loves me! The Bible tells me so! (*LSB* 588:1)

PRAYER

Thank You, Lord Jesus, for caring so much about me. Amen.

E. W. Lichtsinn

God Is Good

Psalm 147:1–11

March is many things. To people who live in the North, March is the return of the robins. In the South, March is green grass and blossoms on flowering shrubs.

Many things in March point to spring. After all, the first day of spring is in the month of March. Since all of us like spring, we all have something to enjoy this month.

Have you ever wondered why you like spring? Your reasons may be like those we listed: robins, green grass, and blossoms. There may be others too, like playing in the warm sunshine or even going barefoot. But there may be a deeper reason. Probably you can't explain it exactly or even put it into words. You just feel it. Spring makes you feel good and makes you feel that God is good. The sun is warm and the grass grows and the birds sing, and somehow you know that God's goodness is the cause of it all.

When someone does something for you, what do you say? Why, "Thanks," of course. And that is what we say to God because it will soon be spring. The writer of today's psalm did that long ago when he said, "Sing to the LORD with thanksgiving! . . . He covers the heavens with clouds; He prepares rain for the earth; He makes grass grow on the hills" (Psalm 147:7–8).

These signs of spring are all signs of God's love. But there is a still greater sign of His love, and this comes in spring too. This greater sign is the story of Lent. In this season, we think of the suffering and death of Jesus. We are sorry for our sins, which put Jesus on the cross.

If we say "Thanks!" for spring, we say "Many thanks!" for Jesus and His love and forgiveness. One Lenten hymn puts it this way: "Thousand, thousand thanks shall be, Dearest Jesus, unto Thee!" (*LSB* 420).

PRAYER

We thank You, God, for all the good things of March, especially because March brings Lent, and Lent tells us the Good News of Jesus and His love. Amen.

Lloyd H. Goetz

Washed Down the Drain

Psalm 131

A special thought: Don't throw in the towel. Pull out a new blueprint.

It was quite a storm! Late in the afternoon, we could see the clouds forming in the southwest. As they came nearer, they looked dark and threatening. Then the winds began to blow. Small branches in the trees began to snap off and fall to the ground.

The rain came suddenly, hard, and lasted for quite some time. Through most of the night, the storm continued. But by morning, God's good earth had been washed and watered.

Near the edge of our patio, we saw some unfortunate results of the storm: nests, several of them, washed out by the rain, washed down through the drain spouts. The nests were shattered, and several baby sparrows were lying around them.

There was only sorrow in our hearts—until we saw the parent birds. They must have realized there was nothing they could do by the patio. So two of the sparrows were already busy bringing in new string and grass to build new nests.

Sometimes even the very best things we try to do go wrong, and we are tempted to give up. Unexpected problems at home or at school suddenly ruin everything. We plan a party with friends and rain spoils everything. Our family starts the day with a fun breakfast, but by bedtime, many angry storms have dampened the fun.

The psalmist must have felt something like that. He said, "My heart is not lifted up; my eyes are not raised too high" (Psalm 131:1). Yet, like the sparrows, he encourages us to start over, to forgive and rebuild. "Hope in the Lord" (v. 3). He will help you live with your problems, large or small—and start each day anew with Jesus, forgiven and restored.

PRAYER

O Lord, when things go wrong, it's good to know that You are there to help me always. I know this for sure because You are my Savior. Amen.

John H. Fischer

L E N T

Grandmother's Love

Psalm 103:10–13

My grandmother died last year. I knew she was in heaven, and I was glad she didn't hurt anymore, but I cried.

My grandmother wasn't a little, round, cookie-making grandmother. She was tall and funny and strong, with beautiful silver hair. She thought I was absolutely perfect.

When I was four, I used to sit at the typewriter and type long lists of jumbled letters to her. Grandmother would write back that she loved my letter and could almost read what the words said.

I loved being the first one to see Grandmother get off the plane for her Christmas visit. She helped my sister and me shake all the presents under the tree and guess what was inside. She made Christmas more fun when she shared Christmas with us.

When my family went to Texas for Grandmother's funeral, we talked with our relatives about the wonderful love she had for people. One of the workers at the hospital where she died asked if he could help carry her casket at her funeral. Grandmother had been telling him about Jesus during her last days on earth.

During the funeral, the pastor told us, "Anna is alive." I knew it was true. When I was small, I thought Grandmother was God's wife. Now she was with Him in heaven.

The love my grandmother had for me is, in a small way, like the love God has for you. When God looks at you, He doesn't see your sins. He sees His Son, Jesus, who washed your sins away. By faith in the Savior, you are His perfect child.

PRAYER

Dear Father, thank You for not holding my sins against me. When I start to feel bad about myself, remind me that because of Jesus, You think I'm wonderful. In His name. Amen.

Ruth Geisler

When Bad Was Good

Romans 8:28

Todd was playing basketball with his friends. They were having a great game. The next instant, Todd was lying on the driveway, holding his ankle.

Painfully, Todd said, "I felt a snap in my ankle, and it hurts like crazy. Somebody better call my mother."

Later, when his ankle was in a cast, Todd listened as the doctor explained, "This is a bad break. I'm afraid you're going to be in a cast for about eight weeks, depending on how quickly it heals."

Todd groaned, "Oh, no! I'm on the tennis team, and I'll miss the big tournament!"

Todd managed to get around on his crutches at school. He used the time at home to read and do his homework. Almost two months later, Todd received his report card and saw five straight A's. Was he ever proud!

While talking with his parents, Todd said, "I could never imagine that anything good would come out of breaking my ankle. I missed the tournament and felt lousy about that. But getting all A's—wow!"

Todd's father suggested, "You must be thinking of that passage you learned: 'We know that for those who love God all things work together for good'" (Romans 8:28).

"Now I know that 'everything' means *everything*," agreed Todd, "even the things we think are bad at the time."

PRAYER

Heavenly Father, sometimes I get disappointed or discouraged with things that happen. Help me understand that You can use everything for my good. Amen.

Carol M. Barton

Rejoice with Mary

Luke 1:46–55

On this day of the liturgical Church Year calendar, we observe the Annunciation of Our Lord. The angel Gabriel announced to Mary that she would be the mother of God's Son.

Let's take a minute to look at Mary. Mary probably wasn't more than fifteen or sixteen years old, and her family certainly wasn't well known. The Bible doesn't give us much information about her, but we know she was engaged to be married to a carpenter named Joseph.

Why did God select a young, poor, and unknown peasant girl? Why didn't He choose someone who would be better able to care for Jesus? Why not a princess or the wife of the Roman governor?

God's choice surprised many people, and it couldn't have surprised Mary more. To think that God had picked her out of all women of all time—what an unexpected honor!

Mary could have taken advantage of this honor. What better way to get attention and gifts from the world? Instead, she opened her heart and sang. Her song was full of love and thankfulness to God. She knew God's gift of a Savior would change the world. This Savior would restore our friendship with God!

Like Mary, we can be happy that God is merciful and kind. He sees us in our sinfulness and takes pity on us. He sends His Son to rescue us from evil and lift us up to glory. With Mary we open our lips and sing, "My soul magnifies the Lord, and my spirit rejoices in God my Savior" (Luke 1:46–47).

PRAYER

Dearest Savior, help my life to be a big thank-You for Your never-ending mercy, grace, and love. You alone are the Lord! Amen.

Beth Firnhaber

LENT
The Annunciation of Our Lord

The Serpent and the Staff

Numbers 21:4–9

A young soldier was very frightened. His friend was lying on the ground close by. A little way off was a dead rattlesnake. "Medic! Medic!" the young soldier cried. The snake had bitten his friend on the hand as they crawled through the brush.

The soldiers were part of an exercise called a war game. Their National Guard unit took part in one of the "games" each year. Getting bitten by a poisonous snake was not part of the game. It was very serious. "Medic!" the frightened man called again.

At last the medic arrived. The bitten person was quickly treated and taken to a hospital. "He'll be all right now," said the medic.

The young soldier noticed that the medic wore a pin. It had a staff with a serpent wrapped around it. He thought about the snake that had bitten his friend. "What does that pin mean?" he asked.

"Well, in the time of the ancient Greeks, it was the sign of Hermes. He was one of their gods. But when I see the sign of the serpent and the staff, I think of a Bible story."

The young soldier looked puzzled. "What story?" he asked.

"The Old Testament tells about God's people getting bitten by snakes. Moses prayed to God that the people wouldn't die. God told him to make a staff with a bronze serpent on it. When the people looked at the staff with the serpent on it, they were saved."

After the medic went away, the young soldier was thinking about the story. It reminded him of something Jesus once said. Read John 3:14–16 to see what the young soldier was thinking about.

PRAYER

Dear Jesus, help us remember that You hung on the cross to save us from our sins. Help us see You on the cross, just as God's people saw the serpent on the staff, so that we will one day live forever with You and the Father and the Holy Spirit. Amen.

Donald S. Roberts

LENT

No Socks for Ducks

Psalm 139:13–16

Sounds silly, doesn't it? Think about it, though. Birds like ducks can swim or stand in near-freezing water, and it doesn't seem to bother them.

If we stood barefoot in ice-cold water, we would endanger our lives. We could get frostbite, or our body temperature could fall (hypothermia). That could kill us. We wear socks and shoes and even waterproof boots when it is cold.

Why don't birds wear socks or shoes? Why don't birds wear waterproof boots? The simple answer is because they don't need to. God created them with a special blood system. The arteries that bring warm blood (106 degrees) from the heart travel next to and are woven together with the veins that bring back the cold blood (37 degrees). The cold veins are warmed by the blood in the arteries. This "wonder net" keeps the bird safely warm-blooded.

Wow! God sure knew what He was doing when He created birds! He also knew what He was doing when He created people! He has given us a special body with intricate systems.

Since the time of Adam and Eve, when man fell into sin, all creation has been marked by sin and suffering. The devil, the world, and our sinful flesh are cold, separated from God. But our re-creating God has provided a warm rescue for us.

God re-created us in Baptism. Through the wonder of Jesus' death and resurrection, we have a new life. Jesus' blood paid the price for our sins. His blood forgave our cold sins and sinfulness. Because of Jesus, we are spiritually healthy. In thanks and praise to God, we can, through God's Holy Spirit, go out into the cold waters of life and do warm, loving things.

PRAYER

Dear God, I see Your hand in all creation. I see Your hand in re-creating me through the wonder of Jesus' sacrifice for me on the cross. Continue to lead and protect me as Your child. In Jesus' name I pray. Amen.

Philip Lang

LENT

Where You Belong

Luke 4:38–44

A king once visited a school. The class was studying natural history. At the end of the hour, the king asked a few questions of the pupils. He wanted to see how well they had learned their lessons.

He pointed to a stone. "To what kingdom does the stone belong?" he asked.

"The mineral kingdom," replied the class.

Holding a flower he asked, "Where does this belong?"

"In the plant kingdom."

"Where does a horse belong?"

"In the animal kingdom."

"And where do I belong?" was the king's last question. He probably expected to hear, "In our kingdom."

But one child stood up and said, "In the kingdom of heaven."

How thankful we can be that this is true, not only for the king, but also for us. We could have been eternally lost in the kingdom of sin, Satan, and death. But Jesus was sent to seek and save the lost. He put His claim on us and made it stick. He is our rightful King. This is good news: our pull away from God was great, but God's pull on us is greater.

In Baptism, God called us by name and said we are His. In faith, we hear His call and respond with joy and thanksgiving.

The king who questioned the class may have been surprised that a pupil would give such an answer to his king. But neither the king nor we should be surprised that the answer was and is true. After all, we know and believe in our Savior, Jesus.

PRAYER

Dear Lord, thank You for making me part of Your kingdom here on earth. Strengthen my faith, and help me boldly speak the Gospel to others, so all may enter the kingdom of heaven. In Jesus' name. Amen.

W. Martin Webern

A Gentle Leader

Isaiah 48:17

Not long ago, my family acquired a new puppy. His name is Rootbeer. As a puppy, he was soft and cuddly, but over time, Rootbeer changed. Each time he went to the veterinarian for some shots, he had gained ten pounds. Rootbeer was quickly becoming a large, strong dog. He pulled me along whenever we walked. We needed to do something soon if we were going to control Rootbeer rather than let Rootbeer control us.

Our solution was to purchase a Gentle Leader head collar. Rootbeer resisted the new collar, but it brought about an immediate change in his behavior. There was no more pulling, lunging, or tugging. He followed our gentle leading.

In many ways, we resist God and attempt to go our own way. We think we know what is best. We don't like being told in the Commandments what we should or should not do.

We can be thankful, however, for a God who cares for us. He gently leads us in the way we should go. Through His gift of Jesus, we have forgiveness of our sins and eternal life.

PRAYER

Heavenly Father, forgive us for those times when we try to leave You. Thank You for Your love for us in gently leading us back to You. Help us accept Your will for our lives. Amen.

James Hahn

Christmas and Good Friday

Matthew 1:21; John 19:30

Pastor Sanders collected many things. His most precious collection was of crosses. When he entered the ministry, his mother had given him a gold cross on a gold chain. Since then, he had added thirty-two more to his unusual collection.

It was Good Friday, a special day for Christians. As Pastor Sanders was going over his sermon for that evening, there was a knock on his office door. "Come in," he called.

Young Jason timidly entered. "Here's something for you," Jason said. He placed a package wrapped in Christmas paper on Pastor Sanders's desk.

"Well, well, a Christmas present on Good Friday," Pastor joked. He opened it and found a crudely carved cross on a shoestring "chain."

"I carved it from the piece of olive wood you brought me from Israel," Jason proudly offered. "I've been working on it since November, but I couldn't finish it for Christmas."

Pastor Sanders held it gently. Then he thought. That's when Good Friday started—on Christmas. When Jesus cried "It is finished," He was giving a cry of triumph. The angel's prophecy to Joseph had now been fulfilled. Jesus had saved His people—*us*—from their sins!

Pastor Sanders felt the crudeness of the cross in his hands. He thought of the pain and humility Jesus had suffered. He thought of love—God's love as He gave His Son to us; Jesus' love as He gave His life for us; Jason's love as he gave his time and gift. This cross would be the most loved of his collection. He thanked Jason warmly—and then rewrote his sermon.

PRAYER

I wonder as I wander, out under the sky,
How Jesus the Savior did come for to die
For poor orn'ry people like you and like I;
I wonder as I wander, out under the sky.

(Traditional Appalachian carol adapted by John J. Niles)

Jewel L. Laabs

LENT

I'm Starving!

John 6:35–40

At Melvin's Diner there are burgers and tacos, salads and pastries, cheesecake and milk shakes. Right after swimming, when your tummy is growling and you know you are *really* hungry, you stop at Melvin's for lots of choices. And when you're finished eating, your hunger is gone. You are satisfied.

Right after sinning, when your conscience is hurting, you are spiritually hungry. You are hungry to hear God's comforting words of forgiveness and everlasting life. His Word tells us we are loved for sure, and we will live forever. To satisfy this kind of hunger, we have God's Word and the Sacraments. We receive absolution, or forgiveness, from our pastor in the Divine Service. We study God's Word in Sunday School and also hear it preached.

When our spirit is hungry because it is lonely, God's Word tells us of our ever-present friend. When we are afraid, God's Word tells us about His great power and might. When we are sick, God's Word tells of His love and healing. When we stray from God's path for us, His Word shows us our sin and our need for a Savior. It tells us that Jesus suffered and died to pay the penalty for our sins. When we face death or despair, God's Word reveals the certain hope of heaven.

We need God's Word every day. As we feed on His Word, God shows us that He loves us and calls us to be His own. He wants to feed us each day and fill us with His love.

PRAYER

Dear Lord, thank You for Your Word, which promises me everlasting life. Help me read it and feed on it daily. I ask it in Jesus' name. Amen.

Mary Ann Berkesch

April Fools

Luke 12:13–21

Have you ever played an April Fools' Day joke? "Your shoe's untied! April fool!"

Did you know that there was an "April Fools' Day trick" in the Bible? One day, a man wanted Jesus to settle an argument about money, but instead of settling the disagreement, Jesus told everyone a parable.

In the parable, a rich man was so wealthy he decided to build bigger barns to hold all of his riches. The man thought that he had everything he needed to live a long and happy life. He said, "I will eat, drink, and be merry!"

But that night, the man died. All of his riches were no good to him anymore, and God said to him, "You fool!"

Why was the rich man a fool? Not because he was rich, but because he was not rich toward God. He was more worried about money than anything else.

Did Jesus say that having nice things is wrong? Not at all! Jesus wanted the foolish man to remember where his wealth had come from. Jesus wants us to remember where all of our blessings come from too.

Do you have a favorite toy or game or even a favorite outfit? I do too! All of those things are fun to have and to wear, aren't they? But what really makes them special is that they are *all* blessings from God, our Creator and Preserver.

James says, "Every good gift and every perfect gift is from above, coming down from the Father of lights" (1:17). On April Fools' Day, we can give thanks to God for the gift of laughter and for all the gifts He gives us, especially the gift of Jesus, who loves us and forgives us, even when we are foolish!

PRAYER

Dear Jesus, thank You for all my blessings. Forgive me when I am foolish and don't trust You to take care of me. Amen.

Nicole Dreyer

The Dogwood Tree

Genesis 1:11–13

In the South where we live, dogwood trees blossom around Easter. We look for their snow-white blossoms to announce spring. Many churches use bouquets of dogwood branches instead of lilies to celebrate Easter.

The legend of the dogwood tree says that its blossoms tell the story of Jesus' crucifixion. The white outer leaves of the dogwood blossoms form a cross, with two long and two short petals. At the center of the outer edge of each petal is a "nail print" of brown rust stained with "blood." In the center of the flower is a "crown of thorns." The white color reminds us of Christ's righteousness and purity.

Of course, legends are just stories. Trees don't tell us directly about Jesus' Passion and resurrection. But we can see God in nature as the almighty Creator. Martin Luther writes in his catechism that God has created everything in heaven and on earth and daily sustains it (explanation of the First Article).

I like to look at the dogwood blossoms and "see" the story of the crucifixion of Christ. Each year, as I see their snow-white blossoms, I am reminded of the new life Jesus gives each of us in Baptism through His painful death and victorious resurrection. How blessed we are to know that Jesus' victory over death brings new life—in all seasons and for all time!

PRAYER

Precious Savior, through Your blood shed on the cross, I wear a robe as white as snow, as white as dogwood blossoms. Thank You for the wonderful new life You have won for me. Amen.

Christine Weerts

The Blessing Tree

Philippians 1:3

Keisha set down the macaroni and cheese and looked at a clay pot sitting on the table. A plain tree branch was planted in the dirt. "Uh, Mom, I hate to tell you, but I think your centerpiece died."

Mom laughed as she lifted Javanti into his high chair. "We thought we'd make some Easter eggs during dinner," she said.

"I hate to ruin your fun," Keisha said, "but if we make Easter eggs today, they may not taste too good by Easter morning."

"We have a different kind of egg in mind," Dad explained. "Rashon, why don't you say our prayer for us, and then Mom and I will tell you what we're going to do."

Rashon prayed, "Dear God, thank You for this good dinner. Thank You for Mommy and Daddy and Keisha and Javanti. Thank You especially for sending Jesus to die for us. Amen."

"There, that's going to be our first egg," Mom said as she brought some paper egg shapes to the table. "Every night at dinner, we're going to write down some blessings from God. You kids are great blessings. We want to thank God for you." On a green oval, Mom wrote, "Thank You, God, that Rashon can pray such beautiful prayers." She tied it to the branch with yellow ribbon.

In today's Bible verse, St. Paul says, "I thank my God in all my remembrance of you." God loves you so much, He sent His Son to die on a cross to take the punishment for your sins. In a few days, you'll be decorating Easter eggs and singing hymns in church, thankful that Jesus died for you and rose again. That's a great blessing!

PRAYER

Dear God, thank You for the many blessings You give me every day, especially the blessing of Your Son, my Savior. In His name I pray. Amen.

Ruth Geisler

Cheers for Jesus

Luke 19:37–38

The parade was short. Jesus was the only one in it. He wasn't riding a tall, proud horse, as some might expect. No, our hero rode a donkey. It did not matter to people who had seen Him do miracles. They cheered for Jesus.

On the first Palm Sunday, more than two thousand years ago, Jesus rode into Jerusalem. A few days later, Jesus would carry His cross out of town. He died on the cross for you and all other sinners. This was God's way of saving you from your sins.

Now you can cheer for Jesus. What do you have to cheer about?

Give one "hooray" that Jesus knows you. He knew that you needed Him to take away your sins even before you were born. He knew who you would be—and He loved you.

Give another "hooray" for your faith. Faith is a gift from the Holy Spirit, who works through God's Word. Faith is what makes you believe that Jesus is your loving Savior.

Give a third "hooray" that Jesus promises in His Word to be with you. Of course, you can't see Him, but faith is what makes you believe that He is always near. You are safe with Him. He will never stop loving you.

Give a fourth "hooray" that Jesus has some work for you. He wants you to show others what He is like. You can do that by helping out around the house. You can show His love by being kind to the kids other kids tease. He has given you lips that smile. Smile at your friends, family, old people, grumpy people, teachers, sad people—and you can probably think of many more.

The best "hooray" for Jesus is when, through His Spirit, you are able to forgive others as He forgives you. Aren't you glad to be so cheer-full?

PRAYER

Hooray for You, dear Jesus. Help me to be just like You. Amen.

Edward Grube

The Donkey's Cross

Galatians 6:14

The cross is a very important symbol for Christians. You see crosses in churches and on steeples. You see cross pins and necklaces. You see crosses in Sunday School classrooms and in the living rooms and bedrooms of Christians. But did you know you can see a cross on most donkeys?

The next time you see a donkey at a zoo or farm, take a good look. A line of dark hair begins at the base of the mane and goes partway down the center of the back. It forms the vertical piece of the cross. The arms of the cross are shaped from darker hair that goes across the shoulders of the donkey.

It is likely that a cross-marked donkey carried Jesus into Jerusalem. Five days later, Jesus carried the sins of the whole world to the cross. He suffered the punishment for our sins and died in our place.

Jesus is stronger than death. His resurrection hands are imprinted with the marks of His love. Now all believers will rise again and live with Him forever in heaven. The cross—wherever we see it—is a reminder of what Jesus has done for us.

PRAYER

Thank You, Jesus, for dying on the cross for my sins and for the sins of all people. Whenever I see a cross, let it remind me of Your gift to me. Amen.

Judy Williams

A Lamb Cake

John 1:25–29

"What's the special occasion?" asked Dad as he walked into the house. On the table was a white decorated cake that looked like a lamb.

"Amber and I needed a project," said Mom. "I got the idea from one of her Sunday School papers. I decided to try that iron mold my grandma used for baking these cakes. I'm surprised how well the lamb shape turned out."

Amber showed her dad the activity sheet. She had colored the picture of a lamb carrying a cross. The lesson explained that Jesus was called "the Lamb of God."

The people of Israel had used lambs in an important religious festival for many years. It started when the Israelites were about to leave Egypt, where they had been slaves.

On a certain night called Passover, they were to roast and eat a lamb. They had to put some of the lamb's blood on the doorways. In other homes, the oldest child died, but the people of Israel were spared. The lamb's blood was a sign for God to pass over the Israelite homes.

The Passover lambs died; God brought His people out of slavery. They went to the good land He had promised them.

Jesus, our Lamb sent from God, gave up His life so that we can escape eternal death. By His blood we are saved. Heaven is our promised land. There we will be part of a great celebration, forever praising the Lamb of God.

PRAYER

O Christ, the Lamb of God who takes away the sin of the world, have mercy on us and give us Your peace. Amen.

Mary Krallmann

Watch and Pray

Luke 22:39–46

Have you ever done something familiar that seemed different? Maybe that's how the disciples felt on that last Thursday night they spent with Jesus before He died. They celebrated the Passover with Jesus like they may have done two other years. The people and the pattern were the same, but the experience was different.

Before supper, Jesus washed their feet. Servants were supposed to do that! But Jesus said they were to serve one another. During the meal, Jesus took the bread and wine and said, "This is My body, which is given for you. . . . This cup [wine] that is poured out for you is the new covenant in My blood" (Luke 22:19–20). The disciples didn't quite understand what Jesus was saying. The whole thing was new and different. Now we know and believe that Jesus gives us His own true body and blood in this sacred act, the Lord's Supper. Through this meal, Jesus brings forgiveness of sins and strengthens our faith.

After supper they all went to Gethsemane. This was a quiet place where they often went to be alone. When they arrived, Jesus said, "Pray that you may not enter into temptation" (v. 40). Then Jesus walked a little farther and prayed. The disciples couldn't hear what Jesus said. But they could tell that His prayers were different. Jesus was suffering as He prayed. The disciples were so upset and exhausted that they couldn't stay awake. Jesus woke the disciples and told them again to "pray that you may not enter into temptation" (v. 46).

Jesus tells us to "watch and pray" too. We have many things that tempt us to disobey God or just to not pay much attention to Jesus. We can't overcome the temptations by ourselves. We pray for help. God hears our prayers and helps us. God does that out of love—the same love that sent Jesus to the cross to die for our sins. In Him we have forgiveness and strength.

PRAYER

Dear Jesus, thank You for all You suffered for me. Help me to watch and pray. In Jesus' name. Amen.

Jeanette Dall

L E N T – H O L Y W E E K
Maundy Thursday

God's Will, Not Mine

Matthew 26:39

"I'm not praying ever again!" Katie shouted. "I've asked God for a lot of things, and He hasn't given me any of them!"

"Calm down, Honey. Let's talk about this. What exactly makes you think God doesn't answer your prayers?" Dad asked.

"I asked for straight A's on my report card, but I didn't get all A's. Then I asked for Grandma to get better, and she didn't. Now I asked God to make the new family across the street have girls my age, and all they have is boys. See what I mean? I'm just not going to pray again!"

"I used to think God didn't answer prayers," Dad said. "Then I realized something. Let's look at what you prayed for. Why did you want straight A's?"

"I wanted everyone to think that I'm smarter than Andrea."

"Why did you want Grandma to get better?"

"That's easy," said Katie. "I knew I'd be lonesome without her."

"And why did you want to have new neighbors who were girls?"

"Well, I guess I wanted . . . Wait a minute. I think I'm beginning to notice something. God knew what was best in each case. He decided to answer my prayers with what *He* thought was best, not what *I* thought was best. Am I right?"

"That's exactly right," Dad said. "Think of what Jesus prayed in the Garden of Gethsemane. He wanted His Father to figure out another way to save the world that wouldn't make it so hard on Him. He prayed that again and again, but He also said He would do whatever His Father wanted. God knew that Jesus' dying and rising again was the way for you and me and everyone else to be saved from sin, death, and the devil."

"Boy, I'm really glad God knows what He's doing!"

PRAYER

Dear God, I'm thankful You know what's best for me. I'm glad You answer my prayers in Your way. In Jesus' name I pray. Amen.

Pat List

LENT – HOLY WEEK
Good Friday

Remember Peter

Luke 22:31–34

Weather vanes have been around for almost two thousand years. The first known weather vane was on top of a temple in Greece. Later, weather vanes spread throughout Europe and were mounted only on castles and cathedrals. In the ninth century, church leaders required that every weather vane be in the shape of a rooster to remind people not to deny their faith as Peter did. Maybe you remember the story. It was on the Thursday evening before Jesus died on the cross. He and His disciples shared the Passover meal and the first Lord's Supper. Then Jesus told Peter He was praying for him. Peter didn't think he needed that prayer. He thought he was strong. He told Jesus he was ready to die with Him. Jesus answered, "I tell you, Peter, the rooster will not crow this day, until you deny three times that you know Me" (Luke 32:34).

Later that night, Jesus stood prisoner before the high priest. Peter warmed himself by a nearby fire. Several people asked if Peter was a disciple of Jesus. Peter was afraid he would be taken prisoner too! Three times Peter said he didn't know Jesus. Then the rooster crowed. Jesus looked at Peter and Peter remembered what Jesus had said. He went out and wept bitterly.

The rooster on the weather vane is a reminder: don't be like Peter! Don't think you're brave enough to stand up for Jesus all by yourself. There might be a time when it is hard to say you are a Christian. Jesus knows our faith needs strengthening. He knows we need His forgiveness when we sin. He gives us courage to confess our sins. He forgives us and strengthens our faith through Word and Sacrament. He still loves us, even when we are weak and deny Him. In prayer, ask Him to help you be faithful.

PRAYER

Give me courage, Lord, to say I am Yours because You made me Yours through the power of the Holy Spirit working in the Word and in the water of Baptism. As You forgave Peter, forgive me when I trust in my own strength or when I deny You. Amen.

Carol Albrecht

LENT – HOLY WEEK
Good Friday

Only God

Psalm 49:7–9

They were all sitting together in one long row. It was a family tradition that Jann and his parents went to church with his grandparents on Good Friday.

The service music and hymns were sad. The windows were dark. The cross was draped in black. Jann was thinking about the sound of the hammer against the nails, about Jesus' sacrifice for his sins, about God's love when . . . bang! The pastor slammed the book, reminding everyone that the tomb was sealed. Now the church was dark and quiet. No one spoke a word as they left.

In the parking lot, Jann asked if he could ride with Grandpa. It was another family tradition to gather at Grandma and Grandpa's to color Easter eggs. Friends and relatives of Grandma and Grandpa who hadn't colored eggs in years would also be there.

Grandma had all the supplies needed to make the eggs special: colors, wax crayons, and stickers. The eggs were already boiled, cooled, and ready to color.

Grandma's rule was that everyone had to color at least one egg. So Ann took charge of most of the egg dyeing, helping others. The last egg Jann colored was for Grandpa. He put a big cross on it with the wax crayon and dyed it yellow.

"Grandpa, this is a resurrection egg," Jann told him. "Yellow is for the sunshine on Easter morning, and the cross is to remind you that Jesus died for you."

Jann and Grandpa both believed that no one can redeem himself from sin. Only God can do that. Only God, through the Good Friday death of His Son, could free people from sin. Only God could turn the sadness of Good Friday into resurrection joy.

PRAYER

Heavenly Father, as I think of the death of Your Son, help me to live my life as Your forgiven child. For Jesus' sake I pray. Amen.

Kim Youmans

LENT – HOLY WEEK
Good Friday

Holy Saturday

Matthew 27:57–66

On the first Good Friday, Jesus died for the sins of the entire world, including our own. On Easter, He rose from the dead. What's the connection between these two days?

That's easy, we say—it's the Saturday that lies between the two. Holy Saturday, many people call it.

The answer is right. Christians have reminded themselves in the confession of their creed and in many other ways that Jesus was in the grave for three days. That's Bible language for a part of three different days: a bit of Friday, all of Saturday, and a tiny portion of Sunday.

The Bible goes to special pains to make clear that Jesus really died and that His burial was truly the burial of a dead man. For if He hadn't really died, God's plan to save us from our sins would not have been fulfilled.

Then His rising from the dead, which we remember on Easter Sunday, becomes all the more important and remarkable. For that is God saying that when He died, He died for you.

In many Christian churches, one of the main occasions for baptizing people is the Saturday between Good Friday and Easter. In the plan of God, the connection between Jesus' death and resurrection is Holy Baptism.

In Baptism, we are glad to know, God gives us a share in the death of Jesus Christ. He died for all people. Our Baptism says that "He died also for *me.*" Baptism gives us a share also in His rising from the dead. It brings Jesus' death and rising together in our own lives and hearts. It makes us the people for whom Christ died and in whom Christ is risen.

Because of our Baptism, we are people who have Good Friday and Easter not just once a year, but every day.

PRAYER

Thank You, Jesus, that You died for me and that You were buried in a grave, to be my Savior and Rescuer. Help me always believe that Your death and resurrection happened for my sake. Amen.

Richard R. Caemmerer

Empty!

1 Corinthians 15:20–23

Most things in this life are better when they are full. We like a full glass of lemonade and a full piggy bank. We are disappointed if we don't have a full stomach at the end of a meal.

Some things, though, are better when they are empty. A pencil sharpener can't do its job well unless it is emptied of its shavings. An empty backpack at the end of the day means no homework. If the trash can is empty, you won't have to take out the garbage for a while.

But do you know what the very best empty thing is? It is Jesus' tomb! The tomb was full on Good Friday. It held Jesus' lifeless body. The disciples didn't expect the grave to be empty on Easter Sunday. The women didn't either. They came with spices to put on Jesus' body. And then, what a surprise! What was supposed to be full of death was empty.

Why is an empty tomb such good news? It is good news because it means death couldn't hold Jesus. It meant that everything He had said about how God was His Father was true. No wonder it was such a surprise!

But there is more good news about that empty tomb. Because Jesus' grave was empty, it means death isn't the winner anymore. Yes, we will die someday. But there is a surprise ahead for us too. Someday Jesus will return. He'll call us from our graves. He'll gather our bodies and take them to heaven. Our tombs will be as empty as Jesus' grave was on Easter morning.

For Christians, *empty* is a wonderful word. An empty tomb means eternal life. Jesus rose from the dead, and we will as well. Hallelujah! Jesus is risen!

PRAYER

I praise You, Lord, for having power over death. Thank You for leaving an empty tomb so I, too, can have eternal life. Alleluia! Amen.

Carol Albrecht

EASTER
Easter Sunday

Sign of Victory

Colossians 2:13–15

Sir Winston Churchill was prime minister of Great Britain during the crucial years of World War II. His speeches inspired his people. Everywhere he went, he held up two fingers in a "V for Victory" salute. This simple gesture became a symbol of faith in eventual victory over the Nazi forces.

But there is a far greater symbol of victory than Churchill's heroic sign. That symbol is the cross of Jesus Christ. It stands for victory in the greatest conflict of all time—the war against sin and death.

The war against death actually began when Adam and Eve sinned. This was a victory for the devil, who is God and man's enemy. Adam's sin brought the penalty for sin set by God Himself: death. Thus everyone on earth who sinned became worthy of death. And all have sinned—so all deserve to die.

But God used a strategic plan to defeat the enemy. He sent His Son to pay this penalty for all people.

Because the decisive battle in the long conflict with Satan was waged on a cross, the cross has become a sign of victory to all who believe in the success of God's plan. Jesus emerged the victor. The resurrection of Jesus three days after His death proclaims that our Lord conquered death for us on Calvary. "Thanks be to God, who gives us the victory through our Lord Jesus Christ" (1 Corinthians 15:57).

PRAYER

Dear Savior, each time I see the cross, remind me of Your great victory over death and the devil. Help me live a life that shows I am really free from the devil's power. Amen.

Myra Wilkinson

EASTER
Easter Monday

Safe in God's Hands

Psalm 37:23–24

The sixth graders were doing a science experiment. Each team designed a box that would keep a raw egg from breaking when it was dropped from the second-floor balcony onto the school parking lot.

Jeremy and his team wrapped the egg in bubble wrap, put it in the box, and then wrapped more bubble wrap around the outside. Jaden's team filled the box with a container of gelatin, which gelled around the egg. Levi's team surrounded the egg with Styrofoam packing peanuts.

One by one, the eggs were dropped, and the boxes were opened. The eggs fell a long way, but not a single one had broken! The boxes protected them.

The Bible tells God's people that they are safe in the hands of God. When we are in God's hands, it doesn't matter if we are sleeping in bed, riding in a car, flying in an airplane, playing with friends, taking a test, or even fighting in a war. God protects us in the best way—in His hands. Dangers may come. Sorrow may come. But through it all, God is our support.

Jesus' strong hands were nailed to the cross so He could die and take away our sins. With His sacrifice, He won the victory over the powers of death and the devil. On the cross and at the empty tomb, we see His eternal care for us. Through His Word, we hear His promise also to care for us while we are here on earth, in our classroom, with our family and friends.

When you feel afraid, remember the words of today's Bible reading. You are safe in God's strong and loving hands, redeemed and forgiven.

PRAYER

Dear heavenly Father, thank You for taking care of me wherever I go. When I am afraid, remind me of Your promise to keep me in Your loving hands. In Jesus' name I pray. Amen.

Carolyn Sims

EASTER

Learning to Slow Down

Matthew 11:28–30

It's raining today as I write this message. Sometimes it rains hard. The big drops of water pop loudly when they hit the metal roof of my office. Sometimes it rains so softly I can't hear or see the raindrops.

I love the rain. It's always seemed to me to be a message from God to slow down and take things a little easier, to rest.

Rest is something that is harder and harder for people to find in our busy world. Everybody is running all the time. Young people have school and sports and clubs and music lessons and dance lessons—all kinds of things that keep them running. Adults have work, home, meetings, and many other things that never let them slow down. Everybody is tired. Instead of getting more out of life, I think life is getting more out of us.

Maybe you could do something, as a young person, to change that pattern. Maybe you could start to slow things down in your life and help the people you love do the same. It would give you time to get to know yourselves and one another.

Jesus wants us to have rest in Him. He said, "Come to Me, all who labor and are heavy laden, and I will give you rest" (Matthew 11:28). The Savior meant not only rest through the forgiveness of sins and rest forever with God in heaven, but rest from our cares and worries. There's no better way to rest than to give our troubles and cares to Jesus.

PRAYER

Heavenly Father, You created time and gave me life. Help me use my time wisely. Teach me to value each day of my life and live it in a way that gives me joy and honors You. In Jesus' name I pray. Amen.

Daniel G. Mueller

EASTER

Peace Officer O'Rourke

John 20:19–20

Chris and Adam were trying to find a new way home but got lost. They passed near an old warehouse with graffiti on the walls and windows broken out. Although they didn't say anything, both boys were breathing hard and were frightened. They froze when they heard the crunch of near-by footsteps. "Stop," said a deep voice. A uniformed man with a silver badge stood in front of them.

"We didn't do anything wrong," Chris blurted.

"I didn't say you did," came a hushed response.

"But you're the police," Adam said.

"I call myself a *peace* officer. My name is Manfred O'Rourke."

The officer motioned for them to walk with him. Then he pointed to silhouettes of men huddled around a fire. "My partners and I are stationed around this area to catch someone."

"You mean we could have walked right into the middle of it?" asked Adam, sweating a little.

Officer O'Rourke nodded and walked the boys to safety.

Jesus is our peace officer. He delivered us from the evils of this world to Himself now and forever through our Baptism. On Good Friday, He stationed Himself on Calvary to conquer sin, death, and the devil. Now when we are afraid, or even when we aren't afraid, we remember Jesus' words: "Peace be with you" (John 20:19). His peace means we no longer need to fear the power of sin or death. It means the devil has no right to hold us hostage. It means that throughout this life of troubles, Jesus is our peace officer.

PRAYER

Dear Jesus, protect me from harm and danger. Thank You for being my peace officer and for leading me to the safe place by Your side. Amen.

Rebecca Spitzack

EASTER

Rest in the Lord

Matthew 14:22–23

The whistle blew. The referee hollered, "Time-out, blue!" The basketball game came to a standstill, and everyone got to rest. The teams could get drinks and rethink their strategies. The fans could relax for a while before resuming their loud encouragement of the players.

"It's recess time!" has been heard in schools all over the world. Students and teachers need some free time to release energy and frustration.

Jesus also became weary at times and went off by Himself to rest. In Scripture we read that He left His disciples and the crowds and retreated to a quiet spot to rest. But He did more than rest—He prayed.

Jesus had been given the hardest job in history. He was to live a perfect life, and Satan was trying hard to ruin it. He was to die an innocent, painful death, loaded down with the sins of the whole world.

Jesus was a true man. That means He grew weary from doing His preaching and miracles. When people didn't listen to Him, He became sad. It would have been very easy, very human, to strike out in some way. But Jesus didn't because He repeatedly asked the Father and the Spirit for help. And by His faithfulness to the tasks before Him, He won salvation for us.

Will going to the Lord for help work for us? Of course it will. When things get to be overwhelming, find a quiet spot. Do whatever relaxes you, but don't forget to rest in the Lord. Pray. Read God's Word and meditate on it. Listen for His leading. It will be very refreshing.

PRAYER

Dear Jesus, our Refuge, help us recognize weariness and stress. Lead us to restful things and places, especially closer to You. Only there can we truly receive the refreshment we need. In Your name. Amen.

Jacqueline Loontjer

EASTER

For Such a Time as This

Esther 4:13–14

Do you know the Old Testament story of Queen Esther? Esther lived in a foreign country called Babylon, where her people, the Jews, were slaves. When the king of Babylon married beautiful Esther, she became the queen.

An evil man named Haman tricked the king into passing a law that would mean death for many Jews. It seemed that Esther was the only one who could persuade the king to save the Jews. Yet Esther was afraid that by speaking out, she might anger the king and also be sentenced to die.

Then Esther's uncle, Mordecai, encouraged her with these words: "And who knows whether you have not come to the kingdom for such a time as this?" (Esther 4:14). Mordecai was suggesting that perhaps God had made Esther queen so that she could save her people.

The story has a happy ending. God gave Esther courage to go before the king, who had mercy on God's people. In the end, it was evil Haman who was put to death.

Like the Jews in Esther's time, we also have been given a death sentence. Because of our sin, we are guilty before God, our King, of breaking His laws. We deserve eternal punishment.

Rejoice! God has provided a happy ending to our story! In His great love, God sent His Son into the world "for such a time as this." Jesus lived a perfect life in our place and died on the cross to pay for our sins. Because of Jesus, we have been granted forgiveness and are now His royal sons and daughters!

PRAYER

Dear Father in heaven, forgive me when I don't think the work I do every day is important. Use me, O Lord, to help others in Your name. I pray in Jesus' name. Amen.

Dawn Napier

EASTER

Words of Value

Luke 1:1–4

Lizzie Charlton, a teenager in 1866, would have never expected that her trail diary would become a historic treasure. Lizzie's words describe the ups and downs of her overland journey from Iowa to Oregon. The diary was recently found in a tin box in a California dump site. It was a treasure in the trash.

It takes time to sit down and write in a diary or journal, but it is a valuable exercise. In a few sentences you can recapture your day for reflection in the future.

The Bible is a kind of diary. It is the story of God's love for His people. Where would we be today without the books of the Bible? We wouldn't know the Gospel and the Epistles (Letters) of the New Testament. We wouldn't have the Law and the Psalms and the history and the prophecies of the Old Testament.

All these words and works are ours because God wants us to have His message. He chose writers like Luke, and through His Spirit, gave him and others the very thoughts and words. God led Luke to write an account of Jesus' life and death and resurrection and the growth of the Early Church. God led Luke to gather words from eyewitnesses and servants of the Word. God worked through Luke to provide an orderly record so that "you may have certainty concerning the things you have been taught" (Luke 1:4).

Thanks be to God for His written Word. The Bible is more costly than silver, more precious than gold.

PRAYER

Lord, thank You for Your Word. Help me to tell others about You and Your love in my life. Amen.

Marilyn Sommerer

EASTER

Are You Sure?

Ecclesiastes 7:21–22

"Hey, where's Raul?" asked James as he looked around the locker room. "He's never late for practice," said Chad. "Man, Raul loves basketball. Wonder where he is?"

"I heard Raul's in trouble," Anton said. "Big, big trouble. Might even get kicked off the team! Frank saw Raul in the principal's office. He must have done something terrible to be in there!"

Chad and James looked at each other. Raul was the star on their basketball team. What would they do without him?

Just then Raul rushed into the locker room. "Sorry I'm late," he said. "Principal Wilson saw me in the hall. He wanted to know how my brother Ramon was doing in college. Told him Ramon was playing on the basketball team. Just like me."

James and Chad high-fived Raul as the three of them hurried to the gym. Anton trailed behind his teammates. Next time, he would get the facts before he opened his mouth.

In Ecclesiastes 7:21, we are told, "Do not take to heart all the things that people say." We can't believe everything we hear or read. Many times people say what they believe is true, when it may not be true at all. Spreading rumors and gossiping can hurt people. Maybe you have had someone say something untrue about you. Then you know how bad it can make you feel.

There is only one place that we can get the whole truth. That is in the Bible. Everything God says is true. There isn't even one word that is untrue. There we can read that God offers forgiveness for people who spread rumors and gossip. God offers forgiveness because His only Son, Jesus, died for sinners. Those are the facts!

PRAYER

Lord, help me to avoid gossip and the hurt it brings to others. For Jesus' sake, please forgive me when I don't. Help me to speak the truth. Amen.

Jeanette Dall

EASTER

The Broken Angel

1 John 1:8–2:2

Holly felt awful. She hadn't meant to break the angel. It slipped right out of her hand and seemed to smash into a thousand pieces. Holly knew her mother was going to be mad. It was one of her favorite angels.

All Holly could think about was hiding the pieces. So she gathered them up, wrapped them in a paper towel, and hid them in the bottom drawer of her dresser.

A whole week passed. Not once had her mother noticed the missing angel. Then, one day after school, Holly came into the kitchen searching for a snack. Her mother was sitting at the table. Holly's hunger suddenly disappeared. On the table lay the paper towel containing the pieces of the broken angel.

"Holly, sit down," Mrs. Dean said. "I want to talk to you."

"I didn't mean to, Mom! It was an accident!" confessed Holly.

"Holly, it's not the broken angel that upsets me. It's the fact that you didn't tell me you broke it, and then you hid it from me."

"Mom, I'm sorry! But I was scared!" cried Holly. "It was one of your favorite angels. I just took it out to look at it, and suddenly it was on the floor in pieces."

"Sweetheart, never be afraid to tell me when something like that happens," said Mrs. Dean. "I love you more than any *thing* that I own. This reminds me of Adam and Eve in Paradise. God loved them so much. But they disobeyed God and then hid from Him because they were scared. Yet He showed how much He loved them by promising to send a Savior to forgive them. Jesus is that Savior. He kept God's Law perfectly in our place so that we, too, might be forgiven for all the wrongs we have done."

"I'm sorry, Mom," said Holly.

"I know you are, Holly," said her mom as she hugged her. "I forgive you. Forgiveness is a job for Jesus—but this broken angel is a job for Super Glue!"

PRAYER

Dear Jesus, thank You for forgiving me when I do something wrong. Help me admit my wrong and trust in Your forgiveness. Amen.

Barrie E. Henke

EASTER

What's Your Worth?

1 John 3:1–3

"See what kind of love the Father has given to us, that we should be called children of God; and so we are" (1 John 3:1).

How much is a human body worth? For years, a story has been going around that the iron, calcium, and other materials in our body are worth ninety-eight cents. Recently a research chemist became curious and began looking up the prices of insulin, hormones, and other chemicals in one's body. He then multiplied the weight of these materials by their cost. He found that the worth of one's body on today's market would be six million dollars!

But if our body had to be made from synthetic materials, then each of us would be worth six *billion* dollars. If the cost of forming tissues and organs like the heart and kidneys were computed, the chemist concluded, "the worth of each human being is priceless."

That's the point John is emphasizing in today's Bible reading. To be named the children of God, God's people, is priceless. Being God's son or daughter means that we have been rescued from the fate of living as orphans. No longer are we separated from God by fear, aloneness, or feelings of guilt and sin.

In Baptism, God unites each of us with Himself. When we were baptized "in the name of the Father and of the Son and of the Holy Spirit," God guaranteed us His love and forgiveness. Martin Luther once said, "Through Baptism, God puts us on the ship of salvation whose captain is Jesus Christ." That kind of gift is priceless. As sons and daughters of God, we have received God's most precious gift!

PRAYER

Lord God, heavenly Father, You have shown Your love to us by giving us a wonderful body and by naming us Your sons and daughters through Baptism. We thank You for this priceless gift. Help us treasure it always. Amen.

Marvin Bergman

EASTER

The Hare and the Tortoise

Proverbs 29:23

The speedy hare bragged about how fast he could run. The tortoise was tired of the hare's noisy words and challenged him to a race. The hare, believing no one could beat him, accepted the tortoise's challenge. The two animals started together. The hare quickly gained a healthy lead. Assuming he would easily win the race, the hare rested by the side of the road near the finish line. The tortoise was slow and steady. Eventually, with his steady effort, he got close to the finish line. Just then, the hare woke up. What do you think the hare saw? He saw the tortoise crossing the finish line, winning the race.

We can laugh at the silly hare and cheer for the slow tortoise, but this fable is also like a mirror. We see ourselves as the silly hare. We are smug, bragging that we are better than someone else. We are faster. We are smarter. We are funnier. We are show-offs.

Today's Bible verse says, "One's pride will bring him low." God's Law is a mirror that shows us our sin. Being a sinner is pretty low. We are help-less and hopeless without Jesus. On the cross of Calvary, Jesus won a race for us. He suffered and died for sinners. His resurrection raised us too. It is proof of the gifts He has won for us. God gives us the forgiveness of sins and life eternal. We have a God like no other. He is the One in whom we can boast.

He is the God who makes us fast runners, enthusiastic singers, and people who persevere like the tortoise. He is a God who forgives. He is a God who gives us power to forgive others. He is a God like no other. Take pride in Him.

PRAYER

Dear Lord, thank You for blessing me with things I can do well. Help me to be confident in You and Your blessings in my life. In Jesus' name I pray. Amen.

Kim D. Marxhausen

EASTER

All the Right Words

2 Timothy 3:14–17

Jerome wandered around the house, searching. He wasn't sure what he was searching for. He figured he would know it when he saw it. Somewhere in his house there had to be something that would give him an idea for his English assignment.

"A three-page story—first draft due tomorrow. The topic is your choice," Mr. Wesley had said. So now Jerome was hunting for his topic. The writing was the fun part, Jerome felt. It was just difficult for him to come up with an idea to get started.

Jerome put on his coat, walked outside, and sat down on the front step. He stared into the sky and wondered if all the writers of all the books he had read had had this same problem. He thought that maybe he could write a story about a boy who had to write a story and didn't know how to start!

The writers of the Bible didn't have to worry about ideas and topics. When they wrote, they were inspired by God. God placed the words into their minds and hearts so that they could write those words down in the way that His message of salvation would be told.

Because of the inspiration of the Bible, we know that it truly is God's Word. We can use it to know His laws and His will for us. We can read about Christ's life and the salvation He earned for us on the cross. We can learn about the Holy Spirit's power and know that He is keeping faith alive in us. We can share God's Word with others who do not believe in Him.

The Bible is a precious possession to be read and studied. Jesus said, "The words that I have spoken to you are spirit and life" (John 6:63). These words were also written "that you may believe that Jesus is the Christ, the Son of God, and that by believing you may have life in His name" (John 20:31).

PRAYER

Dear God, thank You for Your Word. Don't let us ignore it or pretend it can't help us. Help us remember that the Bible is Your voice speaking to us. Amen.

Susan Waterman Voss

EASTER

Fried Bugs and Pickled Pigs' Feet

Acts 10:27–28, 34–36

When I traveled to China a few years ago, I ate delicious but unusual foods. The tables were filled with many dishes of vegetables, fish, chicken, soup, and rice. All of it looked and tasted wonderful.

One night I looked more carefully at one plate. Arranged in circles around the plate were *bugs*—fried bugs. I crunched one.

When I lived in the South, a popular snack was pickled pigs' feet. Just looking at them made my stomach queasy, but I tried them. My neighbors enjoyed them more than I did.

Some former missionaries in Liberia told of the wonderful fruits, vegetables, and rice dishes they enjoyed with their neighbors. But when the missionaries served a favorite food of theirs, spaghetti, their Liberian friends wouldn't touch it. They thought it looked like worms.

In ancient Israel, God gave His people rules about what animals, reptiles, and birds they could and could not eat. In the Bible story of Peter and Cornelius, God revealed to Peter that all kinds of food were now permissible. Peter realized also that the Gospel of Jesus Christ is intended for all nations and peoples. Peter told his Gentile listeners, "Everyone who believes in [Jesus] receives forgiveness of sins through His name" (Acts 10:43).

We may not all share the same taste in food, but God has given us all the same Savior. Since Jesus has won everyone back for God, let's joyfully share this great news with many others.

PRAYER

Come, Lord Jesus, be our guest, and let Your gifts to us be blessed. Amen.

Christine Weerts

EASTER

Jesus, the Bread of Life

John 6:32–35, 51

Many people love to travel overseas. It's fun to visit another country and learn about its culture. France is a favorite destination for many North American vacationers.

One thing you notice when you're in France is the many bakeries there. Every neighborhood seems to have its own bakery filled with fresh pastries.

Perhaps one reason for this is that bread is such an important part of every meal in France. Also, people tend to buy their bread fresh every day. Often boys and girls will help their parents by running down to the bakery to buy bread for breakfast.

This can be a big problem during another French tradition, the long summer vacations. Even stores like bakeries will often close for a whole month while the owners go on vacation. Imagine being hungry for some bread, but your favorite bakery is closed for a month. It may take a lot of searching before you find another bakery that is open.

Praise God that our "bread of life," Jesus Christ, doesn't go on vacation. He is always available to us by the power of the Holy Spirit. Through His Word, our hungry souls are fed.

Unfortunately, we sometimes go on vacation from Jesus when we neglect His Word or stop going to church and Sunday School. It is good to know that He never gives up on us! He is always ready to feed us with His Word, to forgive all our sins, and to guide us on the way to heaven.

PRAYER

Lord Jesus, when we "go on vacation" from listening to Your Word, please forgive us. Send Your Holy Spirit to guide us back to You, the true bread of life. In Your name we pray. Amen.

Jeanne Dicke

EASTER

The Boogeyman

Matthew 28:20

Nancy awoke suddenly in the middle of the night. She knew she had been having a terrible dream. It was all over now, but still she was afraid. She looked around the room. In the dark she could just barely see her sister asleep in the other bed, the dresser, the windows, the door to her mother's bedroom.

I'm at home in my own bed, she thought. But there's something else here, and I'm afraid. Maybe it's the boogeyman.

Once more she glanced around the room. This time her eyes noticed the picture of Jesus over her dresser. It always had been her favorite because it glowed in the dark. She stared, trying to read the words underneath. Nancy knew what it said, but she wanted to be able to read it.

No matter how hard she tried, she could not read the words. So she decided to pick another Bible verse that would fit. The only one I can think of is the one we learned in Sunday School: "Behold, I am with you always, to the end of the age" (Matthew 28:20). Or was it "unto the end of the world"? I always get it mixed up.

"Yes, that one would go nicely with . . ." But Nancy just couldn't keep her eyes open for another minute.

PRAYER

Jesus is among us, with us every day;
Jesus is among us, at school, at work, at play;
Jesus is among us, with us every night—
Therefore we should trust Him—have no need of fright.
Help us to remember, Jesus, Lord of all,
Makes no difference where we are, You are there to call.
As You promised long ago, be with us always—
Yesterday, tomorrow, and of course, today. Amen.

Naomi Bousman

EASTER

Remember Being a Nerd?

Deuteronomy 24:17–22

I used to be a real nerd. You know—the greasy hair, the glasses, the high-water jeans, the clothes that were one or two styles behind. I was a nice enough kid, I think. I had plenty of friends, but I was going through what parents used to call "the awkward age."

Good news for nerds—you grow out of it! The way we look in our junior high yearbook isn't the way we look forever. We get taller, thinner, or smoother-faced. Our older sisters or brothers teach us how to dress. We learn what to say to other people. Before long, we may even find ourselves being "popular," at least with the people who count.

When that day comes, though, I hope we won't forget what it was like being a nerd. Being a nerd may have taught us some lessons worth remembering.

In our Bible reading, Moses tells the people of Israel to remember what life had been like for them. They had been slaves in Egypt, treated very cruelly (just as nerds are sometimes treated cruelly by the kids at school). God wanted the Israelites to remember their past so they wouldn't mistreat strangers or orphans or widows. Certainly they wouldn't want anyone else to suffer as they had.

If we former nerds remember what it was like, we'll surely be kinder to others than some people were to us. We won't joke about them or leave them out. And we'll try to help anyone who needs a break—a new person in our class, a boy of another race, a girl who didn't do well on her last test.

Not all of us are or were nerds, but all of us have a past to remember. We were all lost in our sins until Jesus brought us out. He died to take away our sinful pasts. How wonderful to remember that! And what a wonderful reason to remember somebody else who needs us now!

PRAYER

Dear Jesus, thank You for loving us in spite of our sinful past. Help us remember that others need Your love too. Amen.

Carl C. Fickenscher II

EASTER

Rainbows and Promises

Genesis 9:12–17

In the Midwest where I live, huge black clouds move in from the West without much warning. Soon the thunder rattles the windows, and lightning shoots from the rolling clouds. Wind bends the trees, and rain beats on the house. Then, just as suddenly as it started, the storm is over. As the sun comes out and shines through the moisture from the storm, you might see a gorgeous rainbow.

The very first rainbow appeared after the flood. Talk about a storm! The ark with Noah, his family, and the animals had been bashed with rain for forty days and forty nights. Even after the storm was over, the people and animals bobbed around on the floodwaters for almost a year.

When they landed and came out of the ark, God promised Noah that there would never be another flood to destroy the whole world. To assure Noah of His promise, God said, "I have set My bow in the cloud, and it shall be a sign of the covenant between Me and the earth" (Genesis 9:13). God has kept that promise to this very day.

God also promises to love and care for us. He promises to forgive our sins because of Jesus' death and resurrection and to take us to be with Him in heaven when we die. The next time you see a rainbow, remember that God keeps *all* His promises.

PRAYER

Dear God, sometimes everything seems to go wrong. Help me remember that You are always with me and that all Your promises are true—just like the promise of the rainbow. Amen.

Jeanette Dall

EASTER

Want to Run Away?

Luke 15:11–24

Have you ever wanted to run away from home? If so, you probably remember that things went something like this:

You had been feeling bad, and everything seemed to be going wrong. No one appreciated you. Your mom or dad had been angry with you. You felt like no one loved you, and you began feeling sorry for yourself. Then the final straw broke. You did some small thing, such as breaking a dish. Your mom said something to you about it, and you ran to your room, slamming the door.

No one loves me, you thought. *I'll run away, and then they'll be sorry. They'll miss me and feel bad about how they've been to me. Maybe I'll get lost or hurt. Then they'll really feel sorry. They'll all be crying for me.*

When you have such thoughts and feelings, you're not so much angry as you are lonely. You feel unloved and unwanted. Most of all, you want to know that your parents really do love you.

Jesus told a parable about a boy who ran away. The boy didn't run away because he felt unwanted, but afterward he felt his dad didn't love him anymore. But the father did still love his son. Every day he went out looking for the boy. The dad couldn't stop loving his son, even though the son had hurt him very much.

This is how God feels about us. Like the father in the parable, God always loves us and watches for us. For the sake of Jesus, who gave His life for us, God is always ready to forgive us and take us back.

Because God loves us, our parents love us too. Sometimes we may not think they love us, but they really do. They are ready to forgive us. Sometimes we may not think so, but they are. What a happy feeling to discover that we are wanted and valued and forgiven!

PRAYER

Lord, sometimes we feel very alone and unloved. Please give us the courage to talk with our parents when we feel this way. Help us be confident that You always love us and are with us and forgive us for Jesus' sake. Amen.

Paul W. Wangerin

E A S T E R

May Day

Matthew 28:5–10

Have you had any surprises today? In some places, it is a custom to make May Day baskets for others. These small baskets, filled with spring flowers or other gifts, can be left on people's front porches. They are meant to be secret surprises. You leave them at the front door of a friend or neighbor, knock on the door or ring the bell, and then quickly hide before the person answers the door.

I think God enjoys surprising people with good things. Have you ever had something nice that you weren't expecting happen to you? Maybe a new friend moved in or your grandparents dropped by. Maybe a worry or trouble suddenly went away. Just as a person getting a May Day basket looks around wondering who to thank, we sometimes wonder who to thank for the good things that happen to us.

Our heavenly Father gives us all good gifts. His greatest gift is Jesus, His Son. Jesus' death on the cross was a terrible experience for His friends. When they wrapped His dead body and carried it to the tomb, they were sad. They didn't believe they would ever see Him again. But what a surprise! Three days later, an angel of the Lord rolled back the stone and sat on it. What a *happy* surprise! Jesus had risen. He was alive!

The happy surprise they felt was a little like finding a May Day basket—only much better! And Jesus' resurrection is a happy surprise for us too. Jesus' resurrection gives the power and authority needed to make our old sinful bodies new. Jesus is alive in His Word. He is alive in the promises of Baptism. He is offered in the Lord's Supper. Jesus and His promises are ours on May Day and every day.

PRAYER

Dear Jesus, thank You for the happy surprise You gave Your people when You rose from the dead and for all the happy surprises You give to me. In Your name I pray. Amen.

Eunice Graham

EASTER

It Isn't Fair

1 Samuel 24:8–13

Willie was sure Mr. Murdock disliked him. In class it seemed Mr. Murdock called on Willie to answer the hardest questions. When Willie hesitated, needing just a moment longer to think, he felt his teacher would jump all over him for not studying.

Once Mr. Murdock accused Willie of copying Simon's homework and turning it in as his own. Untrue! But Mr. Murdock just wouldn't listen. Yesterday he took Willie to the school office with threats to call his parents.

What could Willie do? He felt picked on and powerless to defend himself. Would he lose his temper, get angry, and blow up at Mr. Murdock? Would he find some way to get even?

David must have felt as Willie did. King Saul was chasing him. He accused David without reason. When David had a chance to hurt Saul, he refused. Why? David respected the king's authority. He knew that God had appointed Saul to rule His people.

It isn't easy to show respect for someone whom you think is unfair. David did it because the Spirit of the Lord was with him. Willie, too, will need God's Spirit to make him strong, patient, calm, and polite as he tries to work things out with his teacher. Through the Spirit we have daily forgiveness for our sin and strength to live out that forgiveness to others.

PRAYER

Dear Lord Jesus, help us to respect those You put in authority over us. When that is hard, help us to trust You anyway, and give us the patience we need. Amen.

Donna Streufert

EASTER

What God Calls Himself

Exodus 3:10–15

If someone asks you, "Who are you?" you may answer, "I am _____" and give your name. You may also tell something about yourself and where you live.

Long ago, God sent Moses to bring the people of Israel out of Egypt. When Moses asked God "Who are You?" God gave him an unexpected answer. He said, "I AM WHO I AM" (Exodus 3:14).

Is God's name "I AM"? This doesn't really sound like a name, but it gives a good description of God. By "I AM" God meant that He is eternal— that He always was, is, and will be. He also revealed by this name that He is a God of love and mercy. He keeps His promises and forgives the sins of His children.

Jesus also used this name for Himself. Some people think Jesus never existed before He was born at Bethlehem. But Jesus once said, "Before Abraham was, I am" (John 8:58). Jesus, the Son of God, always was, always is, and always will be. At Bethlehem, He became a human being so He could suffer in our place and save us from eternal death.

Jesus often described Himself by using "I am." In the Gospel according to John, He tells us: "I am the bread of life" (6:48); "I am the good shepherd" (10:11); "I am the resurrection and the life" (11:25). In this way, He showed that He, too, is gracious and forgiving toward us and that He is one with God the Father.

The most wonderful part of all this is that Jesus became one of us. The great I AM died and rose so we could say, "I am a child of God. I shall live forever in heaven with Jesus."

PRAYER

Great and glorious God, I praise You for Your power and love. Keep me as Your child through faith in Jesus, that I may share in Your unending life. In my Savior's name I pray. Amen.

Jeanette Haberstock

EASTER

O God!

Psalm 50:14–15

Last spring Nico went to stay with his grandmother in the country for a week. She took him in her new car for a long drive to the grocery store. They were planning to buy some things that he would like to eat while he was visiting. On the way home, Grandmother suddenly became ill and was unable to control the car. Nico took hold of the steering wheel. "O God!" he said.

He unfastened his seat belt and reached over to move her foot from the gas pedal. As the car slowed down, he concentrated on steering to the side of the road. He managed to get his foot on the brake. At first he pushed a little too hard, but soon the car stopped. Then he used the car phone to call 911 and his parents. The ambulance came and took Grandma and Nico to the hospital.

Nico's story was on the news, and he was called a hero. The reporter asked him what made him so brave. Nico gave the honor to God. He said, "God helped me."

Remember the part in the story when Nico said "O God!"? Sometimes God's name is used for no reason at all. But when Nico called out God's name, it was a prayer for help. He knew what God said in today's Bible reading: "Call upon Me in the day of trouble; I will deliver you, and you shall glorify Me" (Psalm 50:15).

God loves us very much. He knows when we need help. After all, He sent Jesus to help us with our greatest problem—sin. God has the power to help with every problem. Just like Nico, we can call on God's name. We know for sure that He will help us.

PRAYER

Thank You, God, for helping me in my times of trouble. Help me to remember to ask You for help and then to give You the glory. Amen.

Elaine Hoffmann

EASTER

Chips and Cupcakes

Titus 2:11–14

"Who packed their own lunch today?" asked Alan.

"Not me!" Rhonda said. "I've got cheese on whole wheat, carrot sticks, and an apple."

"I've got peanut butter and jelly again and the same old celery and banana," Bill complained. "My mother thinks the jelly is dessert."

"Look at my lunch," Alan said as he pulled out chips, cupcakes, pudding, and a chocolate bar. "I know how to pack a lunch!"

"But not all of that is good for you, Alan," Mrs. Schulz said as she came over to stand beside him. "No matter how good it tastes, it's hard to be healthy when you eat like that!"

Like Alan, we sometimes find ourselves wanting things that bring immediate pleasure but prove disastrous over time. Because we are sinners, we desire things that draw us away from our faith in Jesus. We may ask God to help us win one more game so we can be in the tournament that leaves us no time to worship on Sunday. We may pray for wealth that leads us to trust money for our security instead of trusting in our Father in heaven. We may do things that we know are wrong so we can be popular.

God wants good things for us. He hates all sin and every evil. When Adam and Eve disobeyed by eating the fruit in the Garden of Eden, God sent them out of the garden with the promise that He would send a Savior. Jesus was the promised Savior. He took the punishment for our sins when He died on the cross. All who trust in Jesus are forgiven and will rejoice forever in heaven with Him.

What does our Lord desire for us? Love, forgiveness, peace, joy, faith, eternal life, work to do for Him—all things good.

PRAYER

Dear Jesus, forgive me for seeking things that hurt me. Make me eager to do the things that please You. Amen.

Gretchen Gebhardt

EASTER

Transformation

2 Corinthians 3:18

Spring is my favorite time of year. The world is transformed from death to life. Plants come to life. Crocuses begin the parade. Sometimes they bravely bloom while there is still snow on the ground. Next come daffodils, then tulips and flowering trees. Soon the yards, gardens, and orchards look alive again. Birds nest. Gardeners plant. Children delight in outside fun—flying kites and swinging bats.

There was a time when we were as dead and dark as a gray winter day. When sin entered the world, so did death. Sin separated us from God, from His light and life. Our future looked dismal. But God promised a Savior, who would restore life and take sin's punishment.

Christ's death and resurrection brought springtime back into our lives. When Christ died, He took our sin to the cross. When He rose again on Easter, He guaranteed our salvation. Now, through His Spirit, we are transformed from sinner to saint.

In Baptism, our new life began. Through faith in Jesus, we received the forgiveness of sins and life forever. We received God's Spirit, who works God's good in us.

When you look at the flowers and trees around you, let them remind you of God's change in you. As the grass, flowers, and trees transform before your eyes, so God's Spirit transforms you!

PRAYER

Dear Jesus, thank You for transforming me in Baptism from death to a new life of faith. Amen.

Malinda Walz

EASTER

Not Good Enough

Romans 3:20–24

Inspector Mom visited my room on Saturdays. She could spot a stray sock behind the dresser, a toy soldier in the corner, or a dust bunny under my bed. I would think my room was clean enough. But even after two or three inspections, my mom showed me that it wasn't.

That's a little like the Law of God. God's Law inspects our lives even more closely than a mom. When God's Law finds something dirty or disorderly (and it always does), it accuses us. We may think that our lives are good enough, but God's Law always shows that our lives are not perfectly clean.

How do we get the Law to be quiet and stop accusing us? We can't, but Jesus did. He allowed Himself to be inspected by the Law in our place. His life is the only one perfectly clean from all sin and selfishness. His life is the only one that satisfies the Law. We are justified and redeemed because Jesus has stopped the Law from accusing us.

When the Law comes to inspect our lives and accuse us, we can recall that we have been baptized into Christ. He has passed inspection for us and, because of Him, we cannot be accused by the Law any longer. Redeemed and justified in Christ, we will come to enjoy an eternity of playful Saturdays in the clean rooms He has prepared for us in heaven.

PRAYER

Dear heavenly Father, help us to face all our accusers, to confess the truth, and to stand on the Last Day with Your Son, who has redeemed us from the accusations and curses of the Law. In Jesus' name we pray. Amen.

Joel Brondos

EASTER

A Difficult Visit

Romans 14:7–9

"Come on, Susan, it's time to go," Mother called up the stairs. "I promised Grandma we would be there by three o'clock, and it's quarter to three already."

Susan made her way slowly down the stairs. "I don't want to go, Mom," she said.

"Why not, Susan?" Mother said in surprise. "You always like to go see your grandmother."

"Mom, you know Donna's grandma died, don't you?"

"I know, Susan," Mother said. "She was very old."

"But isn't Grandma old too?" asked Susan. "She looks wrinkled."

"Yes," said Mother, "your grandma is getting quite old now."

"And won't she die soon?" asked Susan very carefully.

"Susan, you know everyone dies," said Mother. "Your grandma has lived a long time. She is ready to be with her Savior when the time comes."

Susan looked down. "But I will be so very sad when she dies. I don't want to see her if she's going to die."

Mother hugged Susan. "But think about Grandma. She needs you. She doesn't have much happiness in her life. She gets so much joy from seeing you. Surely you don't want to take that from her."

"But, Mother," Susan said, near tears, "I'll be so sad."

Mother lifted her face. "And we will all be sad. She is very dear to all of us. But Grandma will be happy. We believe, with her, that Jesus will take her to heaven when she dies and make her happier than she has ever been before. Jesus gives us the opportunity to serve Him by helping make Grandma happy until He takes her home to Him." Mother took Susan's hand. "Come on," she said. "Let's go visit Grandma."

PRAYER

Lord Jesus, we belong to You, whether we live or die. Help us comfort one another with this beautiful truth. Amen.

Theodore W. Schroeder

EASTER

A Sword of Words

Ephesians 6:17

Today computerized missiles are capable of hitting a target many miles away. Long-range weapons, armored tanks, fighter planes, submarines, and other sophisticated equipment are tools for waging war.

Battle was much different in Bible times. The most effective weapon was a sharp sword. The soldier depended on that piece of equipment in one-on-one combat. How important, then, for each soldier to be skilled in using it. He depended on it for survival.

Read Ephesians 6:17: "Take . . . the sword of the Spirit," says Paul to the Ephesians. And look again at what that sword is—the Word of God. God's Word is the only weapon we have in our battle with Satan. Whatever we're up against, God's Word comforts, defends, forgives, strengthens, and encourages us. We depend on the sword of God's Word for survival.

When Jesus was tempted by the devil in the wilderness, He answered all of Satan's temptations with quotes from the Holy Scriptures. The Word of God was the only weapon Jesus needed. And He emerged as our victor!

As we spend time in church, Bible study, Sunday School, Vacation Bible School, daily devotions, and Bible camps, we become more familiar with the tool God has given us. These opportunities help us become skilled in using God's Word as our sword. Then we're ready to resist Satan whenever he strikes. Look up Hebrews 4:12. God's Word is living and active. It tells us about Jesus, who is our victor over Satan.

The Holy Spirit keeps God's Word alive and active in our daily lives. The Spirit lives in our heart through Baptism, giving us power to recall His promises when we need them most. This "sword of the Spirit, which is the word of God" (Ephesians 6:17), is in our hand and on our lips.

PRAYER

Dear Lord, You are the living Word. Thank You for the precious gift of the Holy Scriptures. Sharpen my skills as I read and study about Your message of salvation. Amen.

Gloria Lessman

EASTER

The Forgotten Pilot

1 Peter 1:23–25

Captain Charles Nungesser was an ace pilot in the French Air Force. During World War I, he shot down forty-five enemy planes and won a whole string of medals.

In May 1927, Captain Nungesser tried to do something no one else had done before. He tried to fly all the way across the Atlantic Ocean from France to New York. His plane, "The White Bird," took off one day and headed out across the wild North Atlantic. But nobody ever saw the captain again.

A few months ago in Maine, a man was pulling up his lobster pots from the water near his home. He found some wreckage that looked like an airplane's instrument panel. Some people think it is part of "The White Bird." At the time the plane disappeared, there were reports that people heard a plane pass over that same area in Maine.

Captain Nungesser could have been a hero, but now his name has been nearly forgotten. So often a man's efforts to be famous end up in disaster. Even when he succeeds in winning honor and glory, these things soon pass away.

The Bible says, "All flesh is like grass and all its glory like the flower of grass. The grass withers, and the flower falls" (1 Peter 1:24). Grass can quickly dry up and die. So it is with the glory of man.

There is only one thing that does not pass away—God's Word. Jesus said: "Heaven and earth will pass away, but My words will not pass away" (Matthew 24:35). The Word of God is the Good News that Jesus has redeemed us from sin and death. This is the only thing that matters, for it assures us who believe in Jesus that we will live with God forever.

PRAYER

O God, our help in ages past,
Our hope for years to come,
Be Thou our guard while troubles last
And our eternal home! Amen. (*LSB* 733:6)

Robert Randoy

EASTER

Miserable Mondays

Psalm 59:16–17

Chris was having a miserable Monday. First, some bullies cornered him and teased him about his new haircut. Next, all his friends were raving about the class field trip to a big amusement park last Friday. (Chris had gotten sick the day before and missed the trip.) Then he got soaked in a cold downpour just as he headed home from school on his bike. Feeling wet, cold, and friendless, Chris clumped downstairs to his basement bedroom. His spirits were "in the basement" too.

As a young man, David, too, felt miserable at times. His enemies played tricks on him. They lied about him and even tried to kill him. David had to run for his life. He lived outside in all kinds of weather, among rocks and in caves sometimes.

David told God all about it. He wrote songs and poems expressing his feelings about his misery. He told how he sometimes felt like he had fallen into a pit.

But not every day was like that for David. There were days when David danced for joy, like a football player in the end zone. There were days when his spirits soared to the rooftops. Why? Because David knew that God loved him forever. He knew God was stronger than any enemy, any misery. Trusting God's love and power turned miserable Mondays into terrific Tuesdays.

We may sometimes feel like Chris and David. We can talk to God about our feelings. He loved us so much that He sent Jesus to be our Friend and Savior. Jesus defeated our greatest enemy, Satan.

PRAYER

Dear God, thank You for being here beside me every day. You are the greatest! Amen.

Donna Streufert

EASTER

Be Still!

Psalm 46:10

I feel like my life is going in circles, and the circles seem to be spinning—sometimes out of control. I get up in the morning and rush to school. I check and recheck schoolwork to make sure everything gets done. I go to basketball practice or music lessons. When I get home, I do my chores, help with dinner, and do homework. Then it's time for me to fall into bed. The next morning I do it again. Every day as I work harder, the circles spin faster.

Even on Sunday, I might be going in circles—singing in the choir, working in the nursery, helping the Girl Scouts. Even my worship is too hurried!

Some days I break down. I just can't do anymore. I take a vacation day and do nothing. Genesis 2:3 says that "God blessed the seventh day and made it holy, because on it God rested from all His work that He had done in creation."

God knows that we need His refreshment and peace. That's one reason He gave us the commandment "Remember the Sabbath day, to keep it holy" (Exodus 20:8). God wants us to stop spinning in our daily circles. He wants to renew us with His strength. In Psalm 46:10, He tells us, "Be still, and know that I am God."

He wants us to remember that He has taken care of the one thing that we really need in our lives. He has given us salvation by grace through faith in Jesus, who died on the cross for our sins. We are triumphant with the risen Lord. God used His power to take care of everything that really matters—no more circles without His rest.

PRAYER

Dear Lord, please enter my mind as I sit quietly. Bring Your peace and wisdom to me. Show me Your will in the stillness of Your presence. Amen.

Laura Siegert

Feel like a Nomad?

Matthew 18:19–20

Do you know what a nomad is? He's a person who is always moving from place to place. There's no place he can call home for long. Do you feel like a nomad?

Today people move much more often than they did, say, thirty years ago. Some moves are only for a short time, like when we go off on vacation. But if your father is like many fathers today, he gets transferred to a new job every few years. So every few years, you have to pack up and move away. If your father is in the army, you may find yourself moving from one army base to another. Or the move may be shorter—from an older house in the city to a newer one in the suburbs.

Moving to new places can be exciting—seeing new sights, meeting new people. But it can also bring problems. Moving means going to a new school and church where everyone you meet is a stranger—for a while, anyway. It means leaving behind old friends, a familiar neighborhood—just about everything.

There's one, though, you never leave behind, no matter how often or how far you move. Who? That's right: Jesus. He has promised, "Behold, I am with you always, to the end of the age" (Matthew 28:20). He is not like the empty house we leave behind. He goes with us even if we move all the way from New York to California.

So if we must pack up and say good-bye to old friends, let's remember our best friend is going with us. He'll be with us in our new home and school. He'll be with us as we make new friends. And He'll be there among us in church. For He said, "Where two or three are gathered in My name, there am I among them" (Matthew 18:20).

PRAYER

Abide, O faithful Savior,
Among us with Your love;
Grant steadfastness and help us
To reach our home above. Amen. (*LSB* 919:6)

Robert K. Hall

Concentration Troubles?

Philippians 2:5–11

How many more days till summer? Is that all? Won't be long, will it?

How are things going at school? Keeping your mind on work, I hope. I know, it's tough to think about school at all when summer gets this close.

So what *are* you thinking about? Swimming? Sleeping late? Taking a vacation with your family? Where are you headed? Sounds like fun!

You do still have a few weeks of school left, don't you? And a lot of important things still to be done there—like final tests. We can't goof off now, just because something great is coming up later. First things first.

Having trouble concentrating? Then think about Jesus. Nobody was ever better at keeping His mind on the matter at hand. And nobody ever had it tougher.

Think about it. Jesus is God. He'd always been in glory with the heavenly Father. Then He left heaven to become a human being like us. He knew His mission on earth would be for only a little while, and then He would return to the right hand of the Father in heaven. That would be great!

But in the meantime, He had to concentrate on what He was doing here. He had to live a sinless life. He had to suffer all the pains and embarrassment that we do. He had to die a horrible death on the cross. Through all that, He never wandered. He could have skipped right up to the good stuff, but He didn't. He stayed until His job was finished. Some kind of concentration!

Jesus didn't do all this to show us how to concentrate, though. His reason was much more important. He stuck to His task because it was all necessary for our salvation—yours and mine. He had to live the way we should have; He had to die the way we deserved—all for us. His stick-to-itiveness earned forgiveness for our sins. And it earned eternal glory for us—*after* everything God has planned for us here.

PRAYER

Dear Jesus, how did You do it? How could You love us enough to stay with all that suffering? But You did. Thank You! Amen.

Carl C. Fickenscher II

EASTER

Tornado Alert

Psalm 46:1–3

The wind was whistling through the waving tree branches. Gretchen and Kirsten noticed the sky getting very dark and the clouds looking strange.

"We'd better get back home fast," Kirsten said as some dust swirled into her face.

They both were out of breath as they burst into the kitchen, where their mother was holding the door open.

Mrs. Schultz put her arms around both girls to calm them down. "I'm glad you're back. I was just going to call you," she said. "We're supposed to go to the basement. A tornado has been sighted in our area."

They grabbed the portable radio as they quickly moved to the basement.

Kirsten asked, "Is the tornado going to blow our house away?"

"No, don't be silly," said Gretchen. "God is watching over us, isn't He, Mom?"

Mrs. Schultz asked Kirsten, "Remember that Bible verse you memorized for Sunday School? Didn't that tell you about God helping in time of trouble?"

"Yes, I remember. It's Psalm 46, verse 1." Kirsten recited it for them: "God is our refuge and strength, a very present help in trouble."

The music on the radio was interrupted by a voice that said, "All danger has passed. The tornado warning is over."

"Before we go upstairs, let's say a prayer together," Mrs. Schultz suggested.

PRAYER

Thank You for protecting me in time of trouble, heavenly Father. Help me remember that You're always watching over me, even when I'm not aware of it. I'm glad Jesus has made me Your child. Amen.

Carol M. Barton

Nonskid Wax

1 Corinthians 10:12–13

Rod arrived early for catechism class one Saturday morning. His friends hadn't come yet, and neither had Pastor Anderson. Standing outside, Rod saw and smelled the fresh wax on the parish hall floor. He decided to have a little forbidden fun, sliding over the polished tile. Stepping back a few paces, he made a running start for a long glide.

Just inside the door, Rod's feet came to an unexpected stop. The rest of him kept going and fell forward to the floor. Rod groaned. Just as he was getting up, Pastor Anderson walked in the door.

"Good morning, Rod. What happened to you?"

"Oh, I'll be all right, Pastor. It serves me right, though. You told us not to slide on the floors. But what went wrong? The floors look shiny, yet it's sticky."

The pastor smiled. "The new wax is nonskid, Rod. It's meant to keep you from slipping and falling."

The Bible says, "Let anyone who thinks that he stands take heed lest he fall" (1 Corinthians 10:12). A time comes when you think you can "stand" against the temptation to be bad-tempered. Then your little brother loses part of your model airplane. You blow your stack; you "fall." Or your parents give you a watch for your birthday. They hope you'll come home for dinner on time now. But good times tempt you to stay out late; again you "fall."

Our biggest problem is that the devil makes sin look so attractive. God won't allow His children to be tempted past their ability to endure. He supplies the "nonskid wax": "With the temptation He will also provide the way of escape, that you may be able to endure it" (v. 13).

God is faithful even when we are unfaithful. He always lifts us up after we have fallen. Because our sins are daily forgiven for Jesus' sake, we have new strength to overcome temptations.

PRAYER

Dear Lord, protect me from the temptations of the devil. Forgive me every time I give in to him. Thank You for sending Jesus to take away my sins and lift me up again. Amen.

C. Eileen Prole

E A S T E R

God the Podiatrist

Isaiah 52:7

Don't let the title scare you. If you don't know how to pronounce *podiatrist*, here's how: puh-DIE-uh-trist.

Now that you can pronounce it, the next question is "What is it?" A podiatrist is a foot doctor. Foot doctors treat people for painful foot problems. Why would anyone think of God as a podiatrist? If you read Isaiah 52:7, you have a clue.

In that Bible verse, God speaks to you and everyone else who believes in Jesus. Did you hear what He said about your feet? They are beautiful! It's important to know how they got that way.

Imagine you were walking barefoot through mud. (Don't try this at home.) As you squished through the mud, you stepped on a stem from a rose bush. Ouch! As you hopped around in pain, you accidentally kicked a rock with your other foot. Bigger ouch! Now you can only limp around with muddy, bloody, stubby feet.

Before Jesus made our feet beautiful, they looked like the feet in your imagination. Sin makes us ugly, dirty, bruised, and messed up—kind of like those feet. But Jesus cleaned us up. By dying on the cross and rising from the dead, Jesus took away our sins and made us clean—including our feet. Now He helps us to use our beautiful feet to walk around and tell others that Jesus made them and their feet clean too.

PRAYER

Dear Jesus, help me use my beautiful feet to tell others about You wherever I go. Amen.

Edward Grube

EASTER

Struggles

2 Corinthians 4:7–10

"Oh, Jenna, what a pretty cat!" said Lacey. "What's her name?"

"Struggles," said Jenna. "We have three cats, but Struggles is my favorite. Come here, Struggles."

Struggles came bounding over to the girls and leaped into Jenna's arms. The girls laughed as Struggles purred and cuddled against Jenna's body.

"Why is she your favorite cat?" asked Lacey. "And why did you name her Struggles?"

"Well," began Jenna, "Struggles got her name shortly after she was born. Her mother, Fluffy, gave birth to four kittens. The first three were born easily, but both Fluffy and the fourth kitten struggled a long time before she was born. We didn't name her Struggles right away, but the name kind of grew on her. She struggled the first few days just to live; then she struggled for her place to nurse. Later she had to struggle to learn how to walk and leap. Now," laughed Jenna, "she struggles just to stay out of trouble!"

Have you ever thought that your life is something like that of Struggles? Are you always struggling to make friends, learn something new, or stay out of trouble? Sometimes it seems that no matter how hard we struggle to do what is right, we end up doing wrong. Sometimes the wrong kinds of TV shows, magazines, and movies draw us away from Jesus and into trouble.

But Jesus' love is greater than all our troubles and all our struggles. Jesus loved us so much that He was willing to die on the cross and rise again for us. He won the greatest struggle of all time—the battle against the devil, sin, and the world. And because Jesus won the struggle for us, He helps us as we struggle against our troubles in this life.

PRAYER

Dear Jesus, help me give all my trouble to You. Thank You for always being near to help me. Amen.

Betty Moser

EASTER

Brussels Sprouts

Ezekiel 2:8–3:3

I used to hate Brussels sprouts. I don't suppose they tasted so bad, but I was afraid of them. I have to admit now that I didn't give them much of a chance. Fortunately, my mom insisted that we get our vitamins. Brussels sprouts are just loaded with vitamin A or B or something. Well, you know what happened; Mom made me eat them. And believe it or not, they weren't so awful. At first I ate only one at a meal. Now I can eat a whole serving. Brussels sprouts are all right.

Ezekiel was a prophet in the Old Testament. He was a grown man, and I guess he ate all the usual things that people ate in 600 BC. But then God came to him in a vision and asked Ezekiel to eat something *really* strange. God said, "Ezekiel, eat this scroll!" A scroll is an ancient kind of book, a roll of paper. And I thought Brussels sprouts were bad!

The scroll was just part of Ezekiel's vision, but it represented what God wanted him to do. Ezekiel was to speak God's Word to the people, to warn them of their sin. That may have seemed like a hard job to Ezekiel. Most people probably wouldn't listen to him.

God insisted that Ezekiel eat the scroll. To Ezekiel's surprise, it tasted delicious, as sweet as honey. The job of speaking God's Word would also leave a pleasant taste in Ezekiel's mouth, just as Brussels sprouts turned out to be okay for me.

At times we may be afraid to do something for our Lord. We may fear that no one will listen if we share our love for Jesus, or that friends will make fun of us if we're nice to the kid nobody likes. But we know what Jesus did for us. We know that He loves us and died on the cross for us. That makes it neat to serve Him, and He makes it turn out just fine.

We can think of serving Jesus as being sweet, like honey—or tasty, like Brussels sprouts.

PRAYER

Lord Jesus, thank You for giving us important things to try for You. Thank You for making some things turn out better than we ever expect! Amen.

Carl C. Fickenscher II

EASTER

Who's Staying with You?

Acts 1:3–11

"Who's going to stay with me?" the little boy asked every time his parents were getting ready to leave the house. Even before he asked, his mother knew the question would be on his lips as soon as she started dressing to go out.

"Who's going to stay with me?" Perhaps you have felt like asking that question at times. Maybe your parents hired a babysitter to stay with you when you were young. Now that you are older, they may feel you're big enough to stay home alone or with your little brother or sister. But we all still get lonesome sometimes.

Forty days after Easter, many Christians celebrate the Ascension of Our Lord into heaven. Before Jesus disappeared into heaven, He told His disciples, "Behold, I am with you always, to the end of the age" (Matthew 28:20).

So we can always be sure Jesus is near, and He'll gladly stay with us when we want Him to. Furthermore, because of His Son, Jesus, our Father in heaven has said, "I will never leave you nor forsake you" (Hebrews 13:5). This is why we can boldly say, "The Lord is my helper; I will not fear" (v. 6).

You see, Jesus was forsaken by His Father on the cross so that we would never be forsaken by God. Because God will never stop keeping us as His children, we need never feel unloved and alone.

"Who's going to stay with me?" The answer is easy. The Christian can say to the Lord, "Even though I walk through the valley of the shadow of death, I will fear no evil, for You are with me" (Psalm 23:4).

PRAYER

Abide, O dearest Jesus,
Among us with Your grace
That Satan may not harm us
Nor we to sin give place. Amen. (*LSB* 919:1)

Unknown

EASTER
The Ascension of Our Lord

Coming Back

Acts 1:6–11

Jenny and Fernando blinked back tears as they watched their parents' airplane roar down the runway. The plane gained speed and rose like a mighty bird into the air. Their eyes stayed glued to the plane until it entered the clouds and was gone.

"I don't know why I feel so sad," Jenny told her brother. "I was so happy when Mom and Dad told us that a new job would require moving to a new city. But now that they're going to find our new home, I'm lonely and afraid."

"Me too," answered Fernando. "I know they'll come back. And they said our new home will be better than where we now live. But I don't like to be alone. Let's talk to them on the phone tonight, and they won't seem so far away."

On Ascension Day, we remember how Jesus went back to heaven. When we think of Jesus, we may wish we could see and touch Him as children did when He lived on earth. Like Jenny and Fernando, we may feel alone.

But Jesus doesn't want us to be sad. He is getting heaven ready for us, and He promised that our new home will be better than living on earth. We can also talk to Jesus in prayer, and He won't seem so far away.

Though we can't see Jesus, He is still with us. He sees us all the time and takes care of us. We can be happy because we know He loves us. Our happiness includes knowing that He will come back and take us to live with Him forever. We know these things because we have His Word, the Bible. The Bible tells us so.

PRAYER

Lord Jesus, thank You for coming to earth to save us and for caring about us every day. Keep us in Your Word and happy in Your love until You come back to take us to heaven. Amen.

Robert Holst

EASTER
The Ascension of Our Lord

Don't Remove the Label

Matthew 5:17–20

"Do not remove under penalty of law." You know the label that comes on blankets and pillows? I used to be terrified about tearing off one of those.

Well, I did some checking. It's only against the law for the store that sells the item to remove the label. Once the buyers get home, they can do whatever they want with the bedding. Good thing too, because a few months ago, I accidentally tore the label off our bedspread. They're not going to come and arrest me.

God gave us His Law. We read it in the Ten Commandments. The Law tells us what God wants us to do and not to do. Sometimes we may wish God had never given us the Commandments. We would rather do whatever we feel like doing, without having God "bother" us. But God's Law is like the label on a pillow at the store—it may not be removed. We must always follow it. If we don't, there's a serious penalty—eternal suffering.

Unfortunately, we have ignored God's Law. We have "torn off the label" by sinning. We do it every day. That means we deserve the penalty of separation from God.

Since Jesus is God, who gave us the Law, we certainly wouldn't expect Him to forget about it. He couldn't remove the label or pretend it didn't matter anymore. He couldn't pretend that we hadn't sinned by breaking the Law. Still, He wanted to help us.

Jesus helped us by keeping the Law, by obeying it perfectly. Then He took the penalty for us. By paying for our sins on the cross, He took the punishment we deserve.

Jesus doesn't ignore our sins; He forgives them. Now we don't have to suffer the penalty of death. Instead, we're free to serve the Lord joyfully and to live in His grace. Isn't that great?

PRAYER

Dear Lord, we confess that we haven't kept Your Law. We have disobeyed, cheated, hurt others, and lived selfishly. Thank You for not ignoring our sins but forgiving them. Amen.

Carl C. Fickenscher II

EASTER

Kept from Slipping

Psalm 73:1–3, 15–28

In the Philippines (and other countries too), there's a lizard known as the gecko. This six-inch-long, stubby-tailed lizard has little "vacuum cups" on its feet that enable it to cling to smooth surfaces. Most reptiles would have trouble crawling up a windowpane. But because of the many little cups on its feet, the gecko can do it easily. It can even crawl upside down across a ceiling as it catches flies for food. The little suction cups on its feet are God's way of keeping it from slipping.

God has also provided a way to keep His children from slipping away from Jesus and falling from faith. By our own power we couldn't stay in the faith. One of the saddest sentences in the Bible reminds us of this truth. It's about a man named Demas. St. Paul wrote: "Demas, in love with this present world, has deserted me and gone to Thessalonica" (2 Timothy 4:10). Demas had been a believer in Jesus, but sin pulled him away from Jesus and from serving God. He lost his faith and the way to heaven.

God the Holy Spirit has given us faith in Jesus. He also keeps us in the faith through the Word of God. On Sundays, we have another opportunity to hear and study God's Word in church and Sunday School. That Word works like a suction cup, for by it, the Holy Spirit keeps us from falling away from Christ.

The Bible says, "He who began a good work in you will bring it to completion at the day of Jesus Christ" (Philippians 1:6). The "good work" God has begun in us is our faith. He will make it grow stronger until, at last, we meet Jesus face-to-face.

PRAYER

Heavenly Father, I thank You for the gift of Your Spirit. Make me faithful in hearing, reading, and studying Your Word so the Holy Spirit can make my faith grow stronger every day. Amen.

Leonard Aurich

EASTER

School Year Memories

Jeremiah 31:31–34

You are   2 good

           2 be

        ___

        4 gotten

Roses are red,
Violets are blue;
Sugar is sweet,
And so are you!

Have you ever written in anyone's yearbook? At the end of the school year, we may sign autograph books or yearbooks. We share our memories with one another this way. We might write about the day the snake slithered away during science class. We may recall the slumber party where no one slept. By writing memories down, we can remember them longer.

It's fun to think back on the school year. Or is it? Maybe you remember a problem you had with a friend. Perhaps you wish you'd studied harder for some of your classes. Then, too, there may be a teacher to whom you showed disrespect. Who wants to remember those things? You surely wouldn't write about them in a yearbook, would you?

No, most people would just as soon forget the bad memories. God forgives our failures and gives us the opportunity to begin again. Our Scripture reading says He forgives and forgets our sins. Our heavenly Father keeps no list of our mistakes. They are erased from His memory because Jesus suffered the punishment of hell in our place.

God also helps us to forgive a friend. He empowers us to make amends with a teacher. He even works in our lives to help us do better with homework. We ask in faith. God promises to answer.

As we look back, we praise God for the good memories. Perhaps we made new friends this year. Give God thanks! Praise Him for the improvement in grades. Thank Him for that special teacher. Blessings poured down on us this past school year. God promises He will be with us in the coming year too. Praise Him for His goodness and mercy!

PRAYER

Dear Jesus, roses are red, school's almost through.
Thanks for forgiving and blessing me too. Amen.

Gail Marsh

EASTER

God's Writings

John 20:30–31

In the town of Keswick, England, stands the factory where pencils were first made. Long ago near Keswick, a man found some smooth rocks. When he rubbed them, they turned his fingers gray. People learned they could write with the rocks, called graphite.

Some workers ground the graphite to powder, mixed the powder with clay, and made thin rods of the mixture. Pieces of cedar wood were put around the rods to form pencils. Pencils became popular writing tools. People used them to draw, write stories, and share information.

The Bible, God's Word, is a written record of God's actions and teachings. From the Bible we learn what God wants us to know and believe and how He wants us to live. The Bible tells us that when we sin against God in any way, we deserve punishment.

But the Bible also tells us of God's love in sending Jesus, His Son, to save us from our sin, from death, and from the power of the devil. Through His death on the cross, Jesus suffered the punishment for our sins that we deserve. God forgives our sins for Jesus' sake. The apostle John wrote that Jesus' teachings and actions were written down so that we may believe in Him and have life in His name for all eternity.

PRAYER

Thank You, God, for Your holy, precious Word, where I can learn all about You, who so freely gives me life and salvation. Thank You for giving me faith in Jesus, my Savior. Keep me close to You until You take me to heaven. In Jesus' name I pray. Amen.

Philip Otten

EASTER

Warnings and Promises

Jeremiah 7:23–26

The O'Brien family heard a loud, beeping noise coming from the stairway wall. Dad was sure it was a bird caught between the walls. Scott thought it was a cricket. Mom said it was the boards creaking. The beeping was getting louder. Sometimes it kept them awake at night. What was that noise?

Then Scott's friend spent the day. He heard the beeping sound and knew what it was. It came from a smoke detector in the hallway. Dad took it down. The instructions said that a beeping noise would warn when the battery was weak. To keep the smoke detector working, you have to pay attention to the warning sound.

The prophet Jeremiah gives a warning in our Bible reading. He tells how to live God's way. But the people didn't listen to the warning. We don't always listen to God, either. We are diverted by things around us and drawn away from God's Word and way. Does the TV set take up most of our time? Are we too busy at work or play to listen to God? Jeremiah is speaking to us.

Yet, with every warning from God, Jeremiah gives great hope. He points us to Christ as the branch who will be called "The LORD is our Righteousness" (Jeremiah 33:16). Listen to this love message from God: "I will cleanse them from all the guilt of their sin against Me" (33:8). With the warning came the hope of forgiveness.

God sent Jeremiah to His people to teach them His way. He gives us parents, pastors, and teachers to guide us. How God loves us! Listen to His warning and promises, and follow His way. It's the way of forgiveness and hope.

PRAYER

"Give thanks to the LORD of hosts, for the LORD is good, for His steadfast love endures forever!" (Jeremiah 33:11).

LaVerne Almstedt

EASTER

Inside and Out

1 Samuel 16:7

How do you like your eggs cooked? Hard-boiled? Scrambled? Sunnyside up? Perhaps you'd rather have an egg with a bump of cheese in the middle! Huh? Most restaurants wouldn't know what to do with an order of "one egg with a bump of cheese in the middle."

For a first grader named Allie, an order like that makes perfect sense. To Allie, the golden yolk of an egg looks exactly like a bump of cheese. It's the only way she knows how to describe the kind of eggs she likes to eat.

The yolk of an egg does look like cheese. It's easy to understand Allie's confusion. Outward appearances can sometimes be deceiving. Take Samuel, for example. Samuel was chosen by God to anoint a new king to replace King Saul. God sent Samuel to Jesse's house. One look at Jesse's son, Eliab, and Samuel thought he had surely found the new king God had chosen. God's Word in 1 Samuel 16:7 tells us God didn't care how the next king looked on the outside. Rather, God looked at the heart. God did not choose Eliab, but his younger brother, David. David loved God with his whole heart.

What does God see when He looks at you? From the outside, we might think we look pretty good. But God looks right past our outward appearance. God looks inside. There's no doubt He sees sin inside every one of us. But because He loves us, God didn't want us to live with the guilt of our sins. He sent His Son, Jesus Christ, to be the sacrifice for our sin. When God looks at us, He sees the righteousness of Jesus, which clothes us.

PRAYER

Dear Father, thank You for loving us enough to send Your Son to die for our sins. May Your love fill our hearts and be known to others around us. Amen.

Julie Dietrich

EASTER

Salvation History

Isaiah 43:1–7

A Korean orphan came to the United States and was adopted by Christian parents. He attended school and loved to tell his new parents about all the things he learned. One day, he asked his new mother about some unfamiliar expressions he had seen in his history book: "Remember Pearl Harbor." "Remember the Maine." "Remember the Alamo."

His mother explained that these were slogans marking important events in United States history. "Being an American is more than a matter of birth or citizenship," she said. "It also means knowing the history and traditions of our country."

When Ling Koy became an American citizen, all of American history became a part of him. So also, when we become Christians through the power of the Holy Spirit, the history of God's people is a part of our lives.

Our Christian faith centers on the mighty acts God has done for us. We especially remember Jesus' death and resurrection, His institution of Baptism and the Lord's Supper, His words of love, and His miracles of healing. These "Bible history stories" become real and meaningful for us because we believe that they happened for our sake. We remember the many mighty acts God performed for His people in the Old Testament.

Salvation history is important for us because through Baptism, we have become children of God. It points us to and fixes our eyes on Jesus: "But when the fullness of time had come, God sent forth His Son, born of woman, born under the law, to redeem those who were under the law, so that we might receive adoption as sons" (Galatians 4:4–5).

We Christians remember Jesus and His love, especially when we are tempted and our faith is threatened. Our Lord promises, "Fear not, for I am with you. I have redeemed you. You are Mine."

PRAYER

Dear Father, may I never forget Jesus' love for me in coming to earth and dying on the cross to save me from my sins. When I am tempted or in doubt, remind me that I am Your child. Amen.

Charles Reichert

EASTER

The Masks We Wear

Romans 5:8–11

The knights of the Middle Ages wore suits of armor and rode into battle on horses. The armor gave protection, but it was also heavy and uncomfortable. A man wrote that a knight was "a terrible worm in an iron cocoon."

The helmet alone weighed about ten pounds. It consisted of the top covering and a visor to protect the face. This mask made it hard to see and was dark and stuffy inside. It did hide the face, but it could also get in the way.

We all wear masks, and they usually get in the way for us too. Everyone thinks Daemon is cool. He wears cool clothes and tells neat jokes. But Daemon is really unhappy. He has no one to talk to at home. His "cool" mask covers his sadness. Sally is very shy. She doesn't have friends, and the other girls at school call her stuck-up. Her mask says she doesn't care, but she cries at home. Mrs. Ramos wears a mask in front of her third graders. She has arthritis and hurts all the time. She puts on a mask to cover the pain.

We hide behind our masks, but God sees through the masks we wear. Our Bible reading tells us the wonderful Good News that He loves us. He showed that love by sending Jesus to die for our sins. He knows our false faces and forgives us. He knows our fears, sadness, and pain, and He draws us to Himself.

When no one else understands, God is still there. He invites us to come to Him. His love will carry us through the tough days. Jesus gives us the strength to show our best face—praising Him!

PRAYER

Dear Lord, thank You for Your great love, which sees through many masks. Help me live in the joy of Your love and forgiveness. Amen.

LaVerne Almstedt

EASTER

Power to Speak

Acts 2:1–12

Bonjour, Mesdames et Messieurs! Dieu vous aime!
¡Buenos, dias, damas y caballeros! ¡Dios los ama!
Guten Tag, meine Damen und Herren! Gott hat euch lieb!
Do you understand these sentences? If you don't know French, Spanish, or German, you won't. They say, "Good day, ladies and gentlemen! God loves you!"

When someone speaks in a language different from our own, our faces may look puzzled. That's what happened one Pentecost Sunday to Peter and the other disciples. They were in a large gathering with people from all over the world. The disciples wanted to tell everyone that Jesus had died so that they could live forever.

The disciples had one problem. They knew only one language. The Holy Spirit took care of that problem in a special way on Pentecost. When Peter and his friends started talking about Jesus, all the listeners understood them in their own language! It would be as if the French heard French, the Germans heard German, and the Spaniards heard Spanish. How exciting! Some leaders thought the disciples were drunk, speaking strange languages.

Through God's power, Peter could tell everyone how wonderful God is. He preached a powerful sermon about Jesus. By the working of the Holy Spirit, three thousand people believed in Jesus and were baptized.

Those who believe in the Savior through His Word and Sacraments have the Holy Spirit working in them too. God gives believers the amazing, beautiful words to tell all nations about His Son's loving sacrifice on the cross for the sins of all people.

PRAYER

Holy Spirit, help me speak the language of the Gospel as I share Your words of love and forgiveness with people I know. Amen.

Mark R. Rhoads

PENTECOST
The Day of Pentecost

Does God Make Us Sick?

Romans 8:28–32

June caught up with Jackie as they were walking to their Sunday School class. "Why weren't you here last Sunday?" she asked. "We'd have won the banner for perfect attendance if you had been here."

"I had a bad cold," Jackie answered. "My father even had to get a prescription for me from the drugstore."

"I don't know why God had to make you sick," said June. "We lost the banner to Wayne's class."

"God didn't make me sick," Jackie corrected her friend.

"Yes, He did. He decides everything that happens to us."

The girls' teacher overheard them as they came in the room. "What's all this about?" she asked.

"Mrs. Carlson," said June, "didn't God make Jackie sick last Sunday? I think God controls everything in our lives. So He must decide whether we get sick or stay well."

"Isn't there a difference between controlling something and making it happen?" asked Mrs. Carlson. "We get sick because germs are a part of this natural world, not because God wants to make us feel bad. But God can control our sickness so that good comes from it."

"I know that's true," said Jackie. "Last Sunday I had to stay in bed instead of coming to Sunday School. But I learned that Jesus' love is more important than attendance prizes. In a way, I'm glad God let me be sick. Now I'll appreciate Sunday School more."

Mrs. Carlson added, "God says in His Word that 'for those who love God all things work together for good'" (Romans 8:28). "Even sickness is often a blessing in disguise."

PRAYER

Dear Jesus, help me understand that sickness in this world is a consequence of sin. You know about everything that happens in our lives, when we are sick and when we are well. Please forgive us and mercifully heal us of our sicknesses, especially our sin-sickness. In Your name I pray. Amen.

Robert Kerekes

PENTECOST

God Made Me!

Psalm 100:1–3

Today is my birthday. I was born June 1, 1965, in St. Louis, Missouri. When is your birthday? Where were you born?

When you were born, it made your family very happy. You were a tiny baby. You had to be held, fed, and kept warm. Your parents gladly did this because they loved you. You were a gift from God!

Each year we celebrate the day we were born. On our birthday, we thank God for giving us life. Our Bible reading says, "Know that the LORD, He is God! It is He who made us, and we are His" (Psalm 100:3).

He gave us eyes to see His beautiful world, ears to hear birds and animals, legs to run and play, and a mind to learn things. He gave us His Holy Spirit in Baptism so we can have faith in our Lord and Savior Jesus Christ.

Isn't it nice to know that the God who made us still takes care of us? He gave us life, but He didn't stop there. He has also given us, year after year, food, clothing, shelter, and spiritual blessings.

God gave His one and only Son to be our Savior from sin. Because of Jesus, we have a new life that never ends. He gives us a new birth at Baptism and continues to provide the forgiveness of sins each day.

As you remember your birthday, "Give thanks to Him; bless His name!" (v. 4).

PRAYER

Dear God, thank You for forgiveness and for my life now and forever. Lead me to honor You and my parents each day. In Jesus' name I pray. Amen.

Craig Otto

PENTECOST

Sticking Together

1 Corinthians 13:4–7

Rachel was angry at herself, her parents, and her puppy. Rachel's mother, Ruth, opened the screen door and said, "Honey, there's no reason to cry. The incident is over."

Rachel whined, "But, Mom, Dad is mad at me. I'm mad at the puppy and myself. Do we even love each other anymore?"

Hugging her daughter, Ruth asked, "Rachel, what is love?"

The twelve-year-old responded, "I'm not sure. I suppose it means to feel good about someone."

"Do you feel good about your puppy?"

Rachel answered, "Not right now. I didn't think he would ever do his business on the carpet. What a mess! Dad was yelling at both of us. He made me clean everything up. Gross!"

Ruth smiled. "But you still love your puppy, don't you? And I know Dad loves you. Love is more than a feeling. It's a pledge to stick together."

"Stick together?" Rachel echoed. "Even when we're angry?"

Her mom answered with a question: "Do you suppose God gets angry?"

Rachel replied, "I think Pastor read a passage last Sunday about God's anger."

"That's right," Ruth explained. "On Calvary, God gave Jesus the anger we deserve. Our disobedience still angers God, but He daily forgives us."

Rachel said, "I guess love is like Krazy Glue—sticking us together even though we don't always feel good about each other."

Ruth nodded. "Love is cleaning the mess on the carpet even though it was gross. By the way, I see a puppy outside needing love."

"Not anymore," said Rachel as she headed out the door.

PRAYER

Father, through the cross of Your Son, You have overcome Your anger over my sins. You have restored me to Yourself. Let my love for You and for others be like Krazy Glue, never coming undone. In Jesus' name. Amen.

Michael Parris

PENTECOST

First Things First

Luke 10:38–42

When Jonathan was four, he thought farm life was the best. One day he asked a new friend at preschool if she wanted to be a farmer. When she said yes, Jonathan said, "I will teach you. First, you have to get up very early in the morning."

Jonathan's simple answer makes us laugh. He didn't choose caring for livestock, planting crops, or driving a tractor. He thought of first things first—getting up early!

Mary and Martha were entertaining Jesus. What did the two women put first? Mary was listening to Jesus' words. Martha was thinking of jobs. Martha was frustrated with all the preparations and even asked Jesus to send Mary to help her. Jesus told Martha that Mary had chosen what was needed—hearing His Word.

Your future will include days full of choices. What will be first? Like Martha, you might get so busy with your daily tasks that you decide you have no time to listen to God's Word. But Jesus is waiting to spend time with you, just like He did with Mary.

God knew you would give in to sinful thoughts and actions. He knew you would be born with a sinful nature. He put you first, planning for your salvation back in the Garden of Eden. He invites people to come and sit at His feet and listen to His wonderful words. In a church service, in class or family devotions, and in personal Bible reading, you have the same invitation as Mary—to sit at the feet of Jesus.

PRAYER

O Lord, I have so many things to think about. Help me put You before all other things. Guide me and bless me. Amen.

Donna L. Koren

The Power of Stars

Psalm 103:8–12

Nathan charged toward me with a book in his hands. "Mom, read this article about black holes. It's really amazing!" I learned about another wonder of God's creation that day.

Scientists think that when stars die, they collapse inward with a gigantic pull of gravity. They pull other space objects around them into this whirlpool of gravity. Even the light can't escape, disappearing into the black hole.

This is rather like what God does with our sins. The Bible writers describe forgiveness in various terms: washing (Psalm 51:2), casting into the sea (Micah 7:19), sending far away (Psalm 103:12). However you say it, God removes our sins totally. He does this through Jesus' sacrifice on the cross (Hebrews 9:28).

Jesus was sacrificed once for the sins of all people. His love pulled all sins to Himself on the cross, where He atoned for them completely. He took them to the black hole of His grave and burst forth in triumph, alive.

Now Jesus lives and reigns as our bright morning star, drawing all people to Himself (John 12:32). Now, that's *really* amazing! Thanks, God.

PRAYER

Dear God, You sent Jesus to destroy sin. How can we ever thank You enough? Your love has drawn us to You. Help us stay close to You always. We pray in our Savior's triumphant name. Amen.

Jacqueline L. Loontjer

God's Good Advice

Proverbs 1:7

Benjamin Franklin was a wise man who helped form our nation. He was also a respected businessman, writer, printer, and publisher. We can read some of his good advice in *Poor Richard's Almanac:* "A penny saved is a penny earned" and "Early to bed and early to rise makes a man healthy, wealthy, and wise."

Many, many years before Benjamin Franklin, God used King Solomon and others to write good advice for us, His children. These wise sayings are found in the Book of Proverbs. One piece of good advice that God gives us is in Proverbs 1:7: "The fear of the LORD is the beginning of knowledge; fools despise wisdom and instruction." This verse says that if we fear (that is, love and respect) God, it is the start of a wise and godly life for us. The Holy Spirit will work through God's Word to guide us in the decisions we make and help us to make the right ones.

Still, there are many times when we won't make wise decisions because we are sinners. Temptations can be great, and we may choose to follow the ways of the world. That is why God made His wise plan to send Jesus to be our Savior. For Jesus' sake, God forgives us when we fail to live as His children, and He enables us to share His love and forgiveness with others.

PRAYER

Dear God, thank You for the words of wisdom You have given us in the Bible. Help us to study Your Word and live a life pleasing to You. In Jesus' name we pray. Amen.

Diane Maurer

PENTECOST

1 + 1 + 1 = 1

Ephesians 1:3–8, 13–14

Some students these days are learning new answers to old arithmetic problems. It used to be that two and two were always four. But now the answer could be five or some other number, if you use a new way of figuring.

God's math has always been strange. When we learn about the Holy Trinity—the Father, the Son, and the Holy Spirit—we find that one and one and one are not three, but One. The Bible teaches that God is three persons but only one God. The Father is God, the Son is God, and the Holy Spirit is God.

St. Patrick is said to have used a shamrock (a three-leaf clover) to help people understand this. While preaching in a field, he picked a shamrock and pointed to its leaves. He said that as the three leaves make up one plant, so the three persons of the Trinity are one God. Perhaps you have heard other ways of illustrating the Holy Trinity.

But illustrations don't make this marvelous truth altogether clear. Even as people who learned the old math can't understand the new math at first, so we can't fully understand the Trinity. But it will become clear to us in heaven.

In the meantime we can know what a wonderful God our triune God is. We can rejoice in His great love and mercy to us. We can understand that the Father created us and planned to save us, the Son carried out the plan, and the Holy Spirit gives us faith to believe in Jesus Christ and receive His blessings of new life and forgiveness.

That God is Three in One is an important truth for us to learn. But for our spiritual health, it's even more important to realize that through faith in God, *we* are one with Him, now and always.

PRAYER

Dear Father, I believe that You made me and that You keep me safe. Dear Jesus, I believe that You died for me and rose again to save me from my sins. Dear Holy Spirit, I believe that You brought me to faith in Jesus. Thank You, O God, for Your great love to me. Keep me faithful to You and united with You always. Amen.

Albert H. Miller

PENTECOST
The Holy Trinity

God Is Three in One

1 Timothy 2:1–6

Do you know that Islam is the second-largest religion in the world? Only Christianity has more followers. Today, almost a half-billion people, representing one-sixth of the world's population, are Muslims. In some parts of Africa, Muslims are reported to be gaining ten times as many followers as Christians.*

All Muslim beliefs and practices are based on their holy book, called the Qur'an. Muslims believe the Qur'an is the message of God that the angel Gabriel delivered to a man named Muhammad in AD 622–632. The main teachings of Muslims are called "the five pillars of Islam."

The first and most important pillar is the Muslim creed: "There is no god but Allah, and Muhammad is his prophet." To become a Muslim, all you have to do is to say this creed in the Arabic language and to believe it. You don't have to be baptized or go to catechism class.

This creed emphasizes the oneness of God. Again and again, Muslims stress that "God is one" and "God has no partners." They accuse Christians of worshiping *three* Gods—Father, Son, and Holy Spirit.

What would you answer to that? How many Gods are there? Do Christians believe in three Gods? No, of course not! Christians believe in the triune God, that is, the three-in-one God. We admit that this God is a great mystery that our human minds cannot understand.

The second part of the Muslim creed talks about Muhammad as the prophet of God. Muslims give first place to Muhammad as the greatest teacher, prophet, and messenger of God. This is another difference from Christians, who believe in Jesus Christ as true God and true man and the Savior of all people. Here we begin to see what a hard job it is to tell a Muslim the Good News of salvation through faith in Jesus.

PRAYER

O holy triune God, You have sent Jesus Christ as the Savior of all people. Give the blessing of Your Holy Spirit to all Christian missionaries as they try to tell Muslims of Your love in Christ. In His name I pray. Amen.

Robert McAmis

PENTECOST / TRINITY

*Since this devotion was first printed forty years ago, Islam has continued to grow steadily. Today, according to various sources, there are an estimated 1.2 to 1.5 billion Muslims, accounting for approximately 20 percent of the world's population. —Ed.

Sharing Friendship

Colossians 4:5–6

Jim's dad grew yellow squash in his garden. One morning, he picked two big buckets full. "Why don't you see if the neighbors want any, Jim?" he asked. "We'll never use all of these."

Jim knocked at every door, but nobody was home. The last house on the block was old Mrs. Bundy's. She never had visitors. She was a mysterious woman who always looked angry. Her crooked mouth made her look like she was always frowning.

Jim swallowed hard and knocked on the door. At last, Mrs. Bundy dragged the door open and glared at him. Then, with the same glare, she said slowly, "Oh, squash! How nice! Are you selling them?"

"No, ma'am," Jim said, "we're giving them away."

Before Jim left, he had been given cookies and milk. He had looked at pictures of Mrs. Bundy's husband, who had died years earlier. He had held her cat, Pearly. "I'll make squash pickles," Mrs. Bundy said. "You come back in a couple of days. I'll have some ready for you."

"Mrs. Bundy had a stroke," Jim told his dad later. "She can't help how she looks. She's really very nice!"

Jesus often showed kindness to "outsiders." He even called an outsider, the tax collector Matthew, to be His disciple. Jesus didn't just look at the outside of people. He didn't just listen to what other people said about them. He looked inside and saw each person's heart. Jesus died to earn forgiveness for all people. Young or old, pretty or ugly, rich or poor—they are all dear to Him.

PRAYER

Dear Jesus, help me to be a friend to those who need one. Give me courage and wisdom to talk with people I don't know well. Help me to show my faith in You. Amen.

Glenda Schrock

Overcoming Fear

Isaiah 41:10

Ben's legs trembled as he looked down from the diving board. "Now, Ben, jump!" his instructor shouted.

Out of the corner of his eye, Ben could see people watching. Mom and Grandma were there, along with his classmates and his teacher. He knew there was only one more day of class, and he wasn't going to pass until he fulfilled this final requirement. Tears filled his eyes as he stammered, "I just can't." And he ran off the board, into the locker room.

"I don't want to talk about it," Ben warned as he got in the car to go home. But later, when he was alone with his grandma, he did approach the subject.

"I wanted to do it while you were visiting," he confessed to her. "I wanted you to see me. Now you and everybody else think I'm chicken."

"I don't know about anybody else," Grandma assured him, "but I don't think you're chicken. Do you know how many times in my life I felt exactly as you did today? Fear is natural, Ben, and at times, it protects us. It can overtake us, though, unless we conquer it. I'm going to share with you a Bible verse that helps me when I'm afraid."

The next day, Ben stood on the diving board. He blocked out everything else and said to himself, "I can do all things through Him who strengthens me" (Philippians 4:13). He closed his eyes and jumped.

When he bobbed up to the surface, everyone was clapping and yelling, "Good for Ben! You made it!"

Thank You, God, he said silently. Then he asked his instructor, "Can I jump in once more before I take my shower?"

Do you know who the "Him" is in Ben's Bible verse? Yes, it's Jesus, our Lord and Savior. He promises each of us the strength to overcome fear through trust in His love and mercy. With Jesus as our Savior from sin, we can meet life head-on and win.

PRAYER

When I'm afraid, Lord Jesus, help me know You're always near to help in time of need. Amen.

Dorothy J. Haggstrom

PENTECOST / TRINITY

The Right Trail

Isaiah 58:9–11

Did you ever stoop down to watch an ant trail? Maybe you wondered how the ants knew how to go in the right direction. Scientists tell us that it's because of pheromone, a chemical the insects place as they walk along. It helps the ants following to know that they're on the right trail.

Suppose an ant could suddenly grow giant-size and look down at people. What would it see? You guessed it—confusion everywhere, people going in different directions, and most of them not even sure of where they came from or where they're going. And we thought the *ant* had it tough!

We Christians are to stand out from this confusion. When others see us going to church, caring about strangers, sharing with neighbors, and working cheerfully, they see us following a trail. They might ask, "How do you know how to go in the right direction?"

We needn't wait for scientists to try to discover reasons for our behavior. Jesus is the reason. He has saved us from sin—something we could never do on our own. Through His Spirit, He works faith in us. Through His work in us, we tell others about Jesus as the Savior of the world and the only way to eternal life. His work leads us to invite others to church, where they can hear that Jesus is our Savior.

By studying Scripture and by living our faith, we follow God's way. As we walk His trail, St. Paul's words become our guideline: "Walk in love, as Christ loved us and gave Himself up for us" (Ephesians 5:2).

"Come along," we call to those we meet. "Join us! Follow the trail."

PRAYER

Dear Jesus, I thank You for Your guiding Word and Holy Spirit. I ask for strength and wisdom to follow Your way as You guide me through this week. In Your holy name. Amen.

Kristine M. Moulds

Gasoline and God's Word

2 Timothy 3:14–17

What is the longest road trip you have ever taken? Chicago to Orlando? Seattle to Phoenix? Toronto to Vancouver? How many times did you stop for gas? In order for a car to keep going, it has to be refueled regularly.

The same is true for people. Most children can go for about three hours before they need some fuel—a piece of fruit or a slice of pizza. Without that regular refueling, you may feel a little helpless—too weak to push the lawn mower. Your body might even have a breakdown—the kind where you end up sick.

Christians also need regular refueling. The kind of fuel we need, however, does not come from a gas pump. The kind of fuel every Christian needs comes from the Word of God and the Sacraments—Baptism and the Lord's Supper. These are the ways God connects us to His grace, refueling us by the power of the Holy Spirit. Without regular refueling, we are more likely to break down in our Christian walk and be helpless when facing the attacks of Satan.

God offers us the gifts of forgiveness and salvation freely through the means of grace. These means are the "highest octane" around, getting us where He wants us to go!

PRAYER

Lord, thank You for being my source of spiritual fuel. Guide me to regularly "fill my tank" with Your power. In Jesus' name. Amen.

Mindy Walz

An Unbroken Ticket

Romans 8:1–6

Let's pretend that in two weeks, the king of Ionite is giving a party. It's the biggest celebration we could imagine. Cotton-candy trees, peppermint fences, chocolate fountains, and root-beer lakes cover the palace grounds. Everyone in the land is invited to join the celebration.

However, there is one condition. The king has issued everyone a glass ticket. To enter the gates, you must present this unbroken ticket to the gatekeeper. Attached is a warning: one sin, no matter how small, will shatter the ticket. You must be very careful.

As the days go by, you see that everyone's glass ticket has broken because of sin. When the day of the party arrives, there isn't one person who has an unbroken ticket. Desperately you try to glue your ticket back together. Your effort is useless. There is nothing you can do.

Looking back, you see the crowd make way for one who has an unbroken ticket. He makes his way to the gate and presents his ticket. Suddenly he turns and begins handing out new tickets. You are now allowed to enter and join the celebration.

God has invited you to join in eternal life. Yet your sins would keep you from taking part in this celebration. God loves you so much that He sent Jesus into the world. Jesus fulfilled the Law and suffered the penalty for our evil deeds, words, and thoughts. Through faith in this Savior, you receive eternal life. Come, join His celebration!

PRAYER

Heavenly Father, I know that I am sinful and deserving of death. Please forgive my sins. Strengthen me in my belief in Jesus so I, too, may join the celebration of eternal life. Amen.

Katie Hodel-Berg

Tug-of-War

Hebrews 4:14–16

Coming home from work one evening, I found my children and their friends playing tug-of-war in our front yard. They had a rope stretched across our driveway, and kids on each side of the driveway were pulling on that rope as hard as they could. Whichever side stepped on the driveway first would lose.

Just for the fun of it, I joined one side and pulled with them. Because I helped them, that side won. The other side complained that I was unfair.

Every day of our lives, we're all involved in a tug-of-war with our sinful nature. What the Bible calls our "flesh," the part of us that wants to sin, tugs at us to make us do wrong. On the other side, what the Bible calls our "spirit" tugs at us to do what God wants.

This tug-of-war is not much fun. It makes us feel like the rope in the middle as we get pulled from side to side. Part of us wants to do wrong, and part of us wants to do right.

Thank God we're not alone in this tug-of-war. Our Lord Jesus is on our side to give us an advantage. Jesus was tempted to sin the same way that we are tempted. He knows how hard it is to say no to sin and yes to God. When we are tempted, He says to us, "I know how you feel. Let Me help you. We're in this together."

Our Bible reading tells us that Jesus was tempted in every way that we are, but He never sinned. Through His sinless life and innocent death, our Lord Jesus set us free from the power of sin. His victory over sin is our victory.

When our flesh tugs at us to do wrong, we can tug right back to do what God wants. Jesus will be pulling with us, giving us His strength.

PRAYER

Heavenly Father, thank You for sending Jesus to be on my side in the tug-of-war with sin. With His strength to help me, may I obey You more and more. Amen.

Daniel G. Mueller

PENTECOST / TRINITY

God's Mighty Word

2 Corinthians 12:7–9

John Bunyan was a famous Christian who lived long ago. He wrote a book called *The Pilgrim's Progress*, which millions of Christians have enjoyed reading.

This famous Christian tells us one way in which he became strong in faith. Every morning, he would memorize a short verse from the Bible. Then, throughout the day, he would think about what it meant to him.

One morning, Mr. Bunyan was in great trouble. He felt sad and discouraged. Even his Bible verse for that day didn't seem to help him. But he kept thinking about it anyway. What was the verse? "My grace [love] is sufficient [enough] for you" (2 Corinthians 12:9).

Suddenly, just when Mr. Bunyan was so discouraged that he didn't know where to turn, all his sadness went away. He began to laugh. He laughed at himself because, all of a sudden, that Bible verse showed him how silly it was to worry.

"My grace is enough for you," he said to himself. Why, it's Jesus Himself who promised that His grace and love is enough for me. It's like a river saying to a poor little fish, "My water is enough for you," or the earth saying to a man, "My air is enough for you." If Jesus Himself says that His grace is enough for me, this is surely all I need.

God's Word made John Bunyan's faith stronger. The power of God the Holy Spirit working through His Word and the Sacraments makes your faith stronger. In His Word, we hear the Good News of Jesus' death on the cross to take away all of our sins. His resurrection from the dead makes His promise of our resurrection a reality. God's grace is enough for anyone!

PRAYER

O Holy Spirit, thank You for speaking to me in the Bible. Open my heart and mind to Your Word every day, and strengthen my faith. In Jesus' name I pray. Amen.

Earl Gaulke

File 126,430

Psalm 51:1–12

"File 126,430" sounds like the beginning of a spy story. Really, it is the *end* of a story, the end of some people's attempts to make themselves right with the law. This file is in the U.S. Treasury Building. It contains letters sent in by people confessing that they have cheated the government out of money. Each letter is accompanied by the sum of money its writer had stolen.

Some letters contain only a few cents. Others contain as much as thirty thousand dollars. Over the years, more than two million dollars have been sent in by people with troubled consciences. These people knew they had done something wrong, and they wanted to make it right.

Did you ever feel you had done something wrong and had to make up for it? Maybe it was the time you talked back to your dad. Or maybe you got a friend into trouble at school. At such times, you get a guilty feeling inside—a guilty feeling that demands you make up for the trouble you've caused.

Sin makes us feel guilty. This is what makes the message of the Lord to Joseph mean so much to us. He told Joseph that Mary was to have a child and that "she will bear a son, and you shall call His name Jesus, for He will save His people from their sins" (Matthew 1:21).

We can't make up for our sins. No matter how hard we try, we can't undo what we have done. Only Jesus can. Only Jesus can blot out the sins and make our conscience clean.

The times we have sinned against our parents, the times we have shown no love to our families, the times we have failed to use our abilities have all been washed away. We are no longer guilty, for Jesus took our guilt on Himself. Now we are free to serve God with a clean conscience.

PRAYER

Lord Jesus, my Savior, when I feel guilty, help me remember that You earned forgiveness for me by Your holy life and innocent death. Amen.

Lois Vogel

In the Days of the Flood

1 Peter 3:18–22

Try to imagine what the world was like in the days just before the flood. Hardly anybody believed in God. Young men whose parents had loved God married young women from families that didn't even think about God. Most people lived just for the sake of eating and drinking and having fun. They were so wicked that God decided to destroy mankind.

But God still loved the people and gave them 120 years to change. He also sent Noah to preach them a sermon. This was no ordinary sermon, for it was made of wood. By building an ark, Noah was telling the people that God would destroy the world with a great flood.

Perhaps the people in Noah's day were like some people today. They don't see how a loving God can punish anyone. But God finally did let the flood come. Why? Because the people were dead already. Except for Noah and his family, all were "dead in the trespasses and sins" (Ephesians 2:1).

The ark Noah built was a sign of death to others. But it meant life for Noah and his family. The waters of the flood raised the ark higher and higher and thus saved these eight people from disaster.

Strange as it may sound, we are saved by water too. We were once dead in sin, but the waters of Holy Baptism washed away our sin. Through Baptism, God makes us His sons and daughters and gives us eternal life. Because He once punished Jesus in our place, He will never punish us for sin as He did the people in the days of the flood.

PRAYER

Dear God, I confess that I have sinned and that I deserve Your punishment. Have mercy on me through Jesus, my Lord. Help me remember every day that You have washed away my sins in Baptism and that I am Your child. Amen.

Donald Ortner

PENTECOST / TRINITY

Turn Evil Around

Ezekiel 18:30–32

Here's an easy spelling game. All you do is read or write the printed words backward. Just turn around the letters, and you'll get another word. Try it; the first one is done for you.

saw *was* pots _____won _____lap _____

pit _____ but_____tap _____keep _____!

Those were for fun. This next one can teach us something:

evil _____

You have to turn "evil" around to "live." How true! People caught in evil are not living full and happy lives. Sure, they might be rich and have everything they want. But pretty soon, everything is not enough. They want more and more and are never at peace. Evil may start out small, but it grows and can lead to drugs, stealing, depression, cheating, lying, fighting, and more. That is *not* God's abundant way to live.

The only way to turn the evil in your life around is with Jesus. You can't do it alone. When Jesus lives in you and guides you, you are really living. Peace, joy, patience, kindness, goodness, self-control—all are yours! You'll still be tempted and have bad days, but with Jesus, you'll win.

One more game word. Write a "d" in front of "evil": _____ evil.

Now turn that word around: _____. The devil is the leader of evil ways. But we know he has been defeated, conquered by Jesus. Jesus *lived*, died, won eternal life for us, and lives forever. So will we.

PRAYER

Good and loving God, I praise You for Your plan to save me from sin. Help me turn around from evil ways to Jesus' ways. Thank You for Your merciful forgiveness. Amen.

Nancy Carlson

PENTECOST / TRINITY

Our Hiding Place

Psalm 32:7

Men pushed an iron ball into the cannon. Another man stood behind the cannon and lit the fuse. Boom! Swoosh! The cannonball shot across the field.

Lila and her family were watching a reenactment of the Battle of New Orleans. After the Americans won independence from Great Britain, they had a few years of peace. Then Great Britain wanted the American colonies back, and the War of 1812 began on June 18.

The Battle of New Orleans took place in January 1815. On the American side were about twenty-five hundred untrained troops under General Andrew Jackson. On the British side were eight thousand well-trained troops. No one expected the Americans to win.

The British marched across open fields in bright red coats, playing music on their bagpipes. They marched in rows, standing tall, trying to scare their enemies. The Americans didn't fight like that at all. They built dirt walls and hid behind them, shooting from their hideouts.

The battle was short. Many British soldiers died; many Americans were saved by dirt walls.

Battles have gone on for years. In Old Testament days, David was chased by the king and his men. David found a place to hide, and he also found someone in whom he could hide—someone stronger than he was. In our psalm for today, David calls God his hiding place. David turned to God for protection.

You and I have enemies too. Some of them are mighty, mightier than we are. But God is stronger. In His Word and promises, we can hide. When sin or Satan attacks us, we can remember that Jesus has defeated them. Those enemies may march against us and taunt us. They may hurt us, but they can *never* win.

PRAYER

Dear Father, I could never face life's troubles by myself. Thank You for hiding me in Your arms and giving me Jesus' victory. In His name I pray. Amen.

Cheryl Honoree

PENTECOST / TRINITY

"Forgive Us, Lord"

1 John 1:9–10

I'm writing this from a place called Moose Jaw, Saskatchewan, Canada. (When pioneers were moving West, a man fixed a broken wagon by using the jawbone of a moose.) What's the first thing you think about when the name *Canada* is mentioned?

Last year the temperature got down to 45 degrees below zero and the wind blew at 35 miles per hour. That gave us a windchill of 108 degrees below zero. Brrrr! That's cold! The TV weatherman said that we had low temperatures because cold air was coming down from Alaska. When I heard that, I thought that whenever something bad happens, we blame someone else.

I'll show you what I mean. When I lived in the United States, the weatherman said the cold air came from Canada. I live in Canada now, and the weatherman says the cold air comes from Alaska. When I lived in Alaska, they said the cold air came from Siberia. It always seemed to come from somewhere else.

Sometimes, similarly, when we do something wrong, we might try to blame somebody else. How often have you heard yourself say "he made me do it" when you did something bad? We think that blaming somebody else makes us good.

That isn't the way God wants us to be with Him. When we sin against Him, He wants us to admit we are wrong and say, "I'm sorry." God loves us. God forgives us. He is merciful because Jesus took our blame with Him when He died on the cross for sin.

PRAYER

Father, I'm sorry that I have sinned and then tried to put the blame somewhere else. Please forgive me. Thank You, Lord, for hearing my prayer and for taking my sins away. Amen.

Gerald Schienbein

Buzz—Beware!

1 Peter 5:8

They're back, they're relentless, they're irritating, they're . . . mosquitoes. This rather small insect has a bite that leaves a nasty welt and a terrible itch.

Once, mosquitoes were considered to be a problem only at dusk, but now they can be bothersome throughout the day. Even though we can't get rid of these pests, we can protect ourselves from them. We can wear long pants and long-sleeved shirts. We can apply insect repellent.

The devil is relentless and irritating too. The devil is God's enemy, a continual pest. He tempts us to sin, and sin is nasty and terrible.

We can't get rid of the devil, so we ask God to guard and keep us so that we might not be misled into false thinking or become discouraged. God covers our arms and legs, head and heart with the defense of His Word and the blessings of His Sacraments. We find His covering in Bible-based devotions with our family. We find it where the Word of God is proclaimed or taught. We find it in the blessings of our Baptism and in the Lord's Supper.

What do we do when we give in to temptation, when we despair, or when we are misled into wrong thinking about God? God helps us. He leads us to confess our sins and to find forgiveness in His healing Son, Jesus Christ, our Lord. God does not leave us without hope. He relentlessly cares for us.

PRAYER

Dear God, forgive me for the sins I've committed this day. Strengthen me through Your Word that I might be protected from temptation. Amen.

James Hahn

Praying Anywhere and Anytime

1 Kings 8:27–30

One summer, David and his mother were far from home, visiting at his grandparents' farm. At night, when David looked up at the beautiful, star-lit sky, he would think of his dad at home. They both enjoyed looking at the stars on summer evenings.

David often wondered about God's greatness. Dad sees the same sky at home that I see here, he said to himself. God is watching over both of us at the same time, even though we're far away from each other. And I can pray to God here at Grandma's, and Dad can pray to Him at home. God can hear both prayers because He is everywhere at the same time.

Yes, God is great and marvelous. He can hear our prayers anywhere in the world. We can speak to Him wherever we are. The Bible tells us that the heavens and the earth cannot contain Him. And God can hear the prayers of all people at all times, no matter where they are.

It's very comforting to know that we can talk to God anywhere and at any time. Sometimes we like to be alone in a quiet place when we speak to God. Often we want to be with others when we pray. We can talk to God on our way to or from school; we can speak to Him in school or at home. All day long we can feel close to God.

PRAYER

Lord, teach a little child to pray,
And, oh, accept my prayer;
You hearest all the words I say,
For Thou art everywhere. Amen. (*The Children's Hymnal* 285:1)

Elfrieda Miller

Stop, Anthony, Stop!

Galatians 5:16–18, 24–25

The house was quiet. Mom and Dad were in the garden. Anthony picked up a purple crayon and headed for the stairway. He knew that if he wrote on the wall, his parents would catch him, but he did it anyway.

He moved quickly, pausing to write on the wall at each step until he reached the bottom. Then, feeling guilty, he ran to hide.

When his parents returned from the garden, they were shocked. There was scribbling on the whole wall. All the way down the stairs Anthony had written, "Anthony, Anthony, Anthony . . ."

Even though Anthony tried, he couldn't hide from his parents for long. They found him and talked gently but firmly with him. Then Anthony did what he needed to do. He spent the afternoon trying to remove his name from the wall. But the purple color wouldn't come off until his dad repainted the wall.

Like Anthony, we do sins on purpose. And like Anthony when he was done, we feel guilty and want to hide these sins from our holy God. But can we hide anything from God? No!

We can't hide from God or get rid of our sin. No amount of scrubbing will remove our sins. And the penalty for sin is separation from God forever. In order for humankind to be right again with God, someone must pay the penalty. God provided the solution. He sent Jesus to take the punishment that we deserve. On the cross, Jesus paid for all our sins, and in Baptism, He makes the wall of our life clean, now and forever.

PRAYER

Jesus, please forgive me for doing what I know is wrong. Help me be more like You. Amen.

Gretchen Gebhardt

"Full of Scared and Lonely"

Joshua 1:9

The little boy came toddling out of his bedroom for what seemed to be the hundredth time that night. Patiently his father picked him up in his arms and asked, "Son, what's the matter? Why can't you sleep?"

"I don't like my room," the boy answered.

"Why not?"

"Because it's full of scared and lonely," he replied, almost at the point of tears.

The father carried his small son back to the bedroom. After putting him in bed, the father stayed in the room.

"Do you want to hear a story?" the father asked.

"Sure."

The father then told a story about his own boyhood. He recalled the first time his father, a coal miner, had taken him down into the mine where he worked. "As the elevator started its downward plunge, I was suddenly very afraid. 'Daddy,' I cried out, 'hold me tight! I'm scared!' My father held me tightly in his arms until I felt more secure.

"Later, down in the mine, someone asked me if I was still afraid. 'Well, I would be, if Daddy weren't here,'" I said.

"My father looked at me and said, 'You don't have to be scared, son, because even when I'm not around, our heavenly Father will always be with you.'"

Jesus once said about His Father, "He who sent Me is with Me. He has not left Me alone" (John 8:29). Just as God was always with Jesus, so He is also with us. He tells us, "I will never leave you nor forsake you" (Hebrews 13:5).

PRAYER

Jesus, I know You love me and stay beside me every day. I want to remain close to You, my Savior and Lord, and rely on Your comfort and help. Amen.

Thomas Burton

PENTECOST / TRINITY

Daniel and the Lions

Daniel 6:10–12, 16–23

Before our son was born, my husband and I often talked about what we should name the baby. After many discussions, we finally decided on the name *Daniel.*

After Daniel was born, we naturally told everyone the new baby's name. Many people, after hearing our choice, asked about the lions. The first time, it took me by surprise. "What lions?" I asked.

"You know—Daniel in the lions' den. Has this Daniel met up with any lions yet?"

Thankfully, our Daniel has met up with lions only in his books. But I imagine that he will have some more to deal with in his life.

The Daniel in our Bible reading was thrown to the lions because of his faith in God. Christians today do not usually have to deal with the furry, ferocious type of lions. Our lions often take other forms.

When someone makes fun of us because of our faith, we have a "lion" to deal with. If someone treats us unfairly or hurts us because we are Christians, we have another "lion" to fight off.

As we know from the Bible, Daniel didn't fight off those lions. God took care of the problem for him. When we are faced with difficult situations because of our Christian faith, God helps us as well. The Holy Spirit can help us give an appropriate answer to the people who laugh at us or hurt us. He can help us remember just how important our faith is. He can help us see and feel how much God loves us.

God loved Daniel so much that He let him escape the lions. He loves us so much that He gives us salvation through Christ's death and resurrection. He surely will help us fight off our "lions" also.

PRAYER

Dear Lord, thank You for the gift of our faith. Please help us fight off the lions in our lives, and give us the courage to share Your love with others. Amen.

Susan Waterman Voss

PENTECOST / TRINITY

No Less

Luke 15:1–10

One day to me a test in math my teacher did present,
And at the top, in big, bold red, was "99 percent."
An A adorned that paper, so I burst into a song.
A hundred questions on that test; I only got one wrong!

I told my mom, I told my dad, I told my Aunt Louise.
"I'm so much smarter now," I sang. "This math stuff is a breeze!"
In school, it's true that 99 is really quite enough.
Someone who gets a score like that—she really knows her stuff.

But when we're speaking of the Lord, He never is content
When points are sheep—or souls to save—with 99 percent.
He sent His Son to seek and save all 99 plus one,
To live, to die, in each one's place, so victory could be won!

Yes, each is precious to the Lord, and so He sets the goal
So through His Church His news is spread to reach each living soul.
It's not enough for Him to score a 96 or 7.
He died so all would hear His voice and live with Him in heaven.

PRAYER

Thank You, Lord, for finding and saving me. Amen.

Mindy Walz

In the Eye of a Hurricane

Psalm 46

Hurricanes are the most destructive storms known to man. A hurricane is a large mass of air moving rapidly around in a circle. This circle is often 400 miles across and may have winds up to 200 miles per hour. When these storms cross over land, they can cause millions of dollars in damage.

The center of a hurricane is called its eye. This is usually about 20 miles across. The eye is much different from the rest of the hurricane. Inside the eye, the weather is calm and clear. Only light breezes blow there. You can hardly believe that this is the very center of a monstrous storm.

Sometimes life is much like a hurricane. Everything seems to be swirling around us. We hear threats of a nuclear war that could destroy millions of lives. We worry about the grades we will get and what we're going to become in life. We have problems at school, disagreements with our friends, and troubles at home.

These worries and dangers are very real in every Christian's life. But they don't make us give up. We know that "God is our refuge and strength, a very present help in trouble" (Psalm 46:1). And so we live unafraid in the eye of the hurricane.

God doesn't promise to take away the storm. He still permits troubles and worries to enter our lives. But He helps us live peacefully in the middle of them by assuring us that He is with us.

Whenever our life seems troubled and confused, let's remember the words of the psalm: "Be still, and know that I am God" (v. 10).

PRAYER

Dear Lord, I am not afraid when I know You are with me. Help me believe that none of my problems are too big for You. As You have promised, be my strength and help in every trouble. Amen.

Luther Gutknecht

Fire Ants!

Romans 5:8–9

Moving to Florida has provided me with an opportunity to learn many new things. The climate, plants, and animals are certainly different. If you plan to be outside for any length of time, sunscreen is essential. One more thing I've learned painfully is not to walk barefoot in the grass.

In Florida and other Southern states, small insects called fire ants live in the grass. You can recognize a colony of fire ants by the mound of dirt they create. Here's some advice: avoid those mounds! Here's some more advice: wear shoes! The fire ants are so small that you don't notice them until it is too late. When they contact your skin, they swarm and bite. When they bite you, you feel like you were put into a pizza oven to bake. Ouch! Blisters appear. Don't mess with those little guys!

We all need to avoid certain things—many things more troublesome than fire ants. Lying, stealing, cheating, disobedience, and name-calling are mounds of sin. Even when we avoid stepping into those mounds, we sinners walk through our own sinfulness. Ouch! Blisters of guilt appear.

South Florida needs a solution to fire ants. We need a solution for sin's pain, now and forever. Jesus is our treatment. He is our healer and our salve. Through faith in His death and resurrection, we are healed and free to walk a new life.

PRAYER

Father, forgive me for the times I have done things that hurt You. Give me Your Spirit's power to say no to the devil and temptation. Thank You that I am forgiven because of the work of Jesus, in whose name I pray. Amen.

James Hahn

JUNE 28

An Interesting Language

John 15:9–11

When the United States was a young country, the cowboy was an important person in the West. He led a hard life, but he loved the freedom of life on the open range.

Cowboys developed a language all their own. They called an orphan calf a "leppy" and a weak calf a "dogie." "Critters" was another name for cattle. A dust storm they called "an Oklahoma rain." The deadly, rolling winds that dropped the thermometer 50 degrees in one day they called "blue northers."

The head man who gave the cowboys their "powders" (orders) they called "the wagon boss." And they called their songs "Texas lullabies."

It was an interesting language, but to be useful, it was important to know its meaning.

The language of our faith in God also has some interesting words. Perhaps you're learning new ones every day and, in this way, understanding God's message better. Do you know all these?

Regeneration—being born again
Remission—God's forgiveness
Justification—being forgiven
Sanctification—being made holy
Reconciliation—patching up a friendship
Intercession—praying for another
Grace—love that is undeserved
Gospel—Good News about Jesus
Redeem—to buy back

Look at all these words again. There is something very wonderful about them. Although they all look different and sound different and seem to have different meanings, they all have one thing in common: they are always saying, "God loves you."

PRAYER

Dear Father, my heart is full of joy because You love me. Help me share Your love and my joy with everybody. Amen.

Betty Nohl

PENTECOST / TRINITY

The Greedy Fish

2 Corinthians 12:7–9

Scott dropped a pinch of fish food into the middle of a group of sword-tails.

"Didn't you just feed them after lunch?" asked his father.

"Yes, but they're hungry again. I feed them whenever they're in this eating corner."

"They might want some food, son. But do you think it's good for them? The saleslady said to feed them once a day."

"Don't they know what's good for them?"

Scott's dad laughed. "Apparently not. They've gotten a little greedy, and you're going to have to make them wait."

Scott had to do for his fish what was best for them, not what they wanted. God shows this same care for us by the way He answers our prayers. He doesn't always answer them the way we want Him to.

St. Paul found this out when he asked the Lord to remove some physical problem he had. The Lord didn't remove it. He answered in a different way, by giving Paul the strength to bear it. Paul responded, "I will boast all the more gladly of my weaknesses, so that the power of Christ may rest upon me."

Because the Lord doesn't give us exactly what we ask for doesn't mean He hasn't heard or answered our prayers. Even "no" is an answer. His answer is the one that's best for us.

God knows our needs, and He will provide for us. Paul said in another place, "He who did not spare His own Son but gave Him up for us all, how will He not also with Him graciously give us all things?" (Romans 8:32).

PRAYER

Dear Father, thank You for Your wisdom, direction, and care in my life. Help me not to get upset when my prayers aren't answered exactly as I wish. Help me realize Your way is best. Amen.

Barbara Kosinsky

PENTECOST / TRINITY

Notches in the Wood

Matthew 18:21–22

"What are you doing?" Lauren asked Joshua. She watched as he carved on a piece of wood.

"This is my record," he replied. "This is what I'm using to keep track of Jordan's sins. Every time he does something wrong against me, I make a notch in the wood. See?" He held up the thick branch covered with scratches.

"Why would you want to do that?" Lauren asked.

"Because I multiplied seventy times seven. Once I get to 490, I don't have to forgive Jordan anymore. And by the looks of it, he will reach 490 before the weekend!"

Lauren shook her head. "Josh, are you thinking about our Bible reading from the other day?" The boy nodded and continued to carve into the wood. "But you've got it all wrong! Jesus said to forgive our brother seventy times seven as a way of showing unlimited forgiveness. He didn't mean to stop forgiving when you get to 490!"

Lauren sat down next to Joshua as she continued. "I mean, think about it. We sin all the time. If Jesus stopped forgiving us after we had committed 490 sins, we'd be in big trouble. If He kept a count of all our sins and held them against us, none of us would go to heaven. In fact, the only place we'd deserve to go would be to hell. But He died on the cross to take away *all* our sins. And the Bible says that He doesn't count our sins against us. Isn't that wonderful?"

Joshua had stopped slicing on the wood. "You're right, Lauren," he responded. "Now I see what Jesus was saying to us. I know I've done a lot of things wrong. Yet Jesus forgives me. It's fantastic to know you're forgiven. And Jesus wants us to share that forgiveness with others, just like He shares it with us. Do I understand it now?"

"Yes, Josh. So what are you going to do with that piece of wood?"

"This? I'm going to throw it away. That's what Jesus did with our sins!"

PRAYER

Lord Jesus, thank You for Your unlimited forgiveness. Please help us show it to others. Amen.

Carla Fast

PENTECOST / TRINITY

A Big Holiday

Romans 15:5–6

Do you know what happened on this day, July 1, in 1876? That's when the British colonies of New Brunswick, Nova Scotia, and the Province of Canada were united in one government called the Dominion of Canada. So today is a big holiday for people who live in Canada. Each year on July 1, Canada Day is celebrated with patriotic programs and events.

Many brave people worked together to bring about the union of the provinces. Little would have been accomplished if each one had "done his own thing." Unity was important to these Canadians.

When possible, it's even more important for Christians to be united. New believers can become confused when they see Christians arguing and fighting with one another. Because of that behavior, they may find it hard to believe what Christians are telling them about Jesus.

That's what Paul was talking about in today's reading in Romans when he said, "May the God of endurance and encouragement grant you to live in such harmony with one another, in accord with Christ Jesus, that together you may with one voice glorify the God and Father of our Lord Jesus Christ."

Why do we try to agree? Because God had mercy on us sinners and sent Christ Jesus, His Son, to redeem us from sin. Even though we can be disagreeable, He welcomes us to be His children through Baptism and His Word. He loves us with an everlasting love. He wants us to join in the glad celebration in heaven that will last forever. That will be the grandest and greatest holiday of all!

PRAYER

Dear God, help me work with other people and to agree on the important things that help others to know You. In Jesus' name. Amen.

Jeanette Dall

When We Pray

2 Corinthians 12:7–10

This is a true story about a little boy who lived a long time ago. His father was a minister in Georgia. A minister didn't earn very much money in those days, but their children had fun anyway, especially when they could go barefoot in the summer.

Albert, the boy I'm telling you about, longed for a pocketknife more than anything else. So he decided to pray for one. The next day, as he was walking down the dusty road, his big toe stubbed against something hard. Lo and behold, there was the pocketknife he had prayed for! It was not much of a knife—it was rusty, and one blade was broken. But it was a knife! He took it home and cleaned it, and he carried it proudly.

Well, he thought, if God answers prayers so fast, I'll pray for a bicycle. So he prayed for a bicycle. In fact, he prayed night and day. But he didn't get a bike. When Albert told me this story, he said that it was a long time before he realized prayers were not some kind of magic.

God wants us to pray. But He also expects us to use the abilities He has already given us. For example, I've heard children who haven't studied for a test pray, "O God, please let me be able to answer the questions and pass." It's nice those children knew how to pray, but God had already answered their prayer. He had given them minds with which to think and learn. But with their prayer, they were trying to make God responsible if they failed the test. Studying would have been better.

Perhaps this is part of what God wanted Paul to learn in our Bible reading: trust God for everything, and remember that His grace is what we need most. He might, for our own good, say no to a prayer.

Prayer

Dear God, help me to pray wisely and to accept whatever answer You give through Your Son. Amen.

Margaret O. Eser

God Made Turtles Too

Revelation 4:9–11

"Dad, look!" shouted Marty. "A turtle's crossing the road. Can we stop and take him home? Please, Dad! I've always wanted a pet. He wouldn't be much trouble. I'll take care of him, I promise!"

The turtle kept his head inside his shell during the ride home. "He's shy," said Marty's mother. "Give him some time—he'll get used to us."

When Marty got home, he built a cage with scrap lumber. He set out lettuce and water. Then he put his pet turtle, which he named Sporty, inside. Marty continued to watch and wait, hoping Sporty would poke his head out of the shell.

Several hours later, he raced outside to check on his new pet again. There was Sporty, peeking out at Marty. "Well, Sporty, you finally decided to show your face, huh?" Marty was thankful to have a pet to enjoy.

Have you ever had a pet turtle or another pet? God created animals for our use and enjoyment. He loves us and wants us to be happy.

God not only made all the animals, but He made us too. Look at your fingerprints. No one else has fingerprints like yours. God created you unique and special.

God's greatest gift is His Son, Jesus Christ. God sent Jesus to be our Savior. Jesus lived the perfect life we are unable to live. He suffered and died for our sins. Now He offers us forgiveness and everlasting life. Our God is really awesome!

PRAYER

Thanks, Lord, for creating animals I can enjoy and care for—like turtles, rabbits, dogs, and cats. Most of all, thank You for sending Jesus to be my Savior. In His name. Amen.

Kay L. Meyer

Freedom for All

Isaiah 61:1–3

On July 4, Independence Day, we celebrate the freedoms we have in the United States. You may have read about Martin Luther King Jr. in your history book. He is one of the most famous African Americans. At the time he grew up, blacks were treated differently from other people. They had to sit at certain tables in restaurants. They had to sit at the back of buses. They did not have equal opportunities for education or jobs.

Martin Luther King Jr. knew this was wrong. He began a peaceful movement to change the way African Americans were treated. Many people agreed with him and helped him. But some people disagreed with him. One day one of these people shot and killed him. April 4 is the anniversary of that day.

Martin Luther King Jr. died, but his work did not. As a result of his work, the laws of the United States were changed to guarantee equal rights for all citizens.

There is a bigger champion for freedom than Martin Luther King Jr. You won't read about Him in most history books. That person is Jesus, God's Son. He came to earth to make all people free.

The Bible tells us that all people are slaves to sin and are doomed to spend eternity in hell. Jesus came from heaven to live a perfect life for us. He died to take the punishment for our sins. Through faith in Jesus, we have forgiveness of all our sins and new life. Now *that's* real freedom!

PRAYER

Dear God, it is hard to think what life would be like without the earthly freedom we have. It's even harder to think what life would be if Jesus had not died that we might be forgiven, free from sin, death, and the devil. We praise and thank You that we will live with You in heaven eternally. In Jesus' name. Amen.

Judy Williams

Lighten the Load

Matthew 11:28

Jordon was helping Grandpa clean out his garage. They were moving big boxes of old books onto the driveway. A truck from the library was coming to get the boxes. Jordon groaned as he lifted a heavy box from the floor.

"Always bend at the knees when lifting heavy loads," said Grandpa. "That way your legs will do the work."

Jordon found that by bending his knees, it was much easier to lift the boxes. Grandpa was right.

We might bend at the knees in prayer. Perhaps you kneel by your bed to pray before you go to sleep or when you wake up. Maybe you kneel to pray in your church.

We pray to thank God for His blessings. We pray to confess our sins and ask His forgiveness. We pray when our load or problems seem heavy. We pray for others. God has promised to hear our prayers and help us.

Jesus prayed often when He lived on the earth. He knew that talking to His heavenly Father helped Him do what God had planned for Him. Shortly before He was put to death on the cross, Jesus prayed alone in a garden. He asked God if He really had to die. Yet, Jesus' suffering and death were all part of God's wonderful plan. God the Father strengthened His Son for the terrible days ahead. Those terrible days ended when Jesus rose from the grave. Our forgiveness was won!

Jesus did the work for us on the cross. His work gives us salvation. God the Father invites us to bring our burdens to Him. Whether we bend our knees or not, nothing is too big or too small to bring to God. He hears our prayers and gives us strength to go on.

PRAYER

Dear God, remind me to bend my knees and come to You when my load is heavy. In Jesus' name I pray. Amen.

Dawn Napier

Jan Hus, Christian Martyr

Hebrews 11:32–12:2

On October 31, 1517, Martin Luther posted his Ninety-five Theses on the church door at Wittenberg, Germany. The Protestant Reformation traces its official beginning to that famous act.

But the Reformation actually began long before 1517. One of the earlier reformers who influenced Luther's thinking was Jan Hus.

Jan Hus was born in Bohemia (part of modern Czechoslovakia) about the year 1373. He taught at the University of Prague and later became preacher at a church in Prague. Through his fiery sermons, he gained a large following.

Some of Hus's teachings didn't agree with the teachings of the Roman Church. Hus felt that the true head of the Church is Christ, not some people. He felt that "it is not necessary for salvation to believe the Roman Church superior to all others." Because of his views, he was excommunicated—dismissed—from the Church.

Finally, Hus appeared before the Council of Constance. He was ordered to submit to the Church's authority. But the reformer couldn't betray his conscience. He firmly believed that the Bible, not a council of men, should be the standard of truth. Because he wouldn't change his beliefs, Hus was condemned. He was burned at the stake on July 6, 1415.

Since the time of Christ, millions of people have faced death rather than deny their faith. The name Jan Hus belongs on the long list of Christian martyrs.

The Bible tells us, "Since we are surrounded by so great a cloud of witnesses [to the faith], let us also lay aside every weight, and sin which clings so closely, and let us run with endurance the race that is set before us, looking to Jesus, the founder and perfecter of our faith" (Hebrews 12:1–2).

PRAYER

Heavenly Father, thank You for all the Christian martyrs who have dared to stand up for their faith. They were willing to die for You. Help me be willing to live for You. Amen.

Myra Wilkinson

PENTECOST / TRINITY

Hidden on the Inside

Psalm 139:23–24

Jalysa and Kirsten were excited! This was the first year the pear tree in their backyard was producing fruit. They had just brought in the perfect pear to show their mom. Setting it on the kitchen counter, Mom promised the girls she would slice it for lunch.

An hour later, as their mom called for the girls to wash up, Jalysa came running to see if the pear was ready to eat. To her surprise, something was marring their perfect pear. Little brown specks appeared on one side of the pear and seemed to be getting bigger. As Jalysa watched, the specks seemed to spill over onto each other.

"What's happening, Mom?" she asked.

Taking a knife, her mom sliced into the pear. Inside was a tiny grub, working its way out. Carefully, her mother cut away all the bad spots inside and washed the rest of the pear.

"That's just like us and our sins—God cuts them all away and makes us clean again!" said Jalysa with a smile.

In the Bible reading, David asks God to search him and know his heart. Only God can look on the inside. He sees our sins and, by His word of forgiveness, cleanses us from the inside out.

PRAYER

"Create in me a clean heart, O God, and renew a right spirit within me. Cast me not away from Your presence, and take not Your Holy Spirit from me. Restore to me the joy of Your salvation, and uphold me with a willing spirit" (Psalm 51:10–12). In Jesus' name I pray. Amen.

Beverly J. Soyk

PENTECOST / TRINITY

Standing in a Grace Place

Romans 5:1–2a

When we were young, my brother and I had a jumping contest in the living room. It wasn't a good idea. Mom had warned us, "No horseplay, boys! You might break something."

Sure enough, I fell into a plant. Dirt went everywhere. My brother and I were laughing until we heard the garage door open. Our mother was coming! She would see the dirt and her broken plant. She would be disappointed or angry.

I didn't want to be standing there when Mom walked in. I couldn't hide my mess. So I blamed my brother, he blamed me, and we both got in trouble.

This true story sounds like Adam and Eve in the Garden of Eden. God told them not to eat fruit from a certain tree, but they did anyway. When God called to them, they hid because they were afraid. They couldn't hide their sin from God! Adam and Eve blamed each other, and both were sent out of the garden.

We all sin. And our sin is a mess we can't hide. None of us wants to be standing around when God sees what we have done wrong, even when we knew better.

But God surprises us with His kindness. He sent His Son, Jesus, to shed His blood to pay for our sins. Small ones, big ones, accidents, and ones we do on purpose—all our sins are paid for on the cross. So we aren't punished like we deserve. Jesus was punished for us.

This kindness is called *grace*. As children who are baptized into the grace of Jesus Christ, we don't have to be afraid of sin's mess. Jesus cleaned it up. We can stand before God in a grace place.

PRAYER

Thank You, Jesus, for going to the cross to pay for all my sins. Amen.

Craig Otto

PENTECOST / TRINITY

It's Always Sunday

Numbers 6:24–26

Darrin and Lori glared out the window at the pouring rain. "I guess we won't be going on our picnic," their dad said.

"I hate rain!" Darrin said.

"Whoa," Dad said. "Rain is a gift from God."

"If it's a gift, then let's return it," Lori said, winking.

"Mom," Dad called into the kitchen, "we've got a couple of mopers here."

Mom had a solution. "We'll have our picnic right here." She put on a CD of nature sounds. She carried the picnic basket and blanket into the living room. She spread the blanket over the floor, as if it were a real picnic. Together the family recited their mealtime prayer. Then Mom said, "Let's think of some good things about an indoor picnic."

As they ate, Mom, Dad, and Lori called out ideas. "No bugs." "Air-conditioning." "Clean bathrooms." But Darrin remained unconvinced.

"Okay," Dad said, "now let's think of some good things about rain." Again, Mom, Dad, and Lori called out ideas. "Clouds." "Flowers."

"You know," Mom said, "the sun shines wherever you are. Remember the blessing 'The LORD bless you and keep you; the LORD make His face to shine upon you' (Numbers 6:24–25)? The Lord's face shines brighter than the sun ever could. It shines on us because He loves us. Jesus loves us so much He died for us."

"I guess you're right," Darrin said. "With God smiling on us, every day is 'Sun Day.'" He laughed at his own joke.

"More like 'S-o-n Day.'" Lori winked again.

PRAYER

Lord, thank You for a variety of weather. Thank You for blessing me with forgiveness, salvation, and life eternal through Your Son's sacrifice for me. Amen.

Jane Heitman

PENTECOST / TRINITY

The Lamb of God

John 1:29–37

"Behold, the Lamb of God, who takes away the sin of the world!" (John 1:29). John the Baptizer said these words. He was pointing to Jesus Christ. Why did he call Christ "the Lamb of God"? To find the answer, we must turn to the Old Testament.

On the night God led the children of Israel out of Egypt, He gave them some strange instructions. They were to take a perfect lamb, prepare it for eating, smear some of its blood on their doors, and get ready to leave. God told them that the angel of death would pass through Egypt, and any home on which the blood was painted would be spared. In all other homes, the oldest child would die. Painting the blood on the door was a way of saying, "I believe You, God. I will obey You and wait for Your promised deliverance." All the homes that obeyed God were saved from death by the blood of the lamb.

The lamb that spared the children of Israel is a type of the Lamb of God who saves us. An innocent, perfect lamb was sacrificed in Egypt, and they were delivered. The innocent, perfect Lamb of God, Jesus Christ, was sacrificed on Calvary, and we are delivered. Jesus was the Lamb that God supplied. He was not the lamb that protected only the people in one home from earthly death but the Lamb of God who has rescued all men from eternal death.

The last picture of the Lamb in the Bible is in the Book of Revelation. There, Christ is pictured as the triumphant Lamb of God, before whom all His people kneel, and to whom all those who trusted in Him give eternal adoration.

Thinking of all this, Christians have long included in their worship services, whether it is sung or said, the sentence "O Christ, Thou Lamb of God, have mercy upon us." How happy we are that God's Lamb, given for us, will ever have mercy and give forgiveness to all those who ask!

PRAYER

O Christ, Thou Lamb of God, have mercy upon us and give us Thy peace. Amen.

Charles S. Mueller

PENTECOST / TRINITY

Facing a Bear

Psalm 121

When I was young, my family liked to spend summer vacations camping in Yellowstone National Park. Maybe you like to go camping too. Sleeping on the hard ground isn't as comfortable as sleeping at home. However, it's a wonderful treat to roast marshmallows over a flickering fire, to hike through the woods, to view spectacular scenery, and, most of all, to spend time with your family.

One night, Dad and I walked from our campground to an outdoor theater to watch a nature movie. Halfway through the movie, I decided I wanted to go back to our tent. I was smart enough to take the flashlight and remember the trail on which we had come.

However, I came to a stream that had to be crossed on a narrow bridge. As I started to cross the bridge, I looked up. There in the distance, standing nine feet tall, was a huge black bear. He was growling and looking very hungry.

I backed away slowly and went back to my father at the outdoor theater. I would wait and walk home safely, holding my father's hand.

This experience I had with my father reminds me of my heavenly Father. Whenever I face a "big bear" of a problem or temptation, I realize that I need to return to my heavenly Father. In His Word and in Baptism, He gladly promises to be with me. He holds my hand and leads me home safely.

The Lord will keep you safe from all evil of body and soul. He also keeps His promise to be with you through all your problems. May you always turn to your heavenly Father for help and comfort. May you also share with your friends the news of His love and protection.

PRAYER

Dear Lord, thank You that I don't need to face the "big bears" of the devil and sin in my life alone. I believe that You've defeated sin and that You're always watching over me. Amen.

Philip Lang

Cool, Sweet Treats

John 6:35, 37–40

If you are warm today, you may reach into the freezer for a chocolate World's Fair Cornucopia or maybe an orange Epsicle. These are what an ice-cream cone and a Popsicle were called many years ago.

One story says ice-cream cones were invented at the 1904 World's Fair in St. Louis, Missouri. It was a hot summer day, and a vendor soon ran out of dishes for his ice cream. Nearby was a man selling *salabia*, a thin Persian waffle. He quickly rolled a waffle into a cone (or cornucopia) shape and scooped ice cream into it. It was an instant success, and soon everyone was eating ice-cream cones.

At about the same time, an eleven-year-old boy invented another frozen treat. In 1905, Frank Epperson mixed a popular drink—soda water powder and water—and left his stirring stick in it. He put the mixture out-side on a cold night, and the next morning, he had a stick of frozen soda water. When Frank grew up, he began a business, selling seven flavors of Epsicles. Later the name was changed to Popsicles. We still enjoy these treats today.

Do you have an urge to head for the kitchen yet? There is another place to satisfy your hunger. Jesus said that whoever believes in Him will not be hungry or thirsty. What kind of food and drink can offer such satisfaction?

Jesus tells us there is food for our soul. Studying God's Word, hearing His Gospel of forgiveness, believing in Him, and receiving His love will refresh us. If we eat that "food," Jesus says we won't be hungry for the sinful things in the world.

Are you hungry or thirsty? Go to Jesus, who takes away the sins of the world. His love will satisfy you completely.

PRAYER

Dear Jesus, speak Your Gospel to me, that I may hunger only for You. Help me share Your Word with others who are spiritually hungry. Amen.

Doris Schuchard

PENTECOST / TRINITY

Luck or God?

Psalm 37:3–6

Do you know a person who gets upset whenever the thirteenth day of the month is a Friday? Do you know anyone who thinks it's unlucky for a black cat to cross her path? Or do you know somebody who feels safer when he carries a rabbit's foot in his pocket?

There are people all over the world who believe in superstitions like these. But what do they mean to us as Christians? Is there a place for a rabbit's foot or a lucky horseshoe in the life of a Christian? Not according to God's Word if you really expect such things to make any difference in your life.

God tells us in the First Commandment, "You shall have no other gods." This means we should fear, love, and trust in God above all things.

Whatever you put your trust in is really your god. The person who feels safer with a rabbit's foot in his pocket is making the rabbit's foot a god. And the person who believes that a broken mirror means seven years of bad luck is trusting in that superstition rather than in God.

But we Christians know there is no such thing as "luck." We know that God guides and directs our lives. "Commit your way to the LORD; trust in Him, and He will act," the Scriptures tell us (Psalm 37:5).

God loves us so much that He gave His own Son to die for us. That's why we can be sure that He will take good care of us.

And that's why the Bible has so many promises like Proverbs 3:5–6: "Trust in the LORD with all your heart, and do not lean on your own understanding. In all your ways acknowledge Him, and He will make straight your paths."

With such promises, who needs luck?

PRAYER

I trust only You, Lord, for the free salvation You give me because You are gracious and loving. I trust only You to guide me, knowing that You will lead me each day and supply all of my needs. Forgive me when I fail to trust in You alone. In Jesus' name I pray. Amen.

Elmer Luessenhop

PENTECOST / TRINITY

Rejoice in the Morning

Psalm 30:1–5

It's morning again! Oh, what happiness! Birds are chirping, flowers are blooming, and boys and girls everywhere are awaking from sleep. Their eyes are shining, and they are bounding out of bed to start another brand-new, wonderful day of life. Oh, joy of joys—it's morning!

But wait a minute. What's that you're saying? At the stage of life you're in right now, the only joyful mornings you experience are those when you can sleep till ten o'clock?

Well, you'll grow out of it. As you grow older, you'll probably want to wake up earlier. You may even rejoice in the morning—a new dawn offering a chance to experience anew the joys of living.

King David, the author of Psalm 30, felt joy in the morning too. He had known the darkness of night, but in a different way—a spiritual way. He knew what it was like to experience great shame and guilt. His sins of adultery and murder haunted him for more than a year before he repented.

When David says, "Weeping may tarry for the night, but joy comes with the morning" (Psalm 30:5), he is talking about more than an earthly sunrise after ten hours of darkness. He is talking about the weeping that will end when the darkness of sin is gone for good. He sees the bright rays of eternal life spread along the horizon of eternity.

For David, the joy of forgiveness on earth was a beautiful reminder of the joy he would experience in heaven. And so it is for us too. Because of Jesus, we know that our guilt and shame are forever removed.

Rejoice in the morning! Rejoice in Jesus, our Savior and Giver of eternal life.

Prayer

Our Father, we rejoice in the morning of Your forgiveness. Thank You for the gift of Your Son, who enables us to rejoice in the morning of eternal life as well. Amen.

Tom Raabe

Calm Down

Matthew 8:23–27

The disciples in today's reading were in for a shock. While they were on the lake, a storm arose. An approaching storm can be a pretty frightening thing on land. Can you imagine what it's like to be in a little boat with no escape?

It was in such a position that the disciples found themselves. All around was water. Perhaps they tried to row to shore, but the waves were tossing the boat. So the only thing left to do was to hold on tightly—and pray!

That's exactly what they did. Jesus was in the boat with them. He was asleep, but the disciples awoke Him with their prayers of "Save us, Lord! We're going to drown!"

Sometimes you and I may feel like we are drowning too. Troubles and pressures can make us feel tossed about like a boat. Perhaps you're having trouble at school. Maybe your family members are having problems getting along. Or has someone close to you died recently? Living in this world can be anything but calm at times.

Our many troubles can cause us to panic, just as the disciples did. Yet, what did Jesus say—"Why are you afraid?" We are scared because we're sinful. We are afraid because we want to have control over things in our lives. We are afraid because our sin causes us to doubt and trust in God for all things.

Yet, where we are weak, Jesus is strong. He did not abandon the disciples. He does not abandon us. Jesus calms His frightened children. We can be at peace because our Savior is Lord of heaven and earth. We can face the storms in our lives knowing that Jesus has conquered the biggest one of all—death. We can confidently look at the other storms in our lives and say, "Be calm. God is in control."

PRAYER

Almighty God, we praise You for Your goodness. Thank You for calming the storms in our lives. Help us to always trust in You. In Jesus' name we pray. Amen.

Carla Fast

PENTECOST / TRINITY

Blessed for a Reason

Genesis 22:15–18

A small congregation in a rural area was suffering from a drought. Even though their crops weren't doing well and money was tight, the church members took up a special offering to help one of their young men who was studying to be a pastor. He was thinking about leaving the seminary for a while because he needed to earn some money.

As the congregation leaders presented the young man with a check for two thousand dollars, they told him, "We have been richly blessed by God so that we might be a blessing to others. Now we give this gift to you so that you might better prepare yourself to be a blessing to many people."

The young man was so moved by their gift that he couldn't talk. Tears filled his eyes. In his heart, he renewed his promise to follow God's call to serve others.

When God called Abraham to be the father of His people, He promised Abraham that He would bless him. There was a purpose behind God's blessing, as there always is. God blessed Abraham so that, through him, all the nations of the earth would be blessed. Centuries later, Jesus Christ was born into Abraham's family. Through Him, we have received the great gifts of forgiveness and peace with God.

God didn't bless Abraham *because* Abraham was special but *in order that* Abraham might be special. It's just the same today. God blesses you and me so that we might be special blessings to others.

God wants the people of all nations to be His children. He wants them all to know of the salvation that Jesus won for us. He wants them all to share in His wonderful gifts and promises.

Prayer

Lord Jesus, thank You for blessing us with temporal and spiritual blessings. Help us share the wonderful news that You are the Savior of the whole world. Amen.

Rodney Rathmann

Laugh Your Blues Away

Proverbs 17:22

Q. "Why do firemen wear red suspenders?"
A. "To keep their pants from falling off."

Q. "How do you know when an elephant's been sleeping in your bed?"
A. "When he's wearing your pajamas."

When I was in school, my friends and I loved to tell jokes like these. We'd find them in books, or we'd try to make up our own. But one thing was always the same—we loved to laugh.

Have you ever heard the saying "Laughter is the best medicine"? Cases have been reported of very sick hospital patients who began surrounding themselves with things that would make them laugh. They'd listen to tapes of comedians or watch reruns of old comedies like *I Love Lucy* and *Gilligan's Island*. In many cases, their health began to improve when they kept themselves happy and laughing.

But there are times when people make jokes that hurt others. It's never funny when we laugh at the way another person looks or acts. Today's Bible reading says, "A joyful heart is good medicine, but a crushed spirit dries up the bones." When we make fun of others, we "crush their spirit."

We've all had times when we've been tempted to make fun of someone. But we don't have to give in to this desire. God sent His Son, Jesus Christ, to free us from sin and the power of the devil. Jesus enables us to resist temptation.

Joy and laughter are gifts from God. Enjoy these gifts, and let your heart be cheerful!

PRAYER

Dear Lord, thank You for the gift of laughter. Help me use humor and laughter as a way to encourage others, not hurt them. Amen.

Jennifer AlLee

PENTECOST / TRINITY

On the Way to Oz

Jeremiah 29:11–13

Have you seen *The Wizard of Oz*? It's about a journey made by Dorothy and her friends to find the Great Wizard in the far-off Land of Oz. They believed that the wizard could grant their wishes.

In the movie, three travelers go along with Dorothy. The Tin Man desires a heart so that he can love others. The Scarecrow wants a brain so that he can be wise. The Lion wishes for courage so that he isn't so fearful. Dorothy wants to return home so that she can be reunited with her family. They all have needs they cannot meet on their own.

As the four travel, they become friends. By the time they reach the Land of Oz, they are surprised to find that they are not the same as when they started their journey. They have changed.

Sometimes our life's journey doesn't go exactly as we plan. We think we know what will happen, but the journey of life changes us. God tells us that we can trust Him to lead us. He assures us in Jeremiah 29:11 that He knows the plans He has for us—to give us a bright and hopeful future.

Praise God for His power, which gives us peace throughout our days. Praise God for His wisdom, which gives us a bright and hopeful future. Praise God for His love, which changed us from sinners who were separated from God to dearly loved children.

PRAYER

Dear Lord, sometimes I feel afraid or unloved. Sometimes I feel helpless and alone. Thank You that I can trust You to lead me in my journey until I reach my heavenly home. Amen.

Cheryl Ehlers

Palin-what?

John 13:5–9

Do you know what a *palindrome* is? Although the word looks unusual and complicated, it describes a very interesting use of human language. A *palindrome* is a word or words or even sentences that are spelled the same forward and backward. A simple palindrome is the word LEVEL. Read it backward—it is still the same word. Or look at the word SWIMS. It reads the same backward if you turn it upside down.

As a bit of humor someone once said that when Adam was introduced to Eve, he said, "MADAM, I'M ADAM." That is a palindromic sentence.

Knowing what a palindrome is will help you appreciate an even more intriguing sentence. In Greece and Turkey, some baptismal fonts have this twenty-five–letter inscription written in a circle: NIION ANOMHMATA MHMONAN OIIN (NEE-ee-un On-oh-MAY-ma-ta May-MOH-nahn OY-in). You can see that it is a rather giant palindrome. In English, it means, "Wash [my] sins, not only [my] face." We do not know the history behind this sentence. Perhaps the writer of the sentence remembered his parents saying "Wash your hands and face," and Peter saying on Maundy Thursday, "[Wash] not my feet only but also my hands and my head."

This palindrome on baptismal fonts is a reminder of the meaning of Baptism. Through Baptism, God deals with what really soils our lives. He washes not only our bodies, but He also washes away our sins. He creates in us a faith by which we daily seek and receive His forgiveness. That forgiveness washes away the wrongs we do, the evil we think, and the ill we say.

It is no wonder, therefore, that this palindrome surrounds those fonts in Turkey and Greece. And it's no wonder that we, too, because of our Baptism and God's promise, pray, "Wash my sins, not only my face."

PRAYER

Dear God, thank You for washing my sins away in Baptism and giving me forgiveness, life, and salvation that I don't deserve, but that are mine because You love me. Amen.

Richard Hinz

PENTECOST / TRINITY

Zoo Food

John 6:47–51

"Look, Mrs. Grant," said Christopher. "It says here that they feed fresh blood to the vampire bats. Yuck!"

The children in Mrs. Grant's class were discussing some pamphlets they had received from the zoo. They hoped to learn more about the "parents program" that the zoo was sponsoring. An individual or a group could adopt one of the animals for a year by paying for the cost of its food.

"I think I'd like to adopt a Gila (HE-luh) monster," said Linda. "They eat fresh eggs."

"I'd prefer a flamingo," said Lisa. "It needs carrot juice, beet juice, and paprika to keep its pink color."

"Or how about one of the tropical birds?" asked Randy. "They eat oranges, bananas, and grapes."

Some kind of food is necessary for the life of all living things. A well-balanced diet can help us grow up to become healthy adults.

Today's Bible reading tells about food that is necessary for faith. This food is Jesus, the bread of life, who died that we might live. We receive this bread when we read and study God's Word. A regular diet of this food provides the necessary nourishment for our faith. Finally, the best kind of life, eternal life in heaven, will be ours.

PRAYER

Thank You, God, for giving me Your Word of life. Bless me when I hear, read, and study it. For Jesus' sake. Amen.

Arnold E. Schmidt

A Place of Safety

Psalm 121

During 1941, in the early days of World War II, German planes dropped bombs every night for months on major cities in England. Many people were killed or hurt by the explosions, fires, and collapsing buildings. Those terrible days were called "the Blitz."

One night during the Blitz, a father, holding his son by the hand, ran from a building that had been hit by a bomb. In the front yard was a shell hole. The father jumped into the hole for protection and held up his arms for his son to follow.

The boy could hear his father's voice telling him to jump. But he was very scared and couldn't see in the dark. "I can't see you!" the boy cried.

The father looked up from the hole. He could see the outline of his son against the sky, which was glowing red from the burning buildings. "You can't see me, but I can see you. Jump!"

The boy trusted his father and jumped. The bombs kept falling, but he was safe in his father's arms.

Often we cannot see what is ahead. We don't know what will happen after a loved one dies, a parent loses a job, or Mom and Dad are separated. We may be scared about moving to a new city or changing schools. Classmates may treat us badly, or friends may disappoint us. We may feel like we have nowhere to turn.

Our heavenly Father calls us at such times to trust His voice. He calls us to turn to Him and His love and care. He offers us the strength we need to make it through difficulties. He gives us a safe place in the middle of troubles.

Today's psalm offers us these words of hope: "The LORD will keep you from all evil; He will keep your life" (Psalm 121:7).

PRAYER

Dear Jesus, because You died on the cross and rose again, I always have hope in You. I have a place to turn to—someone who will keep me safe. Help me trust Your voice. Amen.

Richard P. Lieske

PENTECOST / TRINITY

A Termite and a Cross

Galatians 6:14

In a stained glass window in a beautiful cathedral in Honolulu is the picture of—a termite!

That's hardly what you'd expect to see in a church window. A termite is a pest. It's an insect that eats its way into wood. If it eats away enough wood, it can cause a building to topple.

Once, a small wooden church stood where the large cathedral in Hawaii now stands. But termites got in. They ate and ate until the building inspector said the church wasn't safe to use.

Sadly, the people tore down the church they loved. But when they rebuilt, they put up this beautiful stone cathedral. Now when they come to worship, they're happy they had to rebuild. If it hadn't been for the termites, they might still be in their little chapel. That stained glass picture of the termite always reminds them of how God turned what was bad into a blessing for them.

In a similar way, the cross reminds us of how God turned an instrument of torture into the means by which Jesus gained our salvation. Evil men plotted against Jesus, told lies about Him, punished Him, and finally even crucified Him. But our heavenly Father meant it all for good, right from the start. He let men nail His Son to the cross so He could suffer the sting of sin and death in our place.

It has all ended well. Jesus, our Savior, rose again and lives eternally in glory. By faith we are free from the evil we have done, and we share with Jesus in a new and victorious life.

Every believer may say with St. Paul, "Far be it from me to boast except in the cross of our Lord Jesus Christ" (Galatians 6:14).

PRAYER

Drawn to the cross, which Thou hast blessed
With healing gifts for souls distressed,
To find in Thee my life, my rest,
Christ crucified, I come. Amen. (LSB 560:1)

Roy Gesch

PENTECOST / TRINITY

Our Shepherd Leads Us

Psalm 23

Suppose you had lived when there were pirates on the seas. And suppose you had been captured by a gang of pirates. They have blindfolded you and tied your hands behind your back, and are making you "walk the plank." One of the pirates guides you so you can walk straight out on the plank. You could say of that pirate, "He leads me." But it wouldn't be a very comforting thought!

Or suppose you have gotten in trouble with the law. A policeman has picked you up and is taking you to the judge. As you follow the officer into court, you could point to him and say, "He leads me." But this wouldn't be very comforting either.

The words "he leads me" don't always cheer us up. It depends on *who* is leading us and *where* he is leading us.

King David made these words famous when he said, "The LORD is my Shepherd. . . . He leads me in paths of righteousness" (Psalm 23:1–3). These were comforting words for David because he knew that God was leading him in a good way.

God is leading us too. The Father provides for us and protects us every day. Jesus, the Good Shepherd, gives us His love and forgiveness. And the Holy Spirit keeps us in true faith.

Where God leads us is also important. He leads us "in paths of righteousness"—that is, in the way of His righteousness—so that we who are unrighteous because of our sin will be saved. We can take comfort in knowing that each day we are in the hands of our Shepherd. We can say with confidence, "*He* leads me."

PRAYER

My Shepherd, I pray that You would take my hand and lead me every day, protecting me and keeping me on the right path of faith in You, so I may live in heaven eternally with You. Amen.

Paul Single

Memory Stones

Joshua 4:20–24

In today's Bible reading, the Israelite families had just witnessed a great miracle. In order to reach the border of Jericho and prepare to conquer the city, they had to cross the Jordan River. The river was very high. The water was at flood level! Yet God took care of His people. He made the waters of the river stand in a heap, and the people safely crossed to the other side.

God told Joshua, their leader, to set up a monument made of stones from the Jordan to help their children and grandchildren remember God's power and His care for them. Each time one of the Israelite families came near the river, they probably pointed out the stones and told the story of how God saved them and brought them to the Promised Land. After they retold the story enough times, just the sight of the "memory stones" may have brought a reminder of their mighty God.

You could be a "memory stone." Your words and actions can remind people that there is a mighty God who cares for you—and for them. In a way, you are very much like the stones Joshua set up. God put you in a special place and time on this earth. When people pass by you, they will see Jesus' kindness as they watch you helping someone. They will see His patience as they watch you wait for your turn. They will see His forgiveness as they see you forgiving others.

You are God's child. He has forgiven your sins because of the suffering and death of His Son, Jesus. God has made you a "memory stone" for Him today.

PRAYER

Dear Jesus, thank You for forgiving me when I fail to be a good witness for You. Help me show others Your love. Amen.

Lisa Hahn

PENTECOST / TRINITY

Sidewalk Chalk

1 Peter 1:18–25

Jake woke up to the sound of rain pelting against his window. In the morning light, he could still see flashes of lightning. He was glad to be inside, where it was dry. He hoped the storm wouldn't cut into his playtime. Jake loved to be outside in the summer.

Suddenly, Jake remembered the sidewalk chalk! Yesterday he and his neighbor Angelo had worked for hours on Angelo's large driveway. They had used the chalk to create a whole town with streets and buildings. They planned to ride their bikes along the path they had created. Now the torrents of rain were washing away their hard work. They would have to start all over.

Like Jake's sidewalk chalk, everything we make on earth will be lost or destroyed with time. All earthly things are perishable. They cannot last forever.

God stepped into our world by sending His Son to redeem all people. Jesus, who is imperishable, offers us a love and forgiveness that will never end. This is the promise of God's Word, and it stands forever. God's love and salvation will last forever. Jesus has permanently washed our sins away.

PRAYER

Dear Lord, thank You for Your love, which will never change. Help me remember that You are always with me. Amen.

Susan Waterman Voss

Two Hanging Trees

John 15:12–17

Many years ago, a robber band lived in the forests of Germany. The band was made up of whole families who went into towns and stole whatever they could. The forests were a good hiding place, and the robbers made a good living.

One day the robber chief called the whole band together. "I have something very serious to talk about," he announced. "Somebody among us is stealing from us. We are going to find this person, and then we will hang him."

In a few days, the thief was found. It was the chief's own mother.

The chief was very sad. He had given an order, and it had to be carried out. If he went against his order, his followers would lose confidence in him and would find another leader.

On the day of the hanging, all the families assembled near the hanging tree and waited for the chief's mother. However, the robber chief himself walked to the hanging tree and announced he would take his mother's place. His love for her was so great that he could not let her die. Can you imagine the love this mother and son had for each other?

Many years ago, another man in another country also went to a hanging tree. His name was Jesus. He, too, died willingly in the place of somebody who deserved to die.

But there was a difference between Jesus and the robber chief. Jesus had no sin. He didn't deserve to die—yet, because He loved us, He gave His life for us. And when He gave His life, He gave us life—eternal life. For such a great love we can only speak words of praise as did the psalmist.

PRAYER

Praise the LORD, all nations!
Extol Him, all peoples!
For great is His steadfast love toward us,
and the faithfulness of the LORD endures forever.
Praise the LORD! (Psalm 117)

Betty Nohl

PENTECOST / TRINITY

Separated from God

Romans 8:35–39

The little boy stood alone in the aisle of a big supermarket. His eyes darted from one face to another as the people passed by. Frightened, he put his hand to his mouth to hold back a cry, and his eyes began to fill with tears.

Then he caught sight of his mother. At once the tears went away, his face lighted up with a smile, and he ran to clutch her skirt so that he wouldn't be separated from her again.

Have you ever thought of what it would be like to be separated from God? We need God much more than the boy in the supermarket needed his mother. If we were separated from God, we would be even more frightened and alone than he was.

Sin separates people from God. The Bible says, "The wages of sin is death" (Romans 6:23). Eternal death means eternal separation from God and His love.

But God loves us so much that He did not want us to be separated from Him. To bring us together, He sent His Son, Jesus, into the world to remove the wall of sin between us and God.

Jesus did more than that. The Bible says, "The Son of Man came to seek and to save the lost" (Luke 19:10). Those who are saved by Him can say the beautiful words of St. Paul in Romans 8:38–39:

"I am sure that neither death nor life, nor angels nor rulers, nor things present nor things to come, nor powers, nor height nor depth, nor anything else in all creation, will be able to separate us from the love of God in Christ Jesus our Lord."

PRAYER

Thank You for Your great love, heavenly Father, that sent Jesus to save me and keeps me always near You. Help me remember Your love so that I never need to be afraid that You will leave me. Amen.

Dorothy Hoyer Scharlemann

Right on Time

Ecclesiastes 3:1–8

What a delight it was to sit on Grandpa's lap when I visited him! Sometimes he'd read from his German Bible or tell me a story about his boyhood in Germany. But Grandpa's special treasure was a beautiful gold pocket watch with a long chain. Whenever the freight trains sped through the small town where he lived, Grandpa would pull out his watch and say, "Train's right on time today." Each afternoon he looked forward to the whistle of that train.

But one afternoon when I was with Grandpa, the train was late. Something as powerful as a locomotive wasn't completely dependable. God *is* dependable. God's time is always right. He's always there when we need Him.

Sometimes we might think God is late. That certain prayer wasn't answered when we thought it should have been. But God heard the prayer. He simply answered in His time. God supplies our needs in His own way. He promises that our times are in His hand.

I loved Grandpa, so I missed him when he died. But I remembered the happy times—little walks and ice-cream-cone times, the gold-pocket-watch times. I could rejoice in his memory. Because Grandpa believed in Jesus, he is spending eternity with Him. So will we. By God's grace, we trust in Jesus as our Savior, and we, too, will someday live with our Lord in heaven.

Only God knows when our time on earth will end. But we can wait in faith and trust, because we know He'll take us home at the right time.

PRAYER

Dear God, when the fullness of time had come, You sent Your Son to be our Savior. We believe in Your promises and trust You for forgiveness and eternal life through Jesus Christ, our Lord. Amen.

Margaret Glasgow

PENTECOST / TRINITY

Mind Fillers

Colossians 3:1–4

Something was coming after her! Terrified, Ellen turned and ran. The faster she ran, the closer the thing got. In the dark, she could barely find her way. She dodged trees and stones. Then she tripped and fell. Screaming in terror, Ellen sat straight up in bed.

"What is it?" asked her father, rushing into the room.

"A nightmare," Ellen answered, feeling like she was going to cry. She wrapped her arms around her knees to stop shivering.

Her father sat on the edge of the bed. His arm was around her shoulders. "Tell me what happened, Ellen."

"It was a monster coming after me. I fell while I was trying to get away. That's when I screamed."

"A monster, huh?" her father commented. "Any idea why you had a dream like that?"

Feeling ashamed of herself, Ellen admitted, "I stayed up to watch a monster movie on TV. I guess it was so scary that I dreamed about it."

"Watching something like that before bed can cause trouble," said Dad. "It's happened to me too. Everyone has nightmares at times, but often it's our own fault. Our minds store up whatever we put in them. Then, at night, those things play back like a movie in our dreams. How do you think we can prevent bad dreams?"

"If we put good things in our minds, it would seem that we'd have good dreams, right?" answered Ellen, smiling at her father.

What Ellen discovered is similar to the advice St. Paul gives us: "Set your mind on things that are above. . . . For you have died, and your life is hidden with Christ in God. When Christ who is your life appears, then you also will appear with Him in glory" (Colossians 3:2–4).

PRAYER

Jesus, thank You for giving us Your Gospel—the *Good* News. Now we don't have to think about *bad* news. Amen.

Karen M. Leet

Draw a Missionary

Acts 26:12–18

Let's draw a missionary. How do you picture missionaries? Where should we start? Isaiah 52:7 starts with beautiful feet—"How beautiful upon the mountains are the feet of him who brings good news, who publishes peace, who brings good news of happiness, who publishes salvation."

Think of fear-filled people waiting in the valley for news of victory. Suddenly the sound of the messenger's feet is heard. These may be young feet or old feet, tired, callused, stubbed, or bruised. Always they are feet in a hurry. Whatever it takes to deliver the message of victory, these feet are ready to go.

Think of remote villages in South America or Papua New Guinea where such feet have traveled. Think of city streets where such feet have dared to go with the Good News. Let's draw running feet.

Next come the lips. When the Lord called missionary Isaiah, Isaiah felt unworthy. "I am a man of unclean lips," he said (Isaiah 6:5). He knew he was a sinner. Quickly, God touched his lips and said, "Your guilt is taken away" (v. 7). When God asked, "Whom shall I send?" Isaiah answered immediately, "Here am I! Send me" (v. 8).

Missionary lips are full of praise. They are full of words about Jesus, who came to save us from dying forever. Draw lips open and filled with messages of salvation for all people.

Missionary hearts are big. "We love because He first loved us!" they say. Make a heart bursting with love for every tribe and nation.

God calls all His saved ones to be His telling ones. Might your name be on this picture? Listen prayerfully to Jesus' words: "I am sending you to open their eyes, so that they may turn from darkness to light and from the power of Satan to God, that they may receive forgiveness of sins and a place among those who are sanctified by faith in Me" (Acts 26:17–18).

PRAYER

Dear Savior, here am I. Send me to share Your love and mercy with many other people, by the power of Your Spirit. Amen.

Mary Lou Krause

PENTECOST / TRINITY

Changed by Grace

1 Timothy 1:12–17

It was hot and dusty on the road that day. The men had traveled since sunup and were getting tired. No one sang to lighten the fatigue of travel. This was not a singing trip. Their job was to capture and bring back some "criminals" and their families. It wasn't going to be easy.

The leader rode in front of the troops. His mind was awhirl with plans. He had wanted the chance to lead these men, and now he was planning how he might catch the lawbreakers and bring them to justice.

The leader's name was Saul. His goal was to capture the Christians in Damascus. How he hated them! But then something happened. He was hurled to the ground, and God Himself spoke to him. From that moment on, Saul's life was changed, and he was an entirely different person.

He made no bones about it. He often said publicly that God had come looking for him and turned his heart to faith. He was so happy God had done this. He could think of no reason for this—except God's grace. In 1 Corinthians 15:10, Saul, who is known as Paul, says, "By the grace of God I am what I am." By this he means that it was only because of God's favor, undeserved by him, that he became a Christian. It was not because of his goodness, for after God touched him, he knew his goodness wasn't worth much. Paul did not become a Christian because God thought he was someone extra special. All people alike are sinners. The only reason God took Paul as His own was because of God's grace. In Ephesians 2:8, Paul tells each of us, "By grace you have been saved through faith." The only reason we believe in Jesus is that the same God who freely gave grace (undeserved favor) to Paul gives us the same thing.

By the grace of God, Paul became a Christian. By this same grace of God, we follow in his footsteps.

PRAYER

Lord, be gracious to me, and change my sinful ways. Thank You for Your gift of salvation through Christ, my Lord. Amen.

Charles S. Mueller

PENTECOST / TRINITY

Our Ladder to the Sky

Acts 17:22–28

"The sky is falling! The sky is falling!" Did you ever hear or read the old fable about Chicken Little? A pebble hit him on the head, and he ran around warning all his friends that the sky was falling. It was a silly story, but there are people living today who have equally strange notions about the sky.

For example, a tribe in Africa believes that in the beginning of time, the sky was very close to the earth. It was so close, in fact, that people of long ago could reach up and touch it. They began to take little pieces out of the sky. They became greedy and cut out bigger and bigger chunks. This angered their god, so he pulled the sky high up out of their reach.

A missionary came to Africa and heard this story. He told the people, "God is not angry anymore, and I know who brought the sky back down to you! The cross of Jesus is your ladder to the sky."

The missionary didn't mean that the people would be able to touch the sky. He meant that Jesus is the one who brings God's love to us. He told the Africans that Jesus came into the world to take away everything that angered God.

That missionary followed St. Paul's example. Paul started with something the people of Athens understood, the statue marked "To an unknown god." He told the people about the true God, who made the world and everything in it.

The missionary to Africa also started with something familiar to the people, the sky. Then he taught them the truth about God's love for them. This is also a good way for us to do missionary work. Start with what a friend understands and then tell him or her about Jesus, the Savior.

PRAYER

Thank You, Jesus, for being my ladder to heaven. Empower me with Your Spirit so that I follow Paul's example and share Your love with others. Amen.

Eleanor Schlegel

The Sand Dollar Legend

John 3:16–18

Taylor and Nicholas were enjoying their day at the beach, building sandcastles and playing in the waves. Later on, they decided to look for seashells. After about thirty minutes of gathering shells, Nicholas cried out, "Hey, look what I found! It's a sand dollar!"

Taylor ran to his side. "That's really cool. You know what? Once I heard my Sunday School teacher say that a sand dollar tells about the story of Jesus."

Taylor pointed to one side of the shell. "See, here's a picture of a Christmas poinsettia to remind us of Jesus' birth. Around the outside are five slits. Four represent the nail holes in Jesus' body from when He was crucified to save us from our sins. The fifth hole represents the mark on His body left by the Roman soldier's spear."

Taylor turned the sand dollar over. "On the back is a picture of an Easter lily to remind us of Christ's resurrection. In the center of the lily is the star that led the Wise Men to Jesus."

Taylor glanced at Nicholas. "You probably don't want to break the sand dollar open, do you, Nicholas?" He shook his head no. "Well, if you shake it, you can hear a rattling sound. Inside are five little pieces that symbolize doves waiting to spread the Good News of Jesus' love."

Nicholas looked at Taylor in amazement. "Who would have thought that a little sand dollar could be such a neat way to tell the story of Jesus?"

PRAYER

I praise You, O God, for Your beautiful creation. Thank You for the sand dollar and other reminders of Your love. Help me share Your message with others. Amen.

Lisa Ellwein

Your Daily Bread

Psalm 145:8–9, 15–16

Have you ever sat down with your mom or dad and watched her or him pay the monthly bills? Right about now is the time they usually do that—around the first of the month.

Ask one of them if you can help pay the bills this month. Perhaps you can address, stamp, or put your return address on the envelopes.

But there's more you can do. Notice where the checks and money are going: the gas company, electric company, doctor's office, telephone company, insurance agency, clothing store, department stores, credit card companies, the mortgage company for house payments.

Now think of all the people who provide services through those companies so that you can enjoy their products. When you think about it, it takes a lot of people to make you and your family comfortable and happy. And it takes a lot of money to pay for those services. You may even hear your mom or dad complain sometimes about how much it costs.

But God has provided your family with all these people and services and the money to pay for them. Martin Luther saw these people and services as being included in the "daily bread" we ask for in the Lord's Prayer. He said daily bread is everything needed for this life (see Luther's Small Catechism, The Lord's Prayer, Fourth Petition).

Our Bible reading tells us why God is so good to us: "The LORD is gracious and merciful, slow to anger and abounding in steadfast love. . . . His mercy is over all that He has made" (Psalm 145:8–9).

Next time you see your mom or dad paying the bills, ask if you can help. Then say a prayer together, thanking God for all the people and services—the daily bread—He has given you.

PRAYER

Thank You, heavenly Father, for all the people and things You provide for us each month to make us comfortable and happy. Bless them all, and bless our family so that we can give honor to You. In Jesus' name. Amen.

Donald R. Haase

PENTECOST / TRINITY

Hang On!

Ephesians 4:11–16

Charlie was small. He was light too. One day, a strong wind came up behind Charlie. His shirt filled with the wind, and he took off like a kite! Charlie's big friend caught him by the foot. Charlie looked down and cried, "Hang on! Don't let go. I could end up in Kokomo!" (Charlie thought himself a poet, even when he was about to fly away!)

Next, Charlie went swimming. The waves were big and strong. Charlie was small and weak. This was not good! Charlie popped up and down like a fishing bobber. Charlie got seasick. Then his big friend came to the rescue. Charlie cried, "Take me to shore! Take me to shore, or I might throw up in Baltimore!" (Seasickness made Charlie a terrible poet!)

Charlie's story might help us understand our Bible reading. It talks about being tossed by waves and blown by wind. These picture words help us to know what happens when people teach us wrong things about Jesus.

People might tell us that Jesus doesn't love children. They might say we must obey God's rules if we want to get to heaven. Maybe they will say that stories about Jesus are not true. Lies like that can make us feel like a kite in a wild wind or a paper boat on the ocean's waves. We need a big and powerful friend to help us hang on to the truth about Jesus!

We have a big and powerful friend. We have the Holy Spirit, who helps us hang on to Jesus. The Holy Spirit works as we read God's Word. He reminds us of what the Bible teaches about Jesus. The Bible says that obeying rules doesn't get us into heaven. That is good news! We could never obey all the rules, so Jesus obeyed them for us. Then He died to take away the sins of the whole world. Just as He came back to life, so will we after we die. Hang on to that good news!

PRAYER

Thank You, Jesus, for taking away my sins. Keep me safe from anyone who tries to teach me anything different. Amen.

Edward Grube

PENTECOST / TRINITY

Wanting? Asking?

Matthew 7:7–8

In Mrs. Krueger's backyard was a huge apple tree with many apples. Sounds good, doesn't it? But there was a problem. Every time Chiwana and his friends tried to sneak over to climb the tree and pick some apples, Mrs. Krueger chased them away.

"I don't understand why she's so selfish," complained Jordan. "There are way more apples there than she could ever use."

"She's just a crabby old lady," added Jathan.

Just then, Chiwana's mother walked by. "Boys, have you ever asked Mrs. Krueger if you could *have* some apples? Let's go see what she says."

The boys were nervous as they walked up to her house. In fact, Jordan almost ran away when they rang the doorbell.

"Mrs. Krueger, the boys were wondering if they could have some apples," said Chiwana's mother.

"Of course," said Mrs. Krueger, "but I get nervous when I see children climbing up in my tree. I'm afraid they will fall. You can have all the apples you want, as long as you use a sturdy ladder."

The boys were surprised. All they had to do was ask, and she was more than willing to give them what they wanted.

God has sent His Son to save us, taking care of our greatest need for a Savior, but He also cares about all our other needs. God wants us to ask Him for these earthly needs in prayer. He is loving and kind. Because of the work of Christ, the Father's ears are always open to hear and answer our prayers.

PRAYER

Heavenly Father, You have told us to come to You with every need. Thank You for hearing and answering all of our prayers for Jesus' sake. Amen.

Pat List

A Big Voice

Jeremiah 1:6–7

Brandon and his parents followed closely behind the tour guide. They were walking through a mangrove forest.

Mangroves are amazingly adaptable trees that live in saltwater marshes. They are found along the coasts of Florida. The unusual, snakelike roots grow partially aboveground so they'll be out of the shallow water. Beneath their roots, living in the water, many small fish, crabs, and animals seek protection from larger predators.

The tour guide was pointing to the unique features of these trees and the animals that lived near them. As the tour guide spoke, Brandon heard many snapping sounds around him. Whispering, he asked his mother, "What is that popping noise?"

The tour guide, hearing Brandon, turned to him. "That sound you're hearing is actually a snapping shrimp. It's a very small creature with a claw on the end. The noises you hear in these woods are those shrimp snapping their claws shut. For a very small animal, it makes a very large noise."

In our passage today, Jeremiah was worried about speaking God's Word to the people around him. He felt he was too young and people would not listen to him. Just like the snapping shrimp, he felt small.

But God had chosen to use Jeremiah. Despite his youth, God would give him the words and the voice to speak. And just like the snapping shrimp, that voice, with God's help, would be heard wide and far, proclaiming God's mercy to the world.

PRAYER

Dear Lord, please help me when I tell others about You. Give me the words to say and help me to say them. Amen.

Cheryl Honoree

The Roaring Lion

1 Peter 5:5–11

Malik liked to sleep with his bedroom window open. Sometimes he heard owls. Sometimes he heard ranch dogs barking to one another. Sometimes he was scared by the sounds of wild dogs and wolves.

Malik knew that wolves killed small animals. It bothered him. Still, he knew that wolves were predators. Their nature was to stalk and kill other animals.

The predator most dangerous to Christians is the devil. The Bible reading for today tells us, "Your adversary the devil prowls around like a roaring lion, seeking someone to devour" (1 Peter 5:8).

It is the devil's nature to tempt us to join him in rebellion against God. He even tried to tempt the Lord! Jesus turned aside the devil's lies and dares by quoting God's truth. Remember the parable of the sower? Sometimes the devil devours a hearer's understanding of the Gospel! He may convince the one who hears the Gospel that it is too good to be true. Or he may whisper that Jesus isn't really God's Son. He tells countless lies; "He is a liar and the father of lies" (John 8:44).

When Jesus died for the sins of all people, He ruined the devil's plans forever. Jesus' sacrifice gave believers the way to be saved from sin. If we believe in the Savior, Satan can still hinder us with problems, but he can't harm our souls. God resists him. He can't stand for a moment against Christ's triumphant power!

PRAYER

Dear Jesus, You are my Savior beyond any doubt. I know that the devil will try to destroy my faith. Give me strength to stand fast and resist his lies. Amen.

Glenda Schrock

An Evening Bike Ride

John 15:12–17

Hannah and Jonathan loved to go biking with their parents. One evening, a stray brown mutt decided to follow them. He was friendly and ran back and forth between the two children.

Halfway through the ride, the family decided to stop and take a rest. They admired the beautiful flowers around them.

Suddenly, a motorcycle roared around a corner straight toward Jonathan. The stray dog leaped at Jonathan, knocking him out of the way.

Hannah and her parents rushed to her brother's side. "I'm okay," said Jonathan, "but what about the dog?"

Going over to where the dog lay, Jonathan's father felt for any broken bones. The dog seemed okay. The family took him home and put an ad in the paper to locate its owner.

When it was time for evening devotions, Father read John 15:12–17. Then he said, "This reminds me of what happened during our biking tonight. That dog sensed the danger and put his life on the line for you, Jonathan.

"We all have a friend who loves us very much. He loves us so much that He gave His life so we would be saved. I'm sure you know the friend I'm talking about is Jesus. He chose us and calls us His friends. We have done nothing to deserve this."

Jonathan added, "I didn't choose that dog to follow us tonight either. But I know that Jesus was looking out for me and taking care of me. I'm so glad He chose me and loved me!"

With tears in her eyes, Hannah said, "Dad, I'm glad that Jesus is our Savior and friend and that Jonathan is okay. Can we thank Jesus for loving us so much?"

PRAYER

Dear Jesus, thank You for laying down Your life to save us and choosing us to be Your very own children. Help me be a faithful friend to others. In Your name I pray. Amen.

Beverly J. Soyk

PENTECOST / TRINITY

The Seas Proclaim!

Psalm 93

Californians have enjoyed the Pacific Ocean and all that it offers for a long time. The Tuna Club of Avalon is the oldest fishing club in the United States, founded in 1898. If you visited California, you could go deep-sea fishing too.

Last summer, I went on an overnight fishing trip on the ocean. From the shore, the water seemed smooth. Aah, we thought, the ocean is calm and safe. But when we got out on the sea, when we really were on the waves, we found out we were wrong. We were rocking and rolling, bouncing and weaving.

When we look at things without knowledge or experience, we might make the same mistake. Those who don't know the true God may just think up ideas about gods without reading the Bible and then try calmly to tell us about God. They might say that there are many gods; "Let's tolerate them all." They make it all sound safe.

But we read in the Bible that there is only *one* Lord. He and He alone reigns. He and He alone is armed with strength and robed in majesty. He and He alone established a throne from eternity.

The Lord is mightier than the seas. He is mightier than sin and death. He is so mighty that He rolls over the devil. In mighty love He sent His Son to die for our sins. His death and resurrection bring salvation's victory to all, and with it, peace. The waters of Holy Baptism and God's Word create in us a new heart, and we proclaim with the seas that there is only one Lord.

PRAYER

Dear Jesus, thank You for Your love, which rolls over me like the ocean tides. Help my actions and speech to pass on the news of Your love to my family and friends. In Your name I pray. Amen.

Bret Taylor

Do You Pay?

Ephesians 2:8–10

The family had just finished dinner, and everyone was quiet. "Well?" Father asked his children.

Paul and Liz had no idea what he wanted. They sat still, wondering what their father would say next.

"Well?" he repeated. "Aren't you going to pay me for the meal?"

"What?" asked Paul.

"Pay you for the meal?" added Liz.

They stared at each other in disbelief, surprised that their father would ask for such a thing. They were used to receiving all kinds of things from their parents at no cost to them.

After a brief pause, Dad explained. "No, I don't really want you to pay for dinner. We give you all you need for free, because we love you. We want you to have all you need and to be happy."

"I'm happy to hear that," Liz answered. "If I had to pay for my meals, I'd be broke by Saturday!"

"In the same way," Dad continued, "our heavenly Father gives us forgiveness, salvation, and every other blessing for free, because He loves us. He wants us to have all we need and to be happy.

"If we had to earn God's blessings, we would already be in debt, with nothing on hand to pay Him. The Bible says, 'By grace you have been saved, through faith. . . . It is the gift of God, not a result of works' (Ephesians 2:8–9). Because Jesus died on the cross for us, all of God's gifts are free."

"Thank God!" Liz and Paul cheered together.

PRAYER

Thank You, dear Father, that salvation and all Your other gifts are free. Help us show that we appreciate them. Help us share them with other people. For Jesus' sake. Amen.

John Juedes

Mike Couldn't Forget

Isaiah 55:10–11

Tom finally got up enough courage to invite Mike to Sunday School. But Mike didn't go for the idea. "I don't believe in all that rot," he said gruffly.

"What makes you think it's rot?" Tom persisted. "How do you know if you haven't been there?"

"Because Christians are all hypocrites," Mike answered. "That's what my dad told me. There's nothing in Sunday School for me."

"Why don't you come anyway and find out?" said Tom.

"Because I don't want to," Mike answered. "Besides, I know where I'm not wanted."

"But you *are* wanted," Tom assured him. "God wants you, and I want you."

"Oh, knock it off, will you?" Mike snapped. Tom could see that he was not getting anywhere.

Mike never did go to Sunday School with Tom. A few months later, Mike and his family moved to another city. But Mike couldn't forget that someone in the Church had cared about him. Several years later, he was invited to Sunday School again, and this time he went.

We don't always see the results of what we do. But God will bring good from our efforts to tell others, in His own way and in His own time.

God promises that His Word will not return empty but will accomplish what He desires. We needn't be afraid to speak of Jesus and His sacrifice for our sins. Since God is with us, our words will bear fruit—if not right away, perhaps at a later time.

PRAYER

Dear God, give us opportunities and the courage to witness for Jesus. Bless the words spoken to bring faith to the hearers. In Jesus' name we pray. Amen.

Alton Donsbach

As Small as Grasshoppers

Numbers 13:25–33

Have you ever looked through a telescope backward? I mean, have you looked through the big lens and out the eyepiece? Instead of things looking larger, they look much smaller. Some people look at themselves that way.

Such people were the Israelites. They had just been told by some spies what a good land God was going to give them. Two of the spies, Caleb and Joshua, said that even though strong people lived there, God would help them move in. The rest of the spies said that moving in would be too hard.

The other spies said that the people who lived in Canaan were giants. "In fact," they said, "next to them, we were as small as grasshoppers." And then they added, "We also seemed that way to ourselves."

Often we look that way to ourselves too. Other people are older, bigger, smarter, faster, richer. The list goes on. We compare ourselves to others by looking through the wrong end of the telescope.

Caleb and Joshua looked at themselves as God did. Caleb and Joshua saw the giants too, but they also saw that God was bigger than the giants. They looked through the correct end of the telescope. They looked at God first, with eyes of faith. They knew that God had promised to help them.

Even though we may be small in our own eyes, we know that God stands right beside us. He has been standing there ever since our Baptism, when He joined us to Christ's death and resurrection. He forgave us then, and He does so now.

With God next to us, holding on to us with His love, we see ourselves as He does—as His sons and daughters, not grasshoppers.

PRAYER

Heavenly Father, I know that I am small. But I thank You for thinking so much of me that You call me Your child. Thank You for sending Jesus to make me Your child. Help me always remember who I am and how much You love me. Amen.

James Klawitter

PENTECOST / TRINITY

Cicadas

1 Corinthians 15:20–23

Cicadas demonstrate one of the most interesting phenomena in the insect world. After living out of sight for seventeen years, they emerge from the ground—first one, then hundreds, thousands, millions. Then the 1½-inch black bugs with iridescent wings climb trees and shrubs, where they shed their crunchy skin and harden to maturity.

Male cicadas sing a whistling love song to attract females for mating. The sound of just one colony's males can drown out a lawn mower! After mating, the females cut slits in tree branches and lay four hundred to six hundred eggs. In a few weeks, the eggs hatch. The young cicadas drop to the ground and burrow in. They will live there for the next seventeen years.

People who study insects knew the cicadas would come out of the ground last summer. They had read the scientists' predictions. When they saw the first cicada rise, they knew that others would follow.

In the same way, prophets long ago wrote that Jesus would come to suffer and die for our sins. He Himself told us that He would rise again on the third day. Because He rose from the grave, we know that we also shall rise. Unlike the cicadas, who live for only 2½ weeks, reproduce, and die, we know that we will live forever with Jesus in heaven.

PRAYER

We praise You, Jesus, for rising from the dead. We know that, although we die, we will one day rise as You did, to live with You forever in heaven. Amen.

Eileen Ritter

We Can Live Forever!

John 12:17–19

How would you react if you had seen Jesus raise Lazarus from the dead? Maybe you would have gone home and said, "Mom! Lazarus is alive! It was so cool—he came out of the tomb when Jesus called him. Jesus is incredible! I've never seen anyone like Him!"

The Jewish people had never seen anyone like Jesus either. It scared them to know that Jesus could make a dead man alive. What would He use His powers to do?

And now big crowds had begun to follow Jesus instead of listening to the Jewish teachers. "Look how the whole world has gone after Him!" they worried.

In the two thousand years since His ministry on earth, we have never seen another person in history who compares to Jesus. He amazed everyone who saw His miracles.

Today, Jesus' power is still at work within the Church, washing away sin in Baptism and pouring out forgiveness through the Sacrament of the Altar. There is power in the Word of God as it is read and preached. His miracles still inspire us!

When Lazarus died, Jesus explained to Lazarus's sister, Martha, that Lazarus had eternal life by knowing and believing in Him. "I am the resurrection and the life," He told her. "Whoever believes in Me, though he die, yet shall he live" (John 11:25).

Because of Jesus' life, death, and resurrection, we can live in heaven with Him forever.

PRAYER

Dear Lord, come soon and bring us to be with You! In Jesus' name I pray. Amen.

Craig Otto

Enjoying the Firstfruits

Deuteronomy 26:1–4; 1 Corinthians 15:20–23

On a Friday in late May when I was growing up in Iowa, our fifth- and sixth-grade teachers would set up a long, rectangular table on the playground. On it they would place thick slices of juicy watermelon for us to enjoy. Can you imagine the sweet juice running down your chin or taking part in a seed-spitting contest?

The firstfruits harvested in our area became available at different times during spring and summer. Fruits bought during those times had that fresh, "just picked" flavor of foods we hadn't eaten in a long time. The firstfruits were always the best!

The ancient Israelites probably would have loved a summer watermelon feast. They had similar festivals of their own. When they arrived in the Promised Land, God wanted them to remember and celebrate the way He had protected them and provided for them on their long journey. So He commanded them to give an offering of their *firstfruits*, the best of their crops.

God still desires our firstfruits. He wants us to serve Him first and foremost in our lives with the best of our abilities and possessions. Yet, because of sin, we can't do this on our own.

Instead, God sent *Jesus* to be our firstfruits. Jesus is the best of the best—God's sinless, firstborn Son. He offered Himself on the cross to pay for our sins. We are no longer required to make sacrifices of animals, grain, or fruits, because Jesus' sacrifice has completed that work once and for all. What is more, Jesus is the firstfruits of those who will rise from the dead on the Last Day!

PRAYER

Dear God, thank You for sending Your one and only Son to pay for all my sins. Forgive me because of Him, and help me offer my firstfruits in service to You. In Jesus' name I ask it. Amen.

Julie Hadler

PENTECOST / TRINITY

Refreshment Time

John 7:37–39

Most of us like to eat. There's nothing quite like making a sandwich after playing a game of ball. And who doesn't enjoy "raiding the refrigerator" during a TV show? One of our favorite times is refreshment time.

Jesus called Himself both "the bread of life" and "the water of life." By these names, He was telling us that He refreshes us with His mercy and kindness. We sing of this in one of our hymns: "O refresh us; O refresh us, trav'ling through this wilderness" (*LSB* 924:1).

We all know what it means to be refreshed. How good that drink of cold water or milk tastes when we're really thirsty! The only problem is that we always get thirsty or tired or hungry again.

Jesus tells us that we'll be refreshed continually when we believe in Him. He promises to satisfy our thirst forever. This is what He means when He says, "Whoever believes in Me, as the Scripture has said, 'Out of his heart will flow rivers of living water'" (John 7:38).

Naturally, Jesus isn't talking about real water. He's speaking about His Spirit given to us in the water of Baptism. When we know and love Jesus, our thirst to be God's child is satisfied. He forgives us every day for all of our sins and gives us eternal life.

This is why the time we spend with our Lord is "refreshment time." Right now, as you read this devotion, you're in "refreshment time." How many other "refreshment times" do you have each week? Visiting with God can be one of your favorite things.

PRAYER

O Jesus, refresh us with the gift of Your Spirit, who assures us we are God's redeemed children. Amen.

David Klumpp

Fantastic Feet

Isaiah 52:7–10

Do you appreciate your feet? Do you think of them as being "swift and beautiful"? Or do you cover them up, neglect them, or take them for granted?

Feet take a lot of criticism. People call them ugly, smelly, and dirty. But feet are a remarkable part of the body. These comparatively small structures support your weight for an entire lifetime. Without your feet, you couldn't walk, run, or jump. You couldn't even stand up.

Each of your feet has twenty-six bones. These bones form three arches that put the spring into your walk. These arches act as shock absorbers to protect your spinal column. Many ligaments and muscles support the arches of your foot. In fact, your feet have as many muscles as your hands.

These fantastic "feats" of God's engineering are able to perform many jobs for Him. Our feet carry us to deliver some cookies and a smile to someone sick. They transport us to the store on an errand for Mother. They support us while we sing in church.

God gave us feet—as well as hands, voices, minds, and whole bodies—to help us serve Him as we serve others in our various vocations. Praise God for His wonderful handiwork!

PRAYER

Take my hands and let them move
At the impulse of Thy love;
Take my feet and let them be
Swift and beautiful for Thee. Amen. (*LSB* 783:2)

Elizabeth Friedrich

The Missing Lepidopteran

Luke 15:8–10

Alex loves lepidoptera, which are better known as butterflies. Alex has butterfly wallpaper, butterfly mobiles, and even a butterfly tie. His favorite items in his collection are seven trays of real butterflies. The trays are mounted on the wall across from his bed.

One morning, Alex noticed that the blue morpho was missing. He scoured the area trying to find it, but he couldn't. At breakfast, he asked his mom to help with the search. "It probably just dropped down onto the floor," she assured him.

After an hour, Mom was ready to give up, but Alex spotted something caught on the windowsill. The breeze from the fan must have blown the missing lepidopteran up there. "Yeah!" Alex screamed. After they put the butterfly back in its place, Alex and Mom had a celebration snack.

Mom told Alex about the woman from today's Bible reading who said, "Rejoice with me; for I have found the coin that I had lost" (Luke 15:9). Jesus goes on to say, "In the same way, I tell you, there is rejoicing in the presence of the angels of God over one sinner who repents."

We were lost because of sin. But God loved us sinners so much that He sent Jesus to die for us to give us eternal life with Him. When the Holy Spirit brought us to repentance and faith in Jesus, there was rejoicing in heaven!

PRAYER

Dear Jesus, thank You for saving me, finding me, and naming me Yours forever. Amen.

Elaine Hoffmann

Mazes

Psalm 27:11

Have you ever played a labyrinth game or walked through a garden maze? A labyrinth game can be as simple as a puzzle on a piece of paper, where you try to find your way from start to finish without coming to a blocked path. Or it can be as difficult as maneuvering a steel ball on a flat sheet of wood, from start to finish, without losing the steel ball in a hole or hitting a blocked path.

Many places in Europe have garden mazes, where hedges have been trimmed to form complex pathways. There are water mazes, where you step from rock to rock, trying not to get sprayed with water. Maybe you have been through a corn maze, where a farmer has created a pathway through a cornfield, with blocked paths along the way.

Life can be like a maze, full of choices. Some choices may lead us to sin—to wander away from following our Lord. These choices lead to a spiritual dead end. By Jesus' death on Calvary and His resurrection from the dead, all who believe in Him as their Savior and repent of their sins will be saved. The Lord turns us from sin toward Him and invites us to repent.

Jesus leads repentant sinners through the maze of this world. Jesus teaches His children His way through Word and Sacraments. Jesus makes our crooked paths level.

PRAYER

Dear Lord, thank You for being near me, to guide me in the way I should go. Lead me for Your name's sake. Amen.

Kathy Johnson

XOXOXO

Ephesians 1:13–14

Do you ever write "XOXOXO" at the bottom of a letter or an e-mail to represent kisses and hugs? The O symbolizes a hug because it looks like someone's encircling arms. But why does the X represent a kiss?

Actually, the practice has been around for hundreds of years. It began long ago, in medieval times. In those days, different signs represented saints. St. Andrew's sign was the letter X.

In order to show trustworthiness, a person placed the sign of St. Andrew after his signature on important papers. Then the signer would kiss the document to guarantee his good faith. The contract was not considered legal unless the signer included St. Andrew's X after the name. Through the centuries, this custom faded away, but people still associated the letter X with a kiss. It's still used that way today.

God has placed His seal, or sign, on you. At your Baptism, He filled you with His Holy Spirit. He owns and protects you. Even when you sin and disobey God, His seal is there, a reminder of His forgiveness. It tells you over and over of His love for you. It shares with you the promise of eternal life with Him in heaven.

God is trustworthy and of good faith. He keeps His promises. When you look at a baptismal font or think about your Baptism, remember that God has His seal on you.

PRAYER

Dear Savior, thank You for the gift of Your Holy Spirit. Thank You for my Baptism and for placing Your seal on me. Forgive me when I stray. I praise You for being trustworthy and always keeping Your promises. Amen.

Lisa Ellwein

Whose Are You?

Ephesians 2:8–10

Do you collect anything special? Maybe you collect baseball or Barbie cards, stamps, seashells, postcards, or marbles. My dad asks people for their business cards and saves all the cards in a big box. Each business card is unique, just as each person and his or her work is unique.

"What do you like best about your work?" Dad asks the people he meets. Most people tell him that the pay is great, the hours are flexible, or they get to travel a lot. Some say they are happy to do work that they enjoy so much. A few reply, "Not one thing!" or "It pays the bills."

Before he leaves, Dad reminds these people that they are God's workmanship. He shakes hands and says, "I am blessed to know you. Remember whose you are. God bless you in your work."

Whose are you? Our heavenly Father created you as His dear child and cares for you each day. He wants the best for you, so He sent Jesus to earth to do His work out of unconditional love for you. He died on the cross for your sins. He kept God's promise to save you and to earn for you a home in heaven.

What's your work? When we believe in Jesus as our Savior, the Holy Spirit helps us do what God has given us to do. We celebrate Christ's work for us by helping others. We wash the dishes because we want to help. We mow the yard because we want to serve. God created us to do good works as our response to the faith He has given us in our hearts.

PRAYER

Dear Father, thank You for making me Yours. Help me show Your love through my work, words, and actions. In Jesus' name. Amen.

Jane L. Haas

Immunizations

Psalm 32:6–7

Terry couldn't wait to start kindergarten. His new clothes were neatly folded in his dresser drawers, and he had packed his new backpack with crayons, scissors, and glue. Every morning he marked off another day on the calendar and counted the days until school started.

Then, one morning, Terry's mother said, "This afternoon we're going to the doctor's office, Terry. Dr. Baker will weigh and measure you and give you a preschool checkup. Then he'll give you a couple shots so you'll be ready for kindergarten."

"Shots!" screamed Terry. "I'm not going! I don't want any shots!"

"But, Terry," Mom explained, "you can't go to kindergarten without shots. Those shots protect you from disease. They'll keep you from getting sick and missing lots of school."

The person who wrote Psalm 32 speaks of a different kind of protection. He says that God will protect him from trouble. He urges everyone who believes in God to pray to Him while He may be found.

Like the psalmist, we pray to God and ask for His protection. We know He can keep us safe from any danger. To save us from the danger of sin and death, He sent His Son, Jesus, to die on the cross in our place. Because He forgives our sin, we are rescued from punishment in hell. And He will protect us from the devil's power so that we may live as His children. Through Christ, we have been immunized against eternal death and the power of sin and Satan.

PRAYER

Thank You, Father, for keeping me safe. Forgive my sins and protect me from the devil, for Jesus' sake. Amen.

Eileen Ritter

God's Heirs

Galatians 4:1–7

Dick Miller was just a common, ordinary fellow. He didn't have too much or too little. He dressed like everyone else, ate like everyone else, and acted like everyone else. If someone had asked Dick whether he thought he'd ever be a rich man, Dick would have laughed. Not much chance of that!

But this changed. A letter came to him from a lawyer in California. The letter said that his father's aunt had died and left a very large amount of money to him, her only nephew.

What a surprise! Dick hadn't even met her. He hadn't even known she was alive. His father had mentioned that the aunt was living across the country, but that had been about all. Now, suddenly, all this money! It all came to him by inheritance.

What made Dick so fortunate? Was he smarter than other young men? No. Was he better than all the others? No. He hadn't in any way earned his inheritance other than by being his father's son. Usually all we have to do to get an inheritance is to be a relative of the one who owned the wealth.

When God speaks to us in Scripture about our great promised inheritance, He even goes a step further. The Bible tells us we are heirs of God, but not because we are natural sons. God has adopted us. We aren't His heirs by birth. He *makes* us His heirs and then gives us the inheritance of life eternal with Him.

In a way, we are all Dick Millers. We have all been notified of what is being given us, not because of what or who we are but because of what and who God is. He is the loving Lord, the Father and Seeker of mankind. He so much wants to give us these great riches. He wants to give them to us as an inheritance. Praise God for His free gift of grace.

PRAYER

Thank You, Lord, for making me Your child and an heir of heaven. You are wonderful! Amen.

Charles S. Mueller

PENTECOST / TRINITY

What Good Is It?

Matthew 19:23–30

What good is that going to do me? Have you ever asked yourself this question? Maybe you couldn't understand a question in your social studies assignment. Or maybe you couldn't understand why you had to practice your music lesson. We don't often want to do things if we can't see how they will benefit us.

We especially don't want to do things that seem unfair to us. If the answer to the social studies question isn't in the book, or if the other kids are out playing while we have to practice, we become frustrated. To find an excuse for quitting, we ask, "What good is that going to do me anyway?"

The apostle Peter once asked Jesus the same question. Jesus had emphasized that only because of God's grace can anyone be saved. A rich person can't buy his way into heaven. So Peter asked Jesus what good it was going to do him to have given up his family and his good fishing business.

Jesus' answer was a real call to be faithful. He promised Peter that those who followed Him faithfully would inherit a treasure that was far more valuable than anything they had given up. That treasure was eternal life.

Do you ever wonder if being a Christian is all that important? Is it worth doing things in a way that will honor Jesus? Is it really important to put Jesus first in your life? What do you think the Lord meant when He said, "Everyone who has [done these things] for My name's sake, will receive a hundredfold" (Matthew 19:29)?

Of course, we can't earn eternal life. That's something we *inherit*—it's a free gift from God, won for us by Jesus' death and resurrection. But we can show our happiness over this gift and share it with others. Then, instead of wondering what good we're going to get, we'll be thinking of how much good others will receive through our witnessing for Christ.

PRAYER

Dear Lord Jesus, strengthen me in the true faith by the power of the Holy Spirit, and empower me that I may serve You faithfully and forever. Amen.

Clarence Berndt

PENTECOST / TRINITY

The Mystery

Ephesians 3:8–9, 12

It was a mystery. Jake's lunch was much better than he had planned or deserved. When his mom reminded him to make his lunch, he said yes, but he got distracted playing the role of a sleuth in a computer game. He did not remember putting anything except an apple in his brown bag. But there in front of him was the apple and also a sandwich, corn chips, and a brownie. How did *that* happen?

God inspired Paul to write about another mystery—the mystery of salvation by God's grace. How did that happen? We didn't plan it or deserve it. We often do things that we shouldn't do, or we don't do things we should do, but God loves us anyway. We live with a sinful condition called original sin, which makes us enemies of God. All this grace is a mystery. Why does God love sinners?

Jake's mom had gotten up early, peeked in the bag, and saw the lonely apple. She decided to surprise Jake. She fixed his favorites and kept her actions a secret.

Like Jake, we receive more than we deserve. We receive all of God's riches because of what Christ did when He took away our sins by dying on the cross.

"Hey, Mom, do you know anything about my lunch?" quizzed Jake as he rounded the kitchen counter with his book bag. When he saw her face, he guessed, "It was you, wasn't it?"

We don't have to guess about God's grace in Christ. It's no secret. God gives us this grace because of Christ's work through the riches of His Word, Baptism, and Holy Communion.

The mystery is solved. God did it in love for Jesus' sake.

PRAYER

Dear God, thank You for Your grace, which sent Your Son to save us. In Jesus' name. Amen.

Heidi Mueller

It's a Mystery

John 3:16

Do you like to read or solve mysteries? Let's try a few. See if you can read this next mysterious sentence.

Ths sntnc sn't hrd f y pt th vwls whr thy blng.

The sentence is confusing and looks strange until you see that all the vowels have been left out. Try putting in all the *a, e, i, o, u's.*

Well, here's another mystery. See if you can read the following:

Fr Gd s lvd th wrld, tht H gv Hs nly Sn.

Add the vowels, and you will have part of John 3:16. We read, "For God so loved the world, that He gave His only Son."

Now, let's consider something else that is a mystery to some people. How do we get to heaven?

Some people think that the way to heaven is to keep every one of the Ten Commandments. So they try very hard not to cheat or curse, to lie or covet. Some people actually think that they are doing a pretty good job. But even kids like you know that no one is perfect—not even your parents.

The way to get to heaven has nothing to do with what we do. It has everything to do with what God has done for us in sending Jesus to suffer and die for our sins. Those who believe in Jesus will be saved. And that's no mystery to those who believe the words of John 3:16.

PRAYER

Dear Jesus, thank You for solving the mystery of how to get to heaven. Help me to tell others how much You love them. Amen.

Philip Lang

A Time to Grieve

Hebrews 4:14–16

Linda was only a baby when her family got Tuffy. Tuffy was a dog, but not just any old dog—he was Linda's. The fun times they shared romping in the yard drew them very close as the years passed.

Linda remembers one special summer when she was about seven years old. The family piled into their car for a ten-hour trip to the town where they would live for the summer. The temperature was over 100 degrees outside, and there was no air-conditioning!

Can you picture a family of five with their belongings and a dog stuffed into a hot car for ten hours? It was quite a trip, but Tuffy didn't seem to mind the heat. After all, he could hang his head out the window to catch a slight breeze.

The following summer was not as enjoyable for Linda. Again, the family would be away for three months. This time Canada was their destination. However, Tuffy was not permitted to go along on this trip. Linda wondered how she would survive for three months without him. At last, summer ended, and Linda was welcomed home by a very happy dog.

Then one day, something happened. After school, Linda had a snack and hurried to the backyard to see her companion. Only this time, Tuffy wasn't there. He had suffered a heart attack and died that morning. Linda was heartbroken.

Maybe you know the grief that comes when a favorite pet dies or a close friend moves away. Someone else knows too, and He cares about you especially at such times. Jesus, our Savior, sympathizes with us—that is, He feels our sadness and comforts us.

We can always come to our Lord and tell Him our sorrows. Because He is gracious and merciful, He can and will help us in times of need.

PRAYER

Heavenly Father, You know I have joys and sorrows in my life. Help me grow as I experience difficult situations. Thank You for allowing a time for all things and helping me through the sad times. Keep me always in the love of Jesus. Amen.

Barbara Juneau

PENTECOST / TRINITY

Meaning of *Concordia*

Psalm 133

Do you get along with your brothers and sisters? Some children fight all the time. How peaceful it is when brothers and sisters get along with, take care of, help, and love one another! The Bible says, "Behold, how good and pleasant it is when brothers dwell in unity!" (Psalm 133:1).

Sometimes Christians, brothers and sisters in the family of God, fight and argue among themselves. They say that they love Christ, that they love one another, that they love their neighbors as themselves. But they don't act like it. Sometimes they act as if they hated one another. How sad! Jesus wants us to love one another as He loves us.

In 1580, a group of Lutheran Christians published a big book. It contained all the important writings and agreements of the fifty-year-old Lutheran Church. These people had had some arguments among themselves about what the Bible said and what they should believe about God. After much debate, study, arguing, and trouble, they had talked over their differences and had come to a complete agreement. They all signed their names to show that they were in "concord" with each other. They were so happy that they called their book *The Book of Concord* ("The Book of Harmony").

Many congregations have called their churches Concordia, which means "hearts together." Some of their colleges are called Concordia. Even a Lutheran publishing house is called Concordia.

The name *Concordia* is a reminder of the agreements of 1580 that help us keep our eyes on Jesus, that we may live together in peace and harmony as fellow disciples of Jesus Christ. He gives us the strength to do this through the Holy Spirit, who lives in us and fills us with His peace.

PRAYER

Dear God, please forgive me for fighting with my brothers and sisters. Help me love them and get along with them. Help me grow closer in Christian love to my brothers and sisters in the Church too, so that we may live as the happy family of God, brothers and sisters of Jesus Christ, our Lord and Savior. Amen.

Wayne Saffen

PENTECOST / TRINITY

Difficult Choices

Genesis 22:1–14

Difficult choices are those that seem to be choices between two good acts. During World War II, a German pastor named Dietrich Bonhoeffer chose to enter prison rather than deny his love for Jesus. By doing so, he was forced to leave his wife and eight children, all of whom he loved dearly. It was not that he loved his family less; it was that he loved his Lord Jesus more. He couldn't make the choice that would cause him to desert his Savior.

God put Abraham to the most difficult test of all when He told Abraham to offer his son, Isaac, as a sacrifice. God asked him to choose between two things: his love for his only child and his love for God. It was a difficult choice.

Choices like that face us too. A boy is employed in a store, packing apples. The manager tells him to put the rotten apples on the bottom and the best ones on top. He must either obey a dishonest employer or lose the job. But suppose that jobs are hard to get, and his family needs the few dollars he earns. He knows he cannot be dishonest, yet he also knows his family depends on his job.

You may have had to decide between telling your best friend that copying homework is dishonest—and possibly losing that person's friendship—or sitting by while God's will was broken. Decisions like that come frequently. There are no easy answers at the back of a book to tell us what to do. We Christians make wise decisions when we call on Jesus in prayer, seeking His help in making the right choice. When we aren't sure, we need to ask God's guidance in reaching a decision. When we have made a wrong choice, we need to ask His forgiveness.

Because Jesus loves us and died for us, we need never worry about wrong choices. Jesus promises to guide us in making right choices and to forgive us when we make poor choices.

PRAYER

Dear Jesus, help me make the right choices in life, choices that please and honor You. Amen.

William C. Beckmann

PENTECOST / TRINITY

Victory Trees

Colossians 2:13–15

Trees have played a part in more than one great victory.

During the American Revolution, the British fleet, together with army regulars and marines, wanted to attack Charleston, South Carolina. But blocking their path were Americans under Colonel Moultrie, stationed at Fort Johnson on Sullivan's Island.

Since the fort was made not of stone but only of sand and earth held together by palmetto logs, few people thought the fort would last long. But the sand absorbed the British cannonballs as a blotter absorbs ink. And other cannonballs bounced off the tough palmetto logs as if the logs had been made of iron. The fort held out, and palmetto trees played an important part in the victory.

A tree played an important part in another victory. The battle wasn't fought on an island but on a hill. The weapons weren't cannon and muskets but hammer and nails. The battle wasn't fought to win freedom for one nation but for all people. In this battle, a tree was used as a cross on which to kill Jesus, God's own Son. But by dying on the cross, Jesus won a complete victory over sin, death, and the devil. And He won this victory for us.

Through the centuries, millions of people have had to fight battles for their freedom. Sometimes they lost their battles. Even when they won, often they lost their freedom again later on. But the freedom Jesus won for us on the tree of the cross—freedom from death and hell—is ours forever. This is His promise to all who believe in Him.

PRAYER

Lord Jesus, we give thanks to Thee
That Thou hast died to set us free;
Made righteous through Thy precious blood,
We now are reconciled to God. Amen. (*TLH* 173:1)

Lois Vogel

Twice Blessed

1 Corinthians 12:4–6

Rob and Darrel were twins, alike in so many ways. They played the trumpet, got A's in math and B's in science, and were acolytes in church. Both boys played Little League baseball and were pitchers.

Over the summer, Rob and Darrel played baseball, went to Vacation Bible School, and took a trip to the Grand Canyon with their family. Then it was time to go back to school. When they got there, a strange thing happened. Darrel decided to play soccer, and Rob decided to play football.

Over the summer, Darrel had grown taller and gotten faster. Rob had grown bigger and gotten stronger. Even though they were alike in many ways, they developed their own talents. Darrel could run and move very quickly. He was good at dribbling and kicking a soccer ball. Rob could dive and tackle. He was good at stopping players from getting a touchdown. Both boys had skills their teams needed.

There are many things we do together as God's family. We go to Sunday School and church. We read the Bible and sing hymns. We pray every day. But God also gives different gifts to the members of His family. One person might be a good singer in the choir. Another might be a good musician and play in the band. You could be good with little children and help in the church nursery. Your friend could be an excellent student and help tutor a classmate.

You are an important member of God's family. It doesn't depend on your talents. Jesus died for all people—people who have many different abilities. Even if you can't sing or play an instrument, even if you don't like to babysit or you don't get straight A's, you can still serve Jesus. Because of what Jesus did for you in His death and resurrection, we are free to serve others, and in so doing, we serve Jesus. You can rake leaves or take out the trash. It doesn't matter how big or how strong you are; there is always something you can do.

PRAYER

Heavenly Father, I want to serve You because You are so good to me. Help me to know my gifts and use them wisely. In Jesus' name. Amen.

Nicole Dreyer

PENTECOST / TRINITY

Lost at the Beach

Luke 15:3–7

"See you down at the beach!" shouted Pastor as he waved and drove out of sight. Confidently, five of us left our campsite and started down the sandy slope to the picnic. We were sure we knew the way to the hot dogs and volleyball.

After ten minutes of hiking, we reached the beach. It wasn't until then that we realized we weren't so sure after all. We didn't know which way to turn. So we went on a hunch and marched to the left. Oops! That beach was closed. Now we were sure we should have gone to the right. Off we went to the right, on and on for half an hour. Would we ever find our friends?

Just when we felt hopelessly lost, we spied Pastor's van in the parking lot. Later, we found out that he was looking for lost people like us. What a relief. What a joy. We had been found!

Sinners are lost too. Often we don't even know it. By ourselves, we can't hike through life and make it to heaven. Not one itty-bitty turn to do something right will get anyone to heaven. Not one carefully plotted path will get anyone from here to eternity. God did the work, and God provided the way. He found us sinners while we were lost. He sent His Son to live on earth, to suffer and die, to rise and prove that He was the one and only Savior.

Sometimes we wander around and forget that in our Baptism, the pastor marked us with the cross of Christ. We forget that through the water and the Word of God, we became children of God. We forget that through God's Word and Sacraments, His Spirit is in us, always working, even through our mistakes. But God doesn't forget us. He is ours, and we are His forever. Heaven is rejoicing.

PRAYER

Dear Jesus, thank You for seeking and finding me. Thank You for rescuing and keeping me forever. Amen.

Philip Lang

PENTECOST / TRINITY

Laboring for the Lord

Colossians 3:23–24

"Work, work, work! All I do is work," said Matthew to his dad as he was raking the lawn. "I sure wish I didn't have to work all the time. I bet I could find a lot of other things to do."

"I'm sure you could," said Matthew's dad. "But you know that some work every day is good for you. If everybody had your attitude, there wouldn't be any factories, offices, or farms. Then there would be no food, clothes, or baseball bats either."

"Oh," Matthew grunted, "I didn't think about that."

Our Scripture reading for Labor Day reminds us that work is an opportunity to serve the Lord. As we grow older and begin to select jobs, we can think of them as ways to honor the One who gained heaven for us. "Whatever you do, work heartily . . . knowing that from the Lord you will receive the inheritance as your reward" (Colossians 3:23–24). Before we do any work, we already have our inheritance from the Lord: salvation from sin, death, and the devil. The work to get our inheritance was done for us by Jesus on the cross. Because of His work, we get the reward. It's already done. Now we can work in thanksgiving to God for Jesus' work on the cross.

It's wise to select a job we like, so that we enjoy our work and don't become bored with it. As we do everyday tasks at home or school, we can already see how God wants us to approach our work. Our chores and even our schoolwork can be pleasurable if we remember that we're laboring for our Lord and Savior.

PRAYER

Heavenly Father, thank You for giving me legs and arms and a mind so I can work. Help those fathers and mothers who don't have a job to get one so they can support their families. Thank You for Labor Day, on which we remember all the workers in our land. In Your Son's name. Amen.

LaVerne A. Janssen

PENTECOST / TRINITY

Jesus at the Wheel

Matthew 18:1–4

Tony Adams, his parents, and his younger brother had spent Labor Day at the home of Tony's grandparents. Now it was evening, and the family was driving home. "This fog is getting bad," said Mr. Adams. "I can hardly see a thing. We'll have to stop if it gets any worse."

Tony leaned forward in his seat. He was anxious to get home, but he was worried about the fog and the heavy holiday traffic. He could feel that his parents were tense too.

Everyone else had forgotten about Bobby. Suddenly, Tony said, "Look at Bobby. He's sound asleep. The fog doesn't bother him a bit."

"I guess Bobby trusts his father," said Mrs. Adams. "He knows he's safe when Dad's at the wheel."

Jesus once said that we need the faith of a little child to enter His kingdom. Bobby had faith that his dad would get him home safely. In the same way, we can trust our Lord Jesus to bring us safely to His eternal home.

We meet many dangers on our pathway to heaven. The devil is also around, trying to lead us off in his direction.

But Jesus is with us all the way. He fought sin and Satan and defeated them. Now we needn't worry or be afraid. Jesus is "at the wheel," guiding our lives. We can relax in His love and "let Him do the driving."

I walk with Jesus all the way,
His guidance never fails me;
Within His wounds I find a stay
When Satan's pow'r assails me;
And by His footsteps led,
My path I safely tread.
No evil leads my soul astray;
I walk with Jesus all the way. (*LSB* 716:5)

PRAYER

Dear God, forgive me for being afraid and failing to trust in You. Guide and keep me on the path to heaven through faith in Jesus. In Jesus' name I pray. Amen.

Les Bayer

PENTECOST / TRINITY

Schooltime

Proverbs 2:1–6

"It's so much fun looking forward to a new school year," beamed Janice at the breakfast table.

"You *would* think so," Bob responded. "I don't think it's fun—all that homework and tests and stuff."

"But think of all the benefits," said Janice. "You learn new things that help you be a better person and know how to take care of yourself."

"How will knowing when Washington crossed the Delaware help me?" Bob argued.

Just then, their mother walked in on the conversation. She said, "Studying history helps you appreciate the things that were done to make our country what it is today. If you didn't learn about these events, you'd probably take a lot of things for granted. For example, Susan B. Anthony worked hard so that women can vote. If history wasn't recorded, we might think women always had the right to vote and hold public office."

"I never looked at it that way," Bob finally admitted. "I guess if you think of why you're studying, it makes more sense."

Have you ever felt, like Bob, that school is a bore or something that gets in the way of your activities? The Book of Proverbs puts going to school in the right light when it says, "Making your ear attentive to wisdom and inclining your heart to understanding; yes, if you call out for insight. . . . For the LORD gives wisdom" (Proverbs 2:2–6). In His Word, God recounts salvation history, and that wisdom makes us wise to salvation. God's Word saves!

Jesus studied and learned when He was young. As we begin another school year, we ask God to bless our study and give us clear minds to concentrate and apply what we learn.

PRAYER

Dear Jesus, thank You for schools, where we can learn, and for teachers who help us. Bless us as we study, so that we can make good use of our time and discover Your will for our lives. Amen.

Betty L. Janssen

PENTECOST / TRINITY

Scared to Go to School

Deuteronomy 33:25–29

David was about to enter kindergarten. He wasn't worried about it. He had some friends who were going, and he knew he could do whatever they could do. He wasn't worried.

But David had some older brothers. One day, at the supper table, they began talking about going away to college. They were happy and excited about leaving home and living and working in a new place.

Suddenly little David began to cry. Everyone looked at him in surprise. But his mother understood. She took him in her arms and held him close.

"Which one are you worried about," she asked, "kindergarten or college?"

"C-college," sobbed little David.

Half laughing, but still holding him close, Mother explained, "But, David, when you go to college, you'll be bigger than I am! You might even be bigger than Daddy! You'll be big enough to do whatever you have to do in college!"

Then David began to feel better. When he discovered he wasn't going to have to do something that he wasn't big enough to do, his worries went away.

"As your days, so shall your strength be," says God in the Bible (Deuteronomy 33:25). God promises that whatever happens to us, whether it be persecution or troubles or hard work or just college, He will give us the strength and wisdom that we need at any particular time. We can trust that promise and never be afraid of what lies ahead.

PRAYER

Thank You, dear heavenly Father, for promising to give me whatever help I need as long as I live with You. Please keep me as Your child through Jesus Christ, my Lord. Amen.

Dorothy Hoyer Scharlemann

Big Dipper

Psalm 147:3–6

One September evening, we took the neighborhood children to see the stars. We drove out a country road, far from town, and looked up. Seeing the vast canopy, we were amazed at the brilliant sparkle of stars.

We showed the children the Big Dipper. Then we used its handle to find the North Star. We told our friends that the North Star guided slaves north to freedom more than a hundred and fifty years ago.

Harriet Tubman was an abused slave. She set her eye on the North Star. One night, she risked her life and fled to freedom. Once she reached freedom, she wanted to help others. She returned to the South several times. Altogether, she led three hundred slaves to freedom.

Harriet knew throughout her journeys that she was never alone. "Oh, dear Lord, I ain't got no friend but You!" she cried out one night, fearing capture. "Come to my help, Lord, for I'm in trouble!"

Through many narrow escapes, Harriet always gave the glory to God, telling people, "It wasn't me. It was the Lord!"

Thanks to God, she could declare that, on her Underground Railroad, she never ran a train off the track, and she never lost a passenger.

As nights get longer, we can look to the sky and remember God's faithfulness. A star at Bethlehem announced the birth of Jesus. Born to save, Jesus suffered and died, delivering us from the slavery of sin. Through His Spirit, we have forgiveness of sins and life everlasting. We also have the Spirit's power to lead others to find freedom in Jesus as their Savior.

PRAYER

Dearest Lord, You are my truest friend. Be my help at all times! In Jesus' name I pray. Amen.

Christine S. Weerts

Lord, Save Me!

Ephesians 6:10–20

When Don was sent to the war in Vietnam, his mother gave him a small pocket Bible. "Carry it with you," she said. "It's God's Word, and it'll help you."

When Don got to Vietnam, he stuck the Bible inside his helmet for safekeeping and forgot about it.

Weeks later, three enemy bullets found Don—one in each leg and one through his helmet. The last one would have killed him, but the Bible saved his life by keeping the bullet from entering his head.

In almost every war, something like this has happened to somebody: a Bible helped save his life. This just shows again that our God can protect people in many different ways.

Unfortunately, some people who hear these stories think the Bible must be some sort of good-luck charm. Actually, the Bible is much more than a bulletproof vest that keeps us from getting killed. It is the story of God's love for us—a love that protects us in our battle with the devil, the world, and our own sinful desires. Those enemies try to destroy our souls. They shoot temptations at us. That's why God's Word tells us to "put on the whole armor of God" (Ephesians 6:11). With His mighty Word, we are able to stand against the devil's clever attempts to make us sin. With His Word and through His Sacraments, we are strengthened in faith. Reading, studying, and hearing about God's love and forgiveness, which He freely gives us because of the work of Jesus, strengthens our faith and helps us with our daily struggles against our enemies. That's why God encourages us to put on His "armor." He loves us and fights the fight for us.

PRAYER

Lord, help me put on the armor of Your Word. Bless my reading, studying, and hearing, and strengthen my faith. In Your name I pray. Amen.

Carl Nitz

PENTECOST / TRINITY

Lost and Found

Luke 19:1–10

My family and I have a small herd of goats on our farm. One afternoon, a mama goat gave birth to twins. The next morning, there was only one baby goat. The other had disappeared!

The dog and I searched every square foot of the pasture. There was no sign of the lost baby. I stood by the pond, thinking, where could that goat be?

Then a weak "Ma-a-a-h" sounded almost under my feet. I dropped to my knees and looked. The little goat had fallen into a hole at the bank of the pond! He was stuck under the ground!

I reached as far into the hole as I could, but I could barely touch the little goat. I dug near the opening, but I was afraid to dig too much or dirt would fall and bury the kid.

So I tried encouragement. "Come on, little goat!" I urged. "Crawl out if you can!" He responded to my voice and wriggled forward. Then I was able to get hold of his shoulders and pull him out. He was a muddy mess!

Without Jesus, you and I would be a lot like that goat. We'd be buried deep in sin's hole. We wouldn't be able to do a thing to help ourselves, not even a wriggle.

But God loved us and didn't want us to die in our sins. He sent His Son, Jesus, into the world to save us. Jesus willingly gave His life on the cross as payment for our sin. Through Baptism, He calls us. He trades our dirty, sinful covering for His righteous white robe. He reaches out for us, pulls us to Himself, and lovingly says, "I came for you. You are Mine."

PRAYER

Dear Jesus, thank You for dying for my sin. Thank You for calling me and reaching out to make me Yours. Help me to live every day for You. Amen.

Glenda Schrock

Bulletin Board Question

Proverbs 2:1–10

Which school subject reminds you most of God? Why?

Social Studies. Because I see God helps people do whatever job they are doing.   Laura, grade 3

Recess. After creation, God rested on the seventh day. Recess lets us rest after working hard too.   Todd, grade 3

Memory Work. I have trouble learning *one* Bible verse. God can remember everybody's name and everything about them.   Mark, grade 4

Science. As I study the universe, I see how large it is. God is powerful. And all the planets stay in their own orbit.   Mike, grade 5

Geography. Studying other lands lets me see how beautiful the whole world is. Mountains, fjords, deserts, jungles, plateaus—each is wonderful in its own way. God created them all.   Lori, grade 5

Health/Physical Education. Our bodies are the most wonderful machines. I am impressed with God's creation.   Debbie, grade 6

Math. Math is accurate and precise—just like God. Our number system reminds me of eternity. It goes on forever.   Eric, grade 7

Addition. If I add up all my good points, I find I'm worthless. I need God.

Subtraction. God says He will never take away His Word.

Multiplication. Grace and peace are multiplied to me from God.

Division. On the Last Day, God will divide the nations into groups—righteous and unrighteous.   Mary, Julie, Phil, grade 7

How would you answer the question on the bulletin board? How does God remind you of His presence daily?

Prayer

Let children hear the mighty deeds Which God performed of old,
Which in our younger years we saw, And which our parents told.
To learn that in our God alone Their hope securely stands,
That they may never doubt His love But walk in His commands. Amen.
(*LSB* 867:1, 5)

                                                        Barbara E. Schafer

---

PENTECOST / TRINITY

Missing the Mark

Psalm 32:1–5

An archer has a quiver of arrows on his back and a strong bow in his hand. He aims at the bull's-eye but he misses. The man looks like a good archer. His form and style are perfect. But no matter how many arrows he shoots, he can't hit the bull's-eye. He keeps on missing the mark.

This is one of the ways the Bible describes sin. Sin is missing the mark. We may look pretty good on the outside. Our clothes, our manners, our speech may be the best. But no matter how hard we try to please the Lord and keep His Commandments, we miss the mark.

Disobeying our parents, telling a "fib" about a classmate, wanting to "get even" with someone who has hurt us—these are ways in which we break God's Law. Because of our sinful nature, we can't hit the target God has put up for us.

What hope is there for us, then? Our hope is in Jesus, the only one who can help us. When we confess our sins to Him, He covers us with the white robe of His own righteousness. Jesus loves us and forgives us even though we continually miss the mark God has set for us.

The Bible says, "Blessed is the one whose transgression is forgiven, whose sin is covered" (Psalm 32:1). We who believe in Jesus have "washed [our] robes and made them white in the blood of the Lamb" (Revelation 7:14). Our sins are forgiven for Jesus' sake, and through Him our lives become pleasing to God.

PRAYER

Lord Jesus,
>Oh, how blest it is to know:
>Were as scarlet my transgression,
>It shall be as white as snow
>By Thy blood and bitter passion;
>For these words I now believe:
>Jesus sinners doth receive. Amen. (*LSB* 609:5)

Charles Reichert

Looks Aren't Everything

1 Samuel 16:6–7

Mercedes and Junior were at the Humane Society, choosing a kitten. "I want the cute one with the black paw," squealed Mercedes.

"I want the big one with the white tail," said Junior.

"How about the little gray one?" suggested their grandmother.

"No way!" Mercedes and Junior said in unison. "That one's too small and ugly."

In today's Bible reading, the Lord sent Samuel to anoint a new king for His people. Samuel followed the Lord's instructions and went to the house of Jesse. When he saw Jesse's oldest son—big, strong, handsome Eliab—Samuel immediately thought he was the one God wanted.

But God had other plans and told Samuel not to choose Eliab. God told Samuel, "The LORD sees not as man sees: man looks on the outward appearance, but the LORD looks on the heart" (1 Samuel 16:6). The Lord had chosen Jesse's youngest and smallest son, David, who later became a great king.

God has not chosen us based on how we look or act. It's a good thing, because we are not able to keep our hearts and minds pure and holy. We are sinful. Yet the Bible assures us that "in Christ Jesus you are all sons [and daughters] of God, through faith" (Galatians 3:26). As His children, we wear the "good looks" that Jesus gave us—His robe of righteousness. We are free to live as God's beautiful children.

PRAYER

Father, create in me a clean heart, and renew a steadfast spirit within me. In Jesus' name. Amen.

Sandy Callahan

More Than Plenty to Pick

Deuteronomy 24:19–22

Have you ever gone blueberry picking? It's a lot of fun! You drive out into the country until you see a sign like this: "U PICK EM." You pull over and find a stand where the owner of the berry field waits. He gives you a bucket, and you just start picking. You put all the berries you pick in the bucket—and then you go home and eat them!

Sound good? In most parts of the country, the picking season is nearly over, so you might want to go soon. Don't worry, though. There are always plenty of berries left. That's the best part! No matter how many people have been out picking before you, you'll still fill your bucket.

As Israelites entered the Promised Land, God gave special instructions about picking their fields. They were not to harvest every last olive or grape or sheaf of grain. They were to leave some, so that poor people could come later and pick the rest.

God would always make sure there was more than enough for every-one. God blessed Israel with rich harvests. An owner could have all he needed and still leave plenty for others.

God always blesses us too, doesn't He? He gives us family, food, clothes, and a home. And more than that, He gives us love and forgive-ness and eternal life through Jesus. Everything we need most. And enough to share.

PRAYER

Dear God, thank You for everything, especially faith in Your Son. Help me to share. Amen.

Carl C. Fickenscher II

Cartwheels and Headstands

Romans 12:1–3

When I was a child, my friends and I loved to perform great feats of acrobatic skill in our grassy front yard. Cartwheels, backbends, and somersaults were just a few of our many talents. Our favorite stunt was the headstand. It took some practice and balance (and finding a level spot), but when it all came together, the headstand felt great. Suddenly the world turned around and we saw everything upside-down.

Sometimes I think the world is turned upside-down. Actors and sport figures get huge salaries; churches struggle to send missionaries to share the Gospel around the world. We judge people by how they look, where they live, or the car their family drives, and not by the kindness or love they show.

We focus on "me" thinking rather than "you" thinking. We see advertisements for things to buy for ourselves. We rarely think about what we could give away or provide for others.

The world hasn't changed; it has always been filled with sinful, self-centered people. Like us. We can't change—not by ourselves. We need our Savior Jesus Christ, who turned the world upside-down. He changes us so we can love those who hate us and give riches away. He calls us to repent, forgive, and live new lives.

The world crucified our sinless Savior, but He overcame the world. In Baptism, God overcomes sin in us. He gives us faith through His Spirit. He transforms our sinful body into a new body—one we offer in service to others. His Spirit gives us power to change.

We can bring God's transforming message to our upside-down neighborhood.

PRAYER

Dear Jesus, in my Baptism, You gave me Your Spirit's power to turn the world and its values upside-down. Direct me to offer myself as a living sacrifice and show my love today. Amen.

Christine S. Weerts

PENTECOST/TRINITY

Cable Car to Heaven

Titus 3:4–7

San Francisco is famous for many things. Tourists come to this city to see the Golden Gate Bridge and the beautiful bay. The cable cars are also a big attraction.

San Francisco is very hilly. Before the invention of the automobile, horses had to do the heavy work of pulling loads up those steep hills. Many horses fell and broke their legs. Others just wore out because of the hard work. The cobblestone streets didn't make the job much easier. Then the cable car was invented.

In 1873, Andre Hallidie ran some heavy steel ropes under the streets of San Francisco. These cables were controlled by a large motor. Attached to the cables were cars on steel rails running along the streets. Ever since then, powerful motors have pulled cable cars up the steep hills through the downtown area.

The road to heaven appears quite steep to many people. They try to pull themselves with their heavy load of sin up to God's kingdom. They try to earn their way to heaven by their own good works.

What they don't realize is that the Bible says, "He saved us, not because of works done by us in righteousness, but according to His own mercy, by the washing of regeneration and renewal of the Holy Spirit" (Titus 3:4–5). Jesus has made the steep hill to heaven easy by His death and resurrection.

The road to heaven is impossible for any of us to climb. We can't be saved by anything we have done or ever will do. It's entirely by God's love and mercy that we have eternal life. Only as the Holy Spirit "hooks" us up to the "cable" of Jesus can we enter the kingdom of heaven.

PRAYER

Thank You, Father, for Your love and mercy. Thank You, Jesus, for Your sacrificial death on the cross. Holy Spirit, work faith in those who do not believe in Jesus so they, too, may know Him as their Lord and Savior. Amen.

Christine Dehnke

PENTECOST / TRINITY

Not Good Enough?

2 Corinthians 5:17–21

Mrs. Monday asked her fourth graders to line up along the wall of the classroom. She challenged them to jump all the way across the room in one leap.

"Wow, I jumped twice as far as Maria did," Carlo bragged.

"But, Carlo, I asked you to jump across the whole room. Did you make it? Were you even close?"

"No, I guess not."

"So you see, you're in the same situation as Maria. You failed! I asked you to do this to illustrate a Bible lesson. God's Law commands us to be perfect."

"That would be impossible, just like jumping across this room in one jump is impossible!" exclaimed Maria.

"So it would seem," said Mrs. Monday. "Maria, try your jump one more time. Go ahead and jump."

When Maria jumped, Mrs. Monday caught her and carried her across the room. Her feet never even touched the floor. She made it in one jump.

"I get it," said Carlo. "We can't do it ourselves. Someone else has to take over."

"That's a *perfect* answer," said Mrs. Monday. "God sent Jesus to be perfect for us. Through His death and resurrection, Jesus lifts the burden of sin from us and carries us all the way to heaven. Through our Baptism, God sees Jesus' perfection in us."

Prayer

Dear Jesus, You died and rose again to make me perfect in God's eyes. Thanks. Be with me so I can live for You. Amen.

Philip Lang

Winter Is Coming

Proverbs 30:24–25

You may know the story of the grasshopper and the ant. The grasshopper played all summer, while the ant prepared for the coming winter. The grasshopper froze, but the ant lived off the food he had stored up for himself.

The Bible verses from Proverbs point out that ants are wise creatures. They are diligent workers, and they have a keen sense of what time it is. Winter is coming.

"Winter" is coming in other ways too. You may become ill or be injured in an accident. You may be concerned about how popular you will be in school this year.

Jesus never promised to make our winter storms go away. He did promise that He will go through them with us. He will *never* leave us, whether it's winter or any other season.

What we need for the winter ahead is Jesus, our Savior. He takes away our sins and makes us whole again. The joy of all this is that Jesus comes to us in His Word and the Sacraments. He grants us new life and salvation. Reading the Bible each day helps us store up God's wisdom for our lives.

PRAYER

Dear Jesus, give me wisdom and strength to depend on You in every hardship I face. Thanks for Your promise to be with me always. Amen.

George T. Zoebl

From Bad to Good

2 Kings 4:32–37

Sometimes I think they should rename the season fall as *Sneeze*. Every fall, many of my friends and I sneeze and sneeze. "How is the weather?" someone will ask.

Sneeze, I reply.

"Would you like to get an ice-cream cone?"

Sneeze, I answer.

"How about a tissue?"

Sneeze, I answer. "Dank you."

I had never thought of my sneezing as much more than a nuisance. That is, until I read about Elisha.

God worked through Elisha in raising a dead boy. That boy awakened from death by sneezing seven times. Wow! God took sneezing and made it a miracle!

God has done miracles in my life! He's taken things that I thought were bad and turned them into something good. In my Baptism, God turned me from being His enemy into being His child. He miraculously gave me forgiveness, life, and salvation as the pastor spoke the Invocation and poured simple water on my head. Through the suffering and death of Jesus on the cross, God gave me, a sinner, good gifts. He continues to work in my life using His Word and Sacraments to strengthen me. Yes, God is changing you and me in all seasons.

PRAYER

Lord, thank You for the miracle of faith through Baptism. Continue to work in me. In Jesus' name. Amen.

Linda L. Hansen

The Chocolate Factory

John 6:35–40

Liquid chocolate poured from the machine into a shallow pan. "Wow, beans at one end and hot fudge at the other!" marveled Adrian. He stood in front of a huge window in a chocolate factory. Everywhere he looked, Adrian saw delicious chocolate—hot chocolate in mugs with floating whipped cream, miniature candy bars, chocolate fudge ice cream.

"Could you use one of your credit cards here, Mom?" he asked hopefully.

"No, Adrian, they only take cash."

"If only you and Dad owned this place, we could always have all the chocolate we wanted," Adrian sighed.

In Jesus' day, people enjoyed eating too. Those who sat in the crowd of five thousand watched Jesus pray over a boy's lunch. They saw a few loaves and fish feed everybody. Some people liked the bread and fish so much that they wanted Jesus to be their king. They followed Him around, hoping He would give them more food. Their idea of a savior was a "bread king."

But Jesus wasn't that kind of king. He told His followers that regular food was good, but it didn't last long. After a person ate it, he or she would get hungry again.

Jesus came to bring us better food than bread, fish, or chocolate. He gives us food that lasts forever—the bread of life, which is found in His Word and the Lord's Supper. Each day He offers us special treats of His love and forgiveness. Eating the food Jesus offers will not only satisfy us but also will enable us to live forever.

PRAYER

Dear Jesus, feed me each day with the best-tasting food of all, Your Word, so my faith will get stronger. Amen.

Ruth Stressow

Men from Outer Space

Psalm 91:9–16

Do you believe there are people living in outer space? The artists who draw comic books often picture men living in outer space.

Even though much that is written about people on Mars or the moon is simply imagined, some scientists seriously believe there might be people on other planets. Whether or not there really are such people is certainly an interesting question.

The Bible does not answer the question for us. But the Bible does tell us that there are beings who live beyond our earth as well as on it. These creatures are called "angels."

One cannot see an angel. Angels are spirits. Spirits usually do not have bodies. We know that they exist because God has told us so in His Word.

The Bible says that some angels are good and others are evil. God tells us that the good angels are His servants whom He sends to watch over His children. "He will command His angels concerning you to guard you in all your ways," says the psalm writer (Psalm 91:11). The evil angels are the servants of the devil.

God wants us always to be safe and happy. That is why He sends His angels to watch over us, to keep us from harm, and to help us.

Isn't it wonderful to know that God's angels are always with us? This is one of many reasons for being glad that we are God's children.

PRAYER

Lord Jesus, may Your holy angels watch over me at all times, to keep me safe from all harm. Amen.

Dale E. Griffin

PENTECOST / TRINITY

Nearer to God

Genesis 28:10–22

In the early 1800s, two sisters wrote many of the hymns sung in their home church in England. Sarah Adams wrote the words, and her sister Eliza composed the music. One week their pastor was searching for a hymn to accompany his sermon on Genesis 28:10–22. Together the sisters produced "Nearer, My God, to Thee," which tells about Jacob's dream of a stairway to heaven.

Two stories show how this beautiful hymn of faith has been comforting people for more than one hundred and fifty years. An assassin shot U.S. President McKinley in 1901. As the president lay dying, his family heard him whisper the chorus of this hymn: "Nearer my God, to Thee, nearer to Thee." A few days later, at his funeral and memorial services, congregations around the country sang the hymn, remembering God's care for His children, including President McKinley.

The second story occurred during the sinking of the *Titanic* on April 15, 1912. There weren't enough lifeboats on the ship to save everyone. More than 1,550 passengers were left on the deck of the ship, facing certain death. As the lifeboats pulled away, the ship's band played "Nearer, My God, to Thee" (*TLH* 533). Hundreds of voices joined in singing the hymn as the sea pounded the battered ship.

The words of this hymn are just as true today as when they were written. The only way you can be nearer to God and eternal life is through Jesus. His death for your sins makes it possible for you to face life and death without fear. You are God's child. You are loved. You are forgiven.

PRAYER

Dear Jesus, because of my Baptism, You have promised to be near me each day of my life. Thank You for Your death on the cross, which made me Your child forever. Amen.

Jeanette Dall

St. Matthew

Matthew 9:9–13

Today is the day the Church remembers St. Matthew. The Bible reading tells us how Matthew came to be a disciple of Jesus. Matthew was doing his job of collecting taxes when Jesus saw him. When Jesus invited Matthew to come and be a disciple, he didn't hesitate, but went with Jesus right away. Later, Jesus and His disciples ate dinner at Matthew's house.

Now, everyone knew tax collectors cheated the people. No one should be friends with a man who had such a bad reputation. The Pharisees were angry with Jesus because He ate with a man who was so bad. Jesus told the Pharisees that God wants His people to show mercy and kindness and forgiveness. And who was it that needed that mercy and would accept it? The Pharisees, who thought they were sinless, or Matthew?

Matthew remembered the words of Jesus. Matthew saw and felt the mercy of Jesus. Because of his experience, he knew that God had forgiven him.

Later in his life, Matthew, inspired by the Holy Spirit, wrote his Gospel of the life of Jesus. He wanted all of us to know the good news that he knew: Jesus does not avoid sinners; He loves them, forgives them, and grants life and salvation to all who believe.

PRAYER

Thank You, Lord, for sending people like Matthew to tell us the Good News. I am glad You forgive me. Help me share my faith with others. Amen.

Edie Gaebler

PENTECOST / TRINITY
St. Matthew, Apostle and Evangelist

The New Parents

Ephesians 6:1–4

Not long ago, a television show told the true story of a Korean orphan girl. Her father and mother had died in a war. She had come to the United States all alone to live with a new mother and father. How afraid she was! She worried, If my new father and mother don't love me, what will happen to me in this new and strange land?

Her new mother met her at the airport, hugged her, and did everything to show the girl she loved and wanted her. "Don't be afraid," she told the girl. But the girl couldn't speak English, so that didn't help. She bought the girl a new dress and shoes and a doll before they started the long bus trip home. But nothing seemed to help. On the bus, the girl was so afraid that she wouldn't let her mother go to sleep. The girl hadn't slept for two whole days herself. And she wouldn't sleep on the bus because she was afraid that her new mother might go away and leave her all alone.

Finally, the tired mother held the girl close and began to sing. For the first time, the girl smiled. She began to sing the *same song* in her own Korean language. This was a song she knew! The song told her that her new mother wouldn't ever leave her. For the song was one most of us learned long ago: "Jesus loves me! This I know, For the Bible tells me so. Little ones to Him belong; They are weak, but He is strong" (*LSB* 588).

You see, the Korean girl was a Christian. When she heard her new mother sing the familiar hymn, she knew her new mother was a Christian too. Then she also knew that Jesus was with her and would take care of her in this new land. Jesus had given her a *Christian* mother and father. Still smiling, the happy Korean girl fell asleep in her Christian mother's arms.

The Bible says, "You [God] have been the helper of the fatherless" (Psalm 10:14).

PRAYER

Lord Jesus, thank You for helping me in every need. Thank You for giving me Christian parents, who love me and have taught me of Your love. Amen.

Earl Gaulke

What You Wear

Colossians 3:12–14

Can you think of different groups of workers who wear uniforms? Sports teams, men and women in the military, police officers and firefighters wear uniforms. Scouts, marching bands, mail carriers, medical workers, mechanics, and even many schoolchildren wear them.

Uniforms identify what people do or to what organization they belong. Uniforms show that people have something in common with those who wear the same uniform.

Several Bible verses talk about what believers in Christ "wear." This spiritual uniform is not made of cloth. You can't buy it or sew it. It was a free gift from our heavenly Father through our Lord Jesus Christ. "He has clothed me with the garments of salvation; He has covered me with the robe of righteousness," reads Isaiah 61:10.

Through Jesus' death and resurrection, our old sinful self was removed, and we "put on the new self, created after the likeness of God in true righteousness and holiness" (Ephesians 4:24).

Today's Bible reading tells what our holy Christian uniform is like: "Put on then, as God's chosen ones, holy and beloved, compassion, kindness, humility, meekness, and patience, bearing with one another. . . . And above all these put on love, which binds everything together."

Wow! How wonderful, that by the power of the Holy Spirit in our lives, we can wear love!

PRAYER

Thank You for my robe of righteousness, Lord. Help me wear it to Your glory each day. For Jesus' sake. Amen.

Dawn Napier

PENTECOST / TRINITY

We'll See

1 John 3:1–3

Those dreaded words, "We'll see."
"Dad, can we go to the Pancake House after church?"
"We'll see."
"Mom, can we get an ice-cream cone after we finish shopping?"
"We'll see."
"Could I have a BB gun for Christmas?"
"We'll see."

Dreaded words. Sometimes they meant "maybe"; there was hope. Mostly they meant "no." Never did they mean "yes." "We'll see" meant we had two chances: slim and none. Oh, how we hated hearing "We'll see"!

Don't you wish your parents would just give you a straight answer? Actually, parents usually do give a simple yes or no if they can. They say "We'll see" because they don't always know what will work out best.

What about our heavenly parent? God is our Father. We are His children. He treats us as a loving father treats his dear children. Our heavenly Father sometimes says the same thing earthly parents say: "We'll see." In our Bible reading, for example, God says, "We'll see."

When God says it, things are different. God is the one parent who always knows what's going to happen. When He says "We'll see," He means "We *will* see." St. John writes, "We know that when He appears we shall be like Him, because we *shall see* Him as He is" (1 John 3:2). God knows that one of these days, Jesus will come back to earth. When He does, we'll see Him in all His glory. We'll see Jesus risen from the dead, bright and shining. He who once hung on the cross to save us will be opening His arms to us. Won't that be something to see! Then God will change our bodies to be perfect and glorious, like Jesus' body.

We'll see. We *will* see Jesus. This *is* going to happen. Our heavenly Father's "We'll see" always means "yes"!

PRAYER

Dear God, we're so happy that You have promised to let us see Jesus someday. Thank You for keeping all Your promises. Amen.

Carl C. Fickenscher II

PENTECOST / TRINITY

Sycamore Christians

Jeremiah 17:7–8

Sycamores are like Christians. What could a tree and a believer in Jesus as Savior of the world have in common?

Those of you who live across the Great Plains of North America can spot a sycamore tree (sometimes called "buttonwood" or "lacewood"). It has white bark and a woody fruit ball in the fall. Those of you who don't recognize this tree, check it out on the Internet.

Hikers use the distinctive bark of the sycamore to locate riverbanks, where these trees like to grow. Along the Mississippi and Ohio river valleys, these trees may grow 175 feet tall. How can they do that in the dry summers? The sycamore survives harsh summers on the prairies because no matter what happens, its water source is nearby. The long roots drink from the water's edge.

Christians are planted near different kinds of water sources. Strength for living as God's children comes from the Word of God and the Sacraments, especially the Sacrament of Holy Baptism. When anger or unkind words lead us to be anxious, we have the gift of faith. When our sinful thoughts and actions nag us, we have the power of God's Spirit to confess them and receive forgiveness. When fears about our future haunt us, we have God's peace.

The words from Jeremiah say we become like trees planted by a never-ending source of water. We stand tall and strong, and we continue to grow because of God. We are like sycamores, growing at the water's edge.

PRAYER

Dear God, thank You for refreshing me with Your Word, strengthening my faith, and using me for Your purposes. Amen.

James Hahn

A House, Not a Museum

Psalm 26

One of the best-known and much-visited buildings in the U.S. is the White House. People stand in line for blocks to be able to see a few rooms in its east wing.

Why? To see some furniture, dishes, and pictures that some presidents used in these rooms over the years? Maybe. But there are lots of things just like that in museums in Washington and elsewhere. Nobody waits in line to see them.

People who go inside the White House know that the president and his family live there. Much of his important work is done there. He meets with people from all over the world in these very rooms. It's not a museum. It's a center of important activity.

Because Americans love their country and are interested in the president and his work, they thrill at the chance of spending a moment in the White House.

In Psalm 26, David tells how excited he was about going to God's house. He loved it because, as he said, God was there. God's people honored and worshiped Him there.

That's why we love our church too—because it is God's house today. God is with us there in His Word and the Sacraments. He talks to us through the pastor as he speaks the words of absolution. The cross in front reminds us that we are saved and have eternal life because of what Jesus did years ago.

Our church is not a stuffy museum. It's a meeting-place with our ever-living and ever-present God. No wonder God's children love it so!

PRAYER

Lord, I, too, "love the habitation of Your house and the place where Your glory dwells" (Psalm 26:8). Amen.

Roy Gesch

PENTECOST / TRINITY

No-See-Ums

1 Peter 5:8

Get out a ruler. Examine one-eighth of an inch. That is the length of a no-see-um, a pesky biting fly. Those little critters are at beach parties and campouts and go unnoticed until you get bitten—a painful bite. The only way to escape is to leave the area.

No-see-um might be a good name for the devil. He seems to go unnoticed, tempting here and there. He sneaks into schools and tempts students to cheat on a test. He sneaks into families and suggests that children lie to their parents. He sneaks into our thinking and suggests that wrong is right and right is wrong.

The devil tempted Adam and Eve centuries ago. When these two people ate the fruit that God had forbidden, they sinned. All people since then have been born with a sinful condition called original sin.

Christians have this condition of sin and also commit sins. Sin disconnects us from God. The no-see-um devil tempts us, hoping to separate us from God. But God does not leave us without help. He promises to help us withstand temptation. With His help, we can walk away from a fight. We can close our eyes in prayer. We can spend quiet time in our room reading God's Word. We can ask an adult, such as our pastor or parent, for guidance.

Because no one can live without sinning, God, in His mercy, sent His Son, Jesus, to save us. Jesus was tempted too, but He was able to resist all of Satan's temptations, every single one. Jesus died to conquer sin, death, and the devil too.

PRAYER

Our Father, give us strength to resist and overcome temptation. Forgive our sins for Jesus' sake. Amen.

James Hahn

PENTECOST / TRINITY

The Lord's Prayer

Matthew 6:5–15

Susan's family often prayed the Lord's Prayer in family devotions. One evening, Susan said, "Mother, why do we say 'Our Father, who art in heaven'? My teacher told me God is everywhere." What do you think?

Susan's teacher was right. God is everywhere. God says, "Am I a God at hand, . . . and not a God far away? Can a man hide himself in secret places so that I cannot see him? . . . Do I not fill heaven and earth?" (Jeremiah 23:23–24).

Jesus told His people to say "Our Father, who art in heaven" when they pray. God loves us and wants us to pray to Him confidently and without fear. He invites us to believe that He is our true Father and that we are His true children.

Long ago, this prayer that Jesus taught His disciples to pray was said only when all the people present were Christians. In Jesus, all believers are children of the one Father and should pray with and for one another. That's why we say "Our Father" when we pray.

When we say "who art in heaven," we are assured that our heavenly Father, as Lord over all, has the power to grant our prayers.

God commands and invites believers in Jesus Christ to speak to the triune God—Father, Son, and Holy Spirit—in words and thoughts. We should pray in Jesus' name and according to God's will, knowing that God hears and answers Christians' prayers in His time and His way. We should pray everywhere, for everyone, and regularly and often, especially in times of trouble. In our prayers, we should also praise and thank God for who He is and what He has done.

PRAYER

Our Father, who art in heaven, hallowed be Thy name, Thy kingdom come, Thy will be done on earth as it is in heaven. Give us this day our daily bread; and forgive us our trespasses as we forgive those who trespass against us; and lead us not into temptation, but deliver us from evil. For Thine is the kingdom and the power and the glory forever and ever. Amen.

Allan Hart Jahsmann

PENTECOST / TRINITY

Angels Everywhere

Psalm 91:9–16

Will you become an angel when you die? Should you pray to angels? Many people would say yes to these questions, but the answer is no. God made angels to watch over us, to protect us, and to care for us. They cannot hear or answer our prayers.

Today is St. Michael and All Angels Day. On this day, we rejoice in God's special gifts of angels. So today, you might ask, "Heavenly Father, how do angels help me?"

"My child, I love taking care of you. You are such a treasure to Me. I watch everything you do, and I guide and protect you. I tell My angels how they are to guard you.

"I say to them, 'This is My special child. Protect this person in playing, learning, and resting. Defend My child against all evil and danger.'

"If you are in danger or harmed in some way, it isn't because the angels were not doing their job. The bad things that happen to you are a result of sin. But remember, when Jesus rose from the dead, He won the fight with the devil. Because Jesus took your punishment, you are forgiven and will someday live in heaven, where bad things never happen. Then you will join the angels in praising Me."

PRAYER

I thank You, my heavenly Father, through Jesus Christ, Your dear Son, that You have graciously kept me this day (night); and I pray that You would forgive me all my sins where I have done wrong, and graciously keep me this night (day). For into Your hands I commend myself, my body and soul, and all things. Let Your holy angel be with me that the wicked foe may have no power over me. Amen.

(Adapted from Luther's Small Catechism, Evening Prayer)

Lisa Hahn

PENTECOST / TRINITY
St. Michael and All Angels

Falling and Rising

Romans 3:21–24

Falling leaves. Falling football players. Falling acorns. Falling temperatures.

The word *falling* can bring many pictures to mind. A baby who is learning to walk might fall down. An older child may fall, trying to ride a bike or skateboard. A soccer player might fall, angling in his body for a great steal. Friends might suddenly tip and then fall over while white-water rafting. Falling can be painful. Falling can be bad.

The fall into sin *was* painful and bad. God's earth was a wonderful place before Adam and Eve did what the devil tempted them to do. Once the forbidden fruit was eaten, sin brought fear and punishment.

God did not leave Adam and Eve without hope. He gave them a marvelous promise. He would send a Savior who would die and rise from death to give us the gifts of His grace—forgiveness and eternal life.

God's Old Testament people saw the coming Messiah with eyes of faith. And we also see Christ the Messiah with eyes of faith. Through the Word of God, we are witnesses to His life, death, and resurrection.

God's Word of Law shows us our sin. God's Spirit uses it to drive us to fall on our knees in repentance. God's Gospel raises us up to celebrate.

PRAYER

Dear Jesus, when I am tempted to fall into sin, pull me back into Your safe, loving arms. Amen.

Jacqueline Loontjer

PENTECOST / TRINITY

Pumpkins Everywhere

Genesis 1:11–12

October is finally here. Quick! What's the first food that comes to your mind? Many people would say pumpkins. You can do a lot with pumpkins. You can make spicy pumpkin pies or pumpkin bread. Some families use pumpkins to decorate their home or table. You might scoop out the inside of a pumpkin and carve a silly face on it. Pumpkins are a versatile food.

But what if pumpkins were the *only* kind of food? What if there were no other fruits or vegetables? Can you imagine how boring it would be? Pumpkin pancakes, pumpkin ice cream, frozen pumpkin yogurt, pumpkin turnovers . . . too much pumpkin would get very old, very fast.

When God created the earth, He could have taken a shortcut. He could have decided to make only one kind of tree, one kind of flower, one kind of bird . . . you get the point. Imagine a world with only pine trees, sunflowers, and doves. Each one is beautiful, but without variety, you'd get tired of seeing them all the time.

How wonderful of God to create a world full of unique and different things. He knows everything we need and everything that makes us happy. We may not *require* a world of variety, but He knew we would enjoy it so much more.

What we need most, though, is salvation, and God provided only one way for that. When it comes to a Savior, there is only One who suffered and died for our sin. Because of the faith God gives us in Jesus Christ, we are free to enjoy the world God made for us. We look forward to the day when we'll live in the perfect home He's prepared for us in heaven.

PRAYER

Thank You, God, for all the wonderful things You've created. Be with me today, and help me notice the variety that's all around me. In Jesus' name I pray. Amen.

Jennifer AlLee

PENTECOST / TRINITY

Big Tex

Deuteronomy 18:15–22

Everything is bigger in Texas. At least, that's what they say. If you're anywhere near Big D (Dallas, that is) in October, you believe them.

For 24 days this month, one of the biggest fairs in the country is here: the State Fair of Texas. The Texas State Fair covers 277 acres. More than three million people attend. Texas fairgoers can ride the biggest Ferris wheel in the nation—212 feet tall! And in the middle of the fairgrounds stands the biggest attraction of all, Big Tex.

Big Tex makes a big impression. Wearing a 75-gallon hat and size 70 boots, he towers 52 feet above the crowd. His remote-control mouth welcomes folks to the fair. His 20-foot left arm points the way to the fair's main entrance.

Big things usually grab our attention, don't they? Several years ago, a well-known man claimed to see Jesus standing 80 feet tall above him. That was a silly claim, but a lot of people listened.

Jesus usually doesn't come on so big. During His life on earth, He didn't try to make a grand impression. He was often quiet and gentle, always humble. He certainly wasn't 80 feet (or even 52 feet) tall. In fact, even His friends didn't always realize how great and powerful He was.

The night before Jesus died on the cross, Philip still hadn't caught on. He asked, "Lord, show us the Father." The disciples expected God to show Himself in a big way. But Jesus explained, "Whoever has seen Me has seen the Father" (John 14:9). In other words, "Even if what I look like isn't any big deal, I am God."

Like Big Tex, Jesus points the way, but He doesn't do it with a 20-foot arm. Jesus is the only way to heaven. When we believe that Jesus Christ died and rose for us, we get in free. That's an even bigger deal than free admission to the Texas State Fair!

PRAYER

Dear Jesus, sometimes I may be disappointed that You don't give me things I think are a big deal. Forgive me. Help me see that You're always really giving me what's biggest and best for me. Amen.

Carl C. Fickenscher II

PENTECOST / TRINITY

Who's Number One?

Philippians 2:3–11

It's October. Leaves are turning colors; the air is turning crisp; the grass is turning brown. And our hearts are turning somersaults of joy every time a Saturday or Sunday rolls around because somewhere, at a field nearby, men or boys are playing football.

And what do men or boys playing football do best? They may tackle and run and throw passes and punt and placekick and block and score touchdowns. But what do they do best? They yell, "We're number one!"

It doesn't seem to matter if the game is for a national championship or a league championship, for the championship of a bowl game or a fifth-grade classroom. Players in any game on any level are always smiling and putting up one lone finger to indicate to all that they are number one.

You never hear anybody yell "We're number two!" because nobody wants to be number two. Everybody wants to be the best.

In football, we want to be number one. But in our Christian life, those of us who try to be number one become number two. There is no way we can become number one in God's eyes through our own effort. No amount of good living, helping our neighbor, obeying our parents, or doing our homework is going to put us first in the eyes of almighty God. His standards are too high for us to meet.

The only person able to meet those standards is the real number one—Jesus. He became first by becoming last. He suffered the worst humiliation so that we might experience glory.

We must become number two. By becoming number two and allowing Jesus to be number one, we become great where it really matters—in God's eyes.

PRAYER

Lord, let me always remember who is really number one. At the name of Jesus I bow, and I give Him all praise, honor, and glory. Amen.

Tom Raabe

Baby Stuff

2 Timothy 3:14–17

How long has it been since you played with a rattle? a brightly colored mobile hanging above a crib? How long since you dived into a box full of Fisher-Price or PlaySkool's finest? Years, right? That's baby stuff!

But what about me? I play with rattles and mobiles every day. And I'm thirty-five! Actually, my daughter Rachel has more fun with her toys than her mommy and I do. Rachel loves baby stuff. Rachel *is* a baby. There are a lot of things Mom and I very much enjoy doing with Rachel, though. We love playing with her on the floor. We love cuddling. We get a kick out of listening to her "talk."

Most of all, we enjoy reading Bible stories and singing Jesus songs with Rachel. Every evening before bed, we have family devotion time together. We read from our favorite book of children's Bible stories. And we sing some of Rachel's favorites—"Jesus Loves Me," "Two Little Eyes," "Praise Him, Praise Him."

Hearing and singing about Jesus is great stuff for babies, isn't it? St. Paul says that Timothy learned God's Word when he was just a little kid. His mother and grandmother read the Bible to him from the time he was a baby. The Scriptures made him "wise for salvation through faith in Christ Jesus" (2 Timothy 3:15). That means by believing in Jesus, we have eternal life. Rachel's not too young to learn that, is she?

And we're never too old. God's Word isn't just baby stuff. The Scriptures were every bit as important to Timothy when he became a man. They equipped him to serve God with his whole life. They always reminded Timothy that he had been saved by Jesus, the rescuer of the whole world. We still need (and love!) to hear about that again at every age.

Like—go on, admit it—you still enjoy a trip to Toys Я Us. Some thirty-five–year–old dads haven't outgrown that yet.

PRAYER

Dear Lord, thank You for taking me in Your arms even when I was a little child. Please help me experience Your wonderful love and forgiveness every day. Amen.

Carl C. Fickenscher II

PENTECOST / TRINITY

Baby Cry

Romans 8:26–27, 32

The first time Sarah and Elizabeth met their cousin, our baby Rachel, they were concerned. "Baby Rachel cry," they told their mommy. Rachel was just fifteen days old then. The twins themselves were only two, but they were alarmed to see their little cousin upset.

"Babies cry," their mother reassured them. "That's what babies do."

Crying is the way babies communicate. They know what they want. They just don't know how to ask for it yet—at least not in words. When a baby cries, it's usually nothing to worry about. It is a challenge, though, for Mom and Dad to figure out what he or she's asking.

We who have learned to speak usually have no trouble asking for things. But maybe even now we have a hard time putting certain needs or requests into words. Maybe we don't always know how to pray—or what to pray about. Maybe we feel shy about praying to God. No need to worry. That's perfectly normal. We don't always know what to ask God for, because often we don't know what's best for us. We can't find the perfect words to use in our prayers, either. No need to be alarmed.

God invites us to pray anyway. We can use any words we choose. We may ask for whatever we think might be good. The Holy Spirit always understands what we're asking, and He always knows what we really need. He brings our prayers to God the Father, sometimes in ways nobody could put into words. Then God answers our every prayer by giving us the very best. We know He gave His Son as our substitute, to suffer and die in our place. So everything else will turn out okay.

Elizabeth and Sarah were satisfied. It's okay when Rachel cries. We're glad she lets us know when she needs something. Likewise, God loves when we cry out to Him in prayer—even when we don't quite know what to say.

PRAYER

Dear God, the things I'd like to ask You for now are . . . Thank You for knowing what I mean and for giving me what's best. For Jesus' sake. Amen.

Carl C. Fickenscher II

PENTECOST / TRINITY

Happy Hunting

Acts 17:10–12

Sometime in the month of October, if it isn't too cloudy, you can see one of God's most beautiful creations. Just after sunset, in the eastern sky on the horizon, you will see a gorgeous full moon traditionally called the Harvest Moon. The October full moon gave farmers of the past the extra light they needed to get the crops harvested and stored in the barns.

Then, the men could think about providing meat for their families to eat during the long winter ahead. The best time to hunt for game was in the light of the next full moon in November, known as the Hunter's Moon. First, the families prayed for a good hunt as they had earlier prayed for a bountiful harvest. Then the men went off to hunt in nearby forests. Under the bright glow of the November full moon that lasted almost all night, the hunters found many animals.

Nowadays, most people don't have to hunt for food. But our Bible reading tells us about a different kind of hunt. St. Luke says that the people in Berea "received the Word with all eagerness, examining the Scriptures daily."

We have the privilege of reading the Word of God often. When we do that, God speaks to us. He shares His wisdom and love with us. In His Word, we are pointed to Jesus, who won salvation for us and gives us eternal hope. All of God's promises to us are fulfilled in Christ.

Today, go on a Scripture hunt and read some promises from God. found in Psalm 50:15; Hebrews 4:16; and Revelation 2:10b. "Capture" one of these verses by memorizing it. This promise from God will then be yours. No one will be able to take it away from you. God bless you as you hunt through your Bible for the Good News of His mercy and grace in Jesus Christ.

PRAYER

Give me, Lord, an eager desire to read Your Word. Bless me as I search the Scriptures to learn more about Your wonderful love for me in Jesus Christ. Amen.

Suzanne K. Schmieding

More Than Just Plywood

Ephesians 2:8–10

Four years ago, I gave my wife a piece of plywood for her birthday. "Some crummy gift," you say? Ah, but this was no ordinary piece of plywood. This was a beautiful 4 x 8-foot sheet of oak plywood. Gorgeous!

Yes, I know. Plywood is made mostly from the chips and sawdust you can't use for other things. Layer upon layer of leftovers all glued together. Cover it with two perfect outer layers of oak, though, and you have something. Oak plywood doesn't come cheap.

Still a pretty disappointing gift, wouldn't you say? But, you see, I never intended for it to remain just a piece of wood. This wood would become a magnificent bedroom chest of drawers. I'm a carpenter on the side. I enjoy building furniture. This wood would soon be shaped by my finest workmanship. Four years later, it's still in the garage. Still just a beautiful sheet of oak plywood—my gift to my very patient wife.

God's gift to us was to make us like beautiful sheets of oak plywood. Because of our sin, we were rejects, good-for-nothings, like leftover scraps of wood. But Jesus took us rejects and made us into something gorgeous. Our sins are covered by the perfect holiness of Christ. That didn't come cheap. It cost Jesus His life. By faith, in believing all this, we aren't sawdust and wood chips anymore. We're plywood!

God didn't intend for us to be just a sheet of plywood. The Bible says, "We are His workmanship, created in Christ Jesus for good works, which God prepared beforehand" (Ephesians 2:10). God has big plans for us. He's already made us into something beautiful. Now He's going to make beautiful things happen *through* us. God will use us, His workmanship, to do other great works. We'll worship Him. We'll tell our friends about Him. We'll love and serve our parents and family and others around us.

By God's grace, we're a magnificent chest of drawers!

PRAYER

Lord Jesus, thank You for dying and rising again to make me beautiful. Help me now to become the finished product You want to make me. Amen.

Carl C. Fickenscher II

PENTECOST / TRINITY

One Little Flame

James 3:5–13

On this very day in 1871, a cow in a Chicago barn kicked over a lighted lantern. The lantern touched off a fire that, because of high winds, leaped from one building to another. By the time the fire stopped thirty hours later, Chicago had lost 17,450 buildings and 300 people. Ninety thousand people were left homeless, and property damage totaled $200 million.

Who could have guessed that the little fire in one lantern could cause so much damage!

St. James tells us about another little fire that can do great damage. "The tongue is a fire," he says (James 3:6). "No human being can tame the tongue. It is a restless evil, full of deadly poison" (vv. 8–9). He surely makes the tongue sound dangerous!

Well, our tongue can produce great harm. With it we can hurt others by calling them bad names or screaming at them in anger. With it we can tell lies that ruin people's reputations. With it we can curse people.

Yet we use our tongues to praise and bless God. James comments, "From the same mouth come blessing and cursing. My brothers, these things ought not to be so" (v. 10).

Some of the most wonderful words we can think of were spoken in a very ugly situation. When people were hurting Jesus—in fact, killing Him—He prayed, "Father, forgive them, for they know not what they do" (Luke 23:34). These words are so wonderful because they bless instead of curse.

These words of blessing are for us too. Jesus gave His life on a cross so that He could bring to every person in the world the forgiveness He prayed for. We need that forgiveness. We need it for our ugly words. We need it so that we, too, can learn to use our tongues to forgive and bless.

PRAYER

Lord Jesus, from Your lips I hear blessing instead of cursing. Please forgive me for the times that my words hurt others. Help me to be mindful of what I think and say so Your glory may be shown. Amen.

Richard Hinz

PENTECOST / TRINITY

A Storytelling Calendar

1 Corinthians 15:1–11

Ellen was talking with Pastor Howard in his office after Saturday class. She noticed an unusual calendar on a wall. The dates were printed in several different colors.

"That's a funny calendar," Ellen said.

"Not so funny at all," Pastor Howard remarked. "It helps us follow the seasons of the Christian Church Year."

"Why are the days colored differently?" asked Ellen.

"I'll try to explain," Pastor Howard told her. "The colors remind us of things that happened in the life of Christ.

"For example, the color for today is green. Green is the color of living things. So the green of the Pentecost or Trinity season represents our growing in faith in Jesus and responding to His good gifts of forgiveness, life, and salvation as we live in our vocations. The color purple is used in the season of Lent and in Advent because it is the color of sorrow, reminding us to be sorry for our sins, which caused Jesus to leave His heavenly home and suffer for us on the cross. On Good Friday, the day of Christ's death, the calendar will be black, the color of death.

"For Easter and the weeks afterward, the color is white. White stands for the joy we have because we know Jesus has risen from the dead. It helps us remember that all who believe in Him are pure and holy in God's sight.

"When we come to Pentecost, the calendar will be red. Remember how the Holy Spirit came to the disciples on that day? Red reminds us of the tongues of fire that were on the heads of the apostles on Pentecost, and of the blood of those who died for their faith."

"This calendar really tells a story, doesn't it?" Ellen remarked.

"Yes, the most important story there is," agreed Pastor Howard. "It's the story of our salvation through the work of the Father, Son, and Holy Spirit."

PRAYER

Lord Jesus, help me remember You as my Savior, not only now in this season of the Church Year, but throughout the year. Amen.

Enno Klammer

PENTECOST / TRINITY

How Come, Lord?

Ephesians 2:4–10

John had quite a day. He had misbehaved in school—so much so that his teacher had telephoned his mother and told her all about it. When John got home, he threw his jacket on the table, knocking off his mother's favorite vase, breaking it into a hundred pieces. Then, walking into the kitchen, he tromped his dirty feet all over the freshly scrubbed floor. His mother was practically in tears when he slipped up to his room.

His parents gave him a good talking-to that night. Later on, as he lay in his bed, he did some thinking and some questioning. "How come, Mom?" he asked. "I've been so bad all day. I've made you and Dad unhappy. Yet you fixed my favorite dinner, and you hugged and kissed me goodnight. How come?"

That's a question every one of us might ask of God. "How come, Lord? Lord, every day I do wrong. How unhappy You must be with me. Yet You still say You want me to live with You in heaven, and You sent Jesus to be my Savior. In spite of everything, You say You still love me. How come?"

The Bible gives the answer to that question: "By grace you have been saved through faith. And this is not your own doing; it is the gift of God, not a result of works, so that no one may boast" (Ephesians 2:8–9).

The secret lies in that one word *grace*. This word emphasizes that we do not deserve God's love and kindness. But God still is loving and kind—not because we are what we are, but because He is what He is.

PRAYER

Heavenly Father, as we come to You, we are both sad and happy. We are sad, for we realize how we sin against You every day. But we are also happy, for we know that You have not rejected us because of our sin. We thank You for loving us so much that through our Lord Jesus Christ, You have saved us. Help us live thankfully and obediently to Your glory. For Jesus' sake. Amen.

Roy Gesch

Trading Places

Philippians 2:5–11

Tim and Andy shared a bedroom. They weren't 100 percent pleased with that setup. Andy was rather neat and took care of his things. Tim was sloppy and seldom put things away. There were many arguments over whose turn it was to clean the room. The boys had a hard time deciding who ought to tidy up the books, model planes, and special keepsakes.

The biggest problem was over the two beds. One was against the wall and the other next to the door. Naturally, both boys wanted to sleep in the bed in the quiet corner. The boy in the bed by the door had to put up with all sorts of noise and interruptions.

An agreement was finally reached. Tim and Andy decided that every two months, they would trade places. Simple solution!

Do you ever think of changing places with someone? Maybe you'd even like to trade families sometimes. And have you ever said, "I wish I were *smart* or *rich* and could do anything I wanted"? Even grown-ups feel that way at times.

However, changing places with someone who is poor or sickly doesn't usually interest us. In a way, that's what Jesus did. He came down from heaven, where He was King. On earth, He became a humble servant. Jesus traded places with us. God wanted us to keep His Commandments perfectly. We couldn't do it, so Jesus did it for us. We deserved death because of our sins. But we didn't have to die; Jesus did it for us. Jesus took our place. What a great exchange!

Isn't it wonderful to know and love such a Savior? He has given us life by His own death. Was that a fair trade? You decide.

PRAYER

He serves that I a lord may be;
A great exchange indeed!
Could Jesus' love do more for me
To help me in my need? Amen. (*TLH* 105:7)

Kay Klinkenberg

Marvelous Discoveries

2 Corinthians 5:17–21

After being turned down by the Portuguese and put off by the Spanish, Christopher Columbus finally obtained the support of Ferdinand and Isabella. They gave Columbus the money he needed. He gathered a group of criminals for his crew and sailed off to find a new and quicker route to the East.

Land was finally sighted after a two-month voyage. Columbus, richly dressed, strode ashore. He took possession of the land, claiming it for Spain. He had, in fact, discovered the islands of Haiti and Cuba off the coast of North America. He died believing that Cuba was the tip of the continent of Asia.

The dictionary says that *discover* means "to obtain knowledge of something for the first time." When we take the word *discover* apart, we find two words: *dis*, meaning "undoing," and *cover*, meaning "a shelter or protection." So *discover* means "to remove from something hidden." Columbus had removed the Western world from its mysterious place in the minds of Europeans. (Of course, to Native Americans, it wasn't mysterious at all.)

You have already discovered many things about yourself. You've found what things make you happy, angry, sad, and disgusted. You know which school subjects are easy and which are difficult. You will probably always be discovering new things about yourself.

How about discovering things about God? To many people, the Bible is unknown or mysterious. Yet it contains all we need to know about God and His glorious plans for us. We can discover wonderful news about God from its pages.

What do you discover about yourself in 2 Corinthians 5:17–21? What do you discover about Christ? By daily exploring the Bible, you will be discovering marvelous things about God and yourself.

PRAYER

Heavenly Father, thank You for making me a new person through Christ. Give me a strong desire to study Your Word. Amen.

Kay Klinkenberg

PENTECOST/TRINITY

Thanksgiving Day Is Today

Psalm 136:1–4

"Today is Thanksgiving Day," said Christie with a little grin on her face.

"Oh, you can't fool me," replied her sister Lorie. "Today is October 13, and Thanksgiving Day isn't till next month."

"Ha! The joke's on you," answered Christie. "You didn't let me finish the sentence. I was going to say, 'Today is Thanksgiving Day in Canada!'"

"Oh, you're very funny," said Lorie as she walked away.

Thanksgiving Day in Canada is always observed on the second Monday in October. But it's also Thanksgiving Day in the United States, in Great Britain, in Germany, and in all the other countries of the world. Or at least it should be.

For Christians, every day is a time for thanksgiving. Every day God forgives our sin for Jesus' sake. Every day He rules the world for our good and helps and guides us.

Every day God gives us food to eat and clothes to wear and air to breathe. Every day He takes care of us and protects us from harm.

Since God blesses us every day, we want to thank Him every day. After every meal, we give thanks. Before we go to sleep at night, we give thanks. Many times during the day, we can think of the goodness of God and say, "Thank You, Lord."

No matter what country we live in, Thanksgiving Day is today.

PRAYER

Praise to God, immortal praise,
For the love that crowns our days;
Bounteous Source of ev'ry joy,
Let Thy praise our tongues employ.
All to Thee, our God, we owe,
Source whence all our blessings flow. Amen. (*TLH* 572:1)

Paul Single

PENTECOST / TRINITY

Undivided Attention

Psalm 33:13–22

My sister Kathy was a "World Series baby." Kathy was born on October 8, at the most exciting time of the baseball season. What a great time of year for a birthday, wouldn't you say? Except . . .

Except that Kathy's birthday parties always had to compete with the television. While Kathy was opening her presents, Dad and I had one eye turned to the series: "Oh, that's a nice new dress, Kath. . . . Come on, Willie, hit it outta sight! . . . Oh, sorry about that, Kathy. Yes, that's a beautiful wrapping. . . . What's the count, three and two?" Kathy was a good sport, but it's too bad she didn't have our undivided attention.

Do you wonder if you have God's undivided attention? He's got so many things to watch, and most of them are a lot more important than baseball. Do you think He's looking in on your big events—birthdays, Scout award dinners, band concerts? Do you think He notices when you're worried about homework or friends or football practice? Or do you suppose He's too busy watching something else?

This is what the Bible says: "The LORD looks down from heaven; He sees *all* the children of man; . . . The eye of the LORD is on those who fear Him, on those who hope in His steadfast love, that He may deliver their soul from death" (Psalm 33:13, 18).

Isn't that amazing? God can keep an eye on everybody all at once. And yet, He doesn't give us just part of His attention. We all have His full attention all the time. He knows what's going on in the World Series, but He also cares about everything going on with us. All of the events in our lives are big to Him. Everything that bothers us He wants to make better. Nothing else is so exciting or important to Him that He forgets about us.

So don't forget to put your hope in God's steadfast love. Through Jesus, He has redeemed us for all time and for eternity.

PRAYER

Dear God, thank You for always paying attention to me and for watching over me in love. Keep me in Your care every day, for Jesus' sake. Amen.

Carl C. Fickenscher II

PENTECOST / TRINITY

Be Constant in Prayer

Matthew 15:21–28

When you ask God for something but don't get it right away, do you quit praying? Do you think God isn't listening to you?

Many people have the idea that prayer is like working a candy machine: you put a dime in, and right away the candy bar pops out. When their prayers aren't answered that fast, they give up on praying.

A woman once asked Jesus to free her daughter from a demon. If she had quit asking when no answer came right away, she would have missed out on a miracle.

First, the disciples wanted Jesus to send her away. Then, the Lord Himself seemed to say He couldn't take time for her. But the woman of Canaan believed that Jesus could help her daughter, so she kept on praying.

Finally, Jesus granted the woman's request. Her God-given faith was strong enough to stand the Lord's testing. Jesus praised her for not giving up: "O woman, great is your faith! Be it done for you as you desire" (Matthew 15:28).

God never fails to answer when we pray. That's why we shouldn't quit, even when He seems to pay no attention. The Bible urges us, "Be *constant* in prayer" (Romans 12:12). That means "*Keep on* praying!" In another place in the Bible, God says, "You will seek Me and find Me, when you seek Me with all your heart" (Jeremiah 29:13).

Of course, the answer to our prayer may not be exactly what we expect. God knows what is best for us, and He will give us what we need most. Above all, He will keep us strong in faith in the Lord Jesus as our Savior from sin.

PRAYER

Lord God, give me the faith to keep on praying to You. Don't let me become discouraged when I don't get an answer to my prayer right away. May Your will be done at all times. In Jesus' name. Amen.

Elizabeth Goerss

PENTECOST / TRINITY

Give God the Glory

Colossians 3:17

Which of the following describes you?
- Soccer star or ball carrier
- Straight-A student or just getting by
- First violinist or kazoo band
- Star of the play or stage cleanup crew
- Budding artist or good at tracing
- Spelling bee champ or spell-check champ
- Champion gymnast or still working on that somersault

Whatever you do, do it to the glory of God. Why give God the glory? Because He gives you the talents and the opportunities. How do you glorify God by what you do? By using your talents and abilities to do something!

"Well," you might be saying, "I do. I am the star, the champ, the expert. Of course, I'm using my talents." Good for you. Then let me ask, to whom are you giving the credit? Are you humbly thanking God for His gracious gift to you? Are you appreciative of those who support and encourage you?

But maybe you're saying, "What's the use? I'm not good at anything, so why even try? The only thing I can do with a ball is trip over it. The only A I ever get on my report card is in my name."

God isn't comparing you to His other creatures such as your classmates or brothers. He is concerned that you know His love and believe in Him as your Savior. God has freed you from your sin, including your need to be better than everyone at everything. Now you can live freely. Now you can use your ability to play the kazoo or trace a picture to the glory of God. It's that easy.

PRAYER

Dear Jesus, thank You for giving me Your best by dying on the cross for my sins. Show me how to give my best to You. Amen.

Valerie Schultz

God Knows It All

Psalm 139:1–4

"I know what you have in your lunch box," Andrea said to Manuel as they sat down.

"Did you look?" Manuel said, holding his lunch box close.

"No," replied Andrea, "but I know. You have a sandwich, chips, and something to drink. That's what you always have."

Manuel opened his lunch box. Andrea was right. "Okay," Manuel grinned, "but what do I have to drink?"

"Cherry Kool-Aid," she said, opening her own sandwich.

Manuel looked worried. Mom gave him cherry Kool-Aid a lot.

He poured out the drink. It was red, but was it cherry? Manuel took a drink. "It's strawberry! Yeaaah!" Manuel cheered for himself.

"Well, only God knows everything." Andrea said.

"How could God know?" Manuel asked. "*I* didn't even know."

"God sees and knows everything," Andrea explained. "He saw your mom pack your lunch. He knows what you're thinking now."

"Does God know when a person lies?" Manuel asked quietly.

"Yes, He knows everything we do wrong. But don't worry. Jesus died for us. He forgives sins. He will forgive you too."

"That's good," Manuel said slowly. "Because I'm sorry that I lied, Andrea. It really *was* cherry. I just wanted to win."

"That's all right, Manuel. I forgive you."

"But will God forgive me too?"

"Well, God already knows that you're sorry. Do you believe that Jesus died for you?"

"Yes, I believe that Jesus died to take away my sins."

"Then God forgives you."

"That's good to know," Manuel said with a sigh.

"It's good to know that God knows everything," Andrea added.

PRAYER

Dear God, You know all things. Forgive all my sins, even my secret sins, because Jesus died to pay for every one. Amen.

Lawrence Eatherton

PENTECOST / TRINITY

St. Luke, MD

Luke 10:1–12

On this day, Christians throughout the world remember the life and work of St. Luke. Unlike many of the other writers of the Bible, little is known about Luke. Almost everyone remembers how Matthew turned from a life of stealing to follow Jesus. John was one of Jesus' twelve disciples and spent much time with Him. Mark and Paul worked together telling the Good News of Jesus' love. But what is there to tell about Luke?

We do know he was a doctor. Paul writes about Luke spending time with him as a friend and helper. Perhaps Luke helped take care of Paul in times of sickness. No doubt Luke learned much about Jesus' life and teaching as he visited with Paul. Luke says he never saw or listened to Jesus in person as many others had done.

God chose this kind doctor to be the writer of two biblical books: the Gospel according to St. Luke and the Acts of the Apostles. In these books, Luke tells us of the love and healing power of Jesus in His life, death, and resurrection. It is Luke's version of the beautiful Christmas story that is so well known.

The four Gospel writers tell about the days Jesus spent on earth. Although each deals with the life of Christ, each one emphasizes different things. Luke relates many of Jesus' miracles of healing. He is also the only writer to tell of Jesus sending out seventy persons to spread the message of salvation.

Notice the advice Jesus gives these travelers as they prepare to meet new people. They are to take no money, and their meals will be only what people give them. They are to preach that Jesus Christ is Savior of all. What a privilege that must have been to be a missionary for Jesus!

PRAYER

Almighty God, You inspired Your servant Luke the physician to write in his Gospel the Good News of life and salvation through Jesus, Your Son. Bless Your Church through the means of grace—Word and Sacraments. Heal sin-sick souls and grant salvation to those who believe in You. Through Your Son, Jesus Christ, our Lord. Amen.

Kay Klinkenberg

PENTECOST / TRINITY
St. Luke, Evangelist

Potato-Chip Dust

Isaiah 61:1–3

Randy, Kordell, and Rashan liked to eat lunch together at school, mainly because they were good friends. They also liked to trade things in their lunches. Usually they could each trade for a lunch they liked better.

One day, Kordell opened his bag of barbecue potato chips and found them crumbled. "Potato-chip dust!" he said sadly.

"That's okay," said Randy. "I'll trade you my chips for your candy bar." Then he opened his chips and said, "Maybe not! Mine are smashed too!"

They both looked at Rashan and then at his bag of chips. "Wait a minute, guys, you don't want mine either! Marcy dropped her math book on my lunch and . . ."

Before he could finish his protest, his hungry friends had torn open his bag. "Dust!" they said with disgust.

Mr. Zehnder, their seventh-grade teacher, came upon the unhappy three and asked, "Who died, guys?"

"Our potato chips!" said Randy.

"I've got a big bag I brought from home," said Mr. Zehnder.

"You'd trade your chips for our smashed ones?" asked Rashan.

"I guess you could call it a trade," said Mr. Zehnder. "But it's really more of a gift. Kind of like God giving us His Son. There's nothing we can trade to God for the wonderful blessings of forgiveness and eternal life He gave through Jesus."

Mr. Zehnder ate some potato-chip crumbs as he went back to his desk. Then Rashan had an idea. "Say, Mr. Zehnder, my sandwich is smashed too."

"Forget it, Rashan," said his teacher, smiling and crunching more crumbs. "God's grace is endless, but my lunch isn't."

PRAYER

Dear Jesus, thank You for taking away my sin and guilt and giving me Your love and forgiveness. Amen.

Richard P. Lieske

Good Outweighs Bad

Romans 8:18–21

How do you remember a day? Do you recall the things that went right or the things that went wrong? Let me tell you about Valerie.

Yesterday was her father's birthday. Mother held a surprise birthday party. Grandma and Grandpa came; even one uncle and aunt were there. And Valerie couldn't have been happier. Everything was just perfect. The weather was great; the food was delicious; and best of all, her favorite relatives were there.

After supper, while the men shot pool in the basement and the ladies did dishes, Valerie went to the school playground. She hadn't been gone but a few minutes when she ran back screaming and hollering, holding her arm that now looked like a corkscrew. Valerie had tried to do a flip on the chinning bar. Instead, she fell off and broke her arm in two places.

Valerie's mom took one look at Valerie's arm and let out such a horrifying scream that, even in the basement, her husband knew something terrible had happened. He bounded out of the basement three steps at a time. After one quick look, he yelled, "Get in the car!" and made one fast trip to the hospital.

Within two hours, the doctor had Valerie's arm straightened and in a cast. And even though she still had some pain, Valerie was thrilled to have her cast, her "badge of courage," to show at school.

The day was filled with much happiness and tragedy. Yet, at the end of the day, Valerie and her family had many good things for which to be thankful. They were not sure how God could use the tragedy for good, but they were not worried. That was God's job.

That night, Valerie's entire family gave a special prayer of thanks to God for having been with them through the good and bad. Can you do the same? Will you do so now?

PRAYER

Dear Jesus, some things went wrong (or will go wrong) today, and some things went right. We truly thank You for being with us through the day, and we ask You to watch over us in our sleeping hours. Amen.

Orlan Zuberbier

PENTECOST / TRINITY

A, E, I, O, and U

Matthew 6:14–15

"What are nouns?" asked Mrs. Miller.

Sara waved her hand enthusiastically and answered, "A, E, I, O, and U are nouns." A few giggles started around the room as Sara realized what she had just said. "Oh, I mean nouns are words that name people, places, or things."

But it was too late. The whole class was laughing, even Kim, her best friend. Sara felt her face get hot, and she wished she could somehow disappear. As the laughter quieted down, Sara felt angrier and angrier. After all, the others made mistakes too. Why did everyone have to laugh at her?

At lunchtime, Sara avoided talking to the other girls and sat by herself. After a while, Kim came over to share her orange with Sara. But Sara just got up and moved away. Sara was miserable. All day she carried her grudge against her friends and found herself doing little things to hurt them back. Pretty soon everyone was miserable. Sara felt worse than ever.

Have you ever had a day like this? Have you ever tried to hurt others because they hurt you? Have you nursed a grudge until you've forgotten what even caused the fight in the first place?

People in Bible times had problems like this too. St. Paul told his friends at Ephesus, "Be angry and do not sin; do not let the sun go down on your anger, and give no opportunity to the devil" (Ephesians 4:26–27).

Paul also told his Christian sisters and brothers in Colossae, "If one has a complaint against another, forgiving each other; as the Lord has forgiven you, so you also must forgive" (Colossians 3:13).

We all get angry sometimes. It's what we do about our anger that makes the big difference. Grudges and more hurt? Or love and forgiveness in the name of Christ our Savior?

PRAYER

Dear Lord, forgive me for trying to hurt others when I'm angry with them. Help me to get over my anger quickly and to forgive others just as You have forgiven me. Amen.

Elizabeth Friedrich

An Ocean Crossing

Joshua 1:7–9

Fourteen-year-old Justina stood on the bobbing, wooden deck of the ship *Copernicus* on her way to the New World. The year was 1838. Ocean spray was cold and damp, and the swaying deck made her stomach queasy. She pulled Mama's patchwork quilt tighter around her shoulders. Staring past the wake of the ship at the horizon, she could no longer see land. Her old home was gone for good! Justina wiped a tear from her face as her new friend Wilhelm stumbled over. The ship's deck heaved up and down on the Atlantic waves, and Wilhelm hadn't gotten his sea legs yet.

"Hello, Justina. Aren't you excited? In eight weeks, our families will be in America!"

"But we're leaving Germany, Wilhelm. We're leaving so much behind!" Justina sighed. She didn't expect a *boy* to understand.

"Yes, but we're headed for a new life, like Moses and Joshua headed for the Promised Land!"

"I suppose," agreed Justina, snuggling into her quilt. "Papa says we will have great freedom in America. We Lutherans will be able to preach and teach what we want there. But I miss our old home."

Wilhelm wanted to comfort Justina in his arms, but he was too shy. Instead he said, "Don't be afraid. God loves us. He sent Jesus to pay for our sins and bring us new life. He won't desert us now."

Like Justina and Wilhelm, we sometimes don't know whether to look back or forward. The Bible says, "This is God, our God forever and ever. He will guide us forever" (Psalm 48:14). Of course, most of us aren't really on the sea, but God promises to guide us—not to America, but to a wonderful relationship with Him and to our home in heaven!

In the winter of 1838, 665 Saxon Lutherans sailed from Germany on five ships. Four ships—the Copernicus, *the* Republik, *the* Johann George, *and the* Olbers—*arrived safely in New Orleans. One—the* Amalia—*was lost at sea.*

PRAYER

Lord, thank You for being with me in all circumstances. Help me remember Your constant love. In Jesus' name. Amen.

Kristine M. Moulds

PENTECOST / TRINITY

1842

Isaiah 55:10–12

Wilhelm stared from his bedroom window at the oak sapling. He'd planted an acorn he had brought from Germany.

It will grow well here, Wilhelm thought. Through the churches and schools we build, God's Word will grow here too. With that conviction, Wilhelm returned to his Bible to finish the chapter.

Meanwhile, in her own home not far away, Justina lay in bed under Mama's patchwork quilt. Wilhelm had been right. Life in America wasn't so bad! Their new house was fast becoming home. Best of all, the government didn't control their churches. The preaching and teaching were faithful to God's Word.

In one corner of Mama's quilt, through a tiny hole between the stitches, Justina had hidden a paper from Wilhelm on which he had written a Bible verse. "[God says,] 'My Word . . . shall not return to Me empty, but it shall accomplish that which I purpose, and shall succeed in the thing for which I sent it'" (Isaiah 55:11).

Remembering this verse made Justina feel safe and secure. God had kept the promises of His Word in many ways, especially in sending His Son, Jesus, to rescue them from sin.

The freedom to worship God and to teach the truth of His Word encouraged many to make new beginnings in nineteenth-century America. For the Saxons in Missouri, and for many others then and now, God's Word was a great treasure. It revealed to them—as it does to us— that our sins are forgiven.

It really happened. The Saxon immigrants traveled up the Mississippi from New Orleans and founded many towns. They built churches and schools in which to teach and preach God's Word, including what later became Concordia Seminary in St. Louis, Missouri.

PRAYER

Heavenly Father, thank You for Your Word and for my opportunities to study it freely. Amen.

Kristine M. Moulds

PENTECOST / TRINITY

An Early Arrival

1 Peter 3:21

Carolyn (or Carrie as her family calls her) will be nine years old in a few days. When she was born, her head was about the size of an orange. She weighed only three pounds one ounce. She was a premature baby, born two months early. Carrie's mom and dad and her doctors were quite concerned whether she would live. The doctor had never seen such a small baby survive. Carrie was baptized by a nurse within a few minutes after her birth.

But Carrie had a long way to go. When she breathed, her tummy seemed almost to cave in. The nurses would try to feed her an ounce of milk in forty-five minutes. If she didn't finish it all in that time, they would stop. Otherwise she would use more energy in sucking than she would get from the milk she swallowed.

But Carrie got stronger and bigger every day. After two months in a special hospital, she was able to come home. She weighed 5½ pounds. Today it's impossible to tell she was once so small.

No matter what our age or size, Baptism is a very important event in our life. God tells us that all who believe and are baptized will be saved. Baptism usually takes place when the pastor pours or sprinkles water on a person three times while saying, "In the name of the Father and of the Son and of the Holy Spirit." As this happens, the Holy Spirit works faith in that person. From then on, the person is a child of God, receiving all the blessings of Baptism—forgiveness, life, and salvation.

This means that Carrie became God's child a few minutes after she was born. This made her parents very happy. If Carrie had died, she would have gone to heaven. There she would have enjoyed everlasting life with Jesus. That is why her middle name is Grace!

PRAYER

Dear Jesus, thank You for dying on the cross for my sins. Dear Father, thank You for giving us Baptism as a means to receive faith. O Holy Spirit, thank You for making me a child of God. Keep me always in Your grace. Amen.

Robert M. Toepper

PENTECOST / TRINITY

Pull Together

Acts 2:42–47

It was a cool Saturday morning, the last day of the fall festival. Pickup trucks and horse trailers were parked at the end of a field. Farmers had brought their best plow horses for the pulling contest.

Matthew hitched up his first team of two horses and pulled five tons of cement blocks—good enough for third place. An hour later, he tried again, hitching up his two other horses. They strained, but pulled only four tons of blocks.

The last event was the four-horse pull. Matt harnessed both teams together. Would they be able to pull their scores from the first round even though they were tired? A nine-ton pull might win a ribbon. Imagine his surprise. His four horses pulled an amazing twelve tons to win first place!

God does amazing things through His people. The Bible reading tells about the work and worship of believers in the Early Church. They worshiped God and told others about Jesus. This was the beginning of the congregation of believers pulling together in Jerusalem. In a world where people selfishly took care of only themselves, God strengthened the believers through Word and Sacrament so they could then show the love of Jesus wherever they went.

Christian Churches today are like that. Young and old gather to hear and study God's Word, receive forgiveness of sins, and enjoy the fellowship of other believers. God puts us in His Church. There we praise God and receive His strength to help others. He tells us to pull together and even gives us the power to do amazing things!

PRAYER

Dear heavenly Father, thank You for keeping all believers close to You through Jesus and helping them reach out to others with Your strength. Amen.

Suzanne Ramsey

Bread of Life

John 6:35–40

One crisp fall morning, Kelsey and Mrs. Lawton were in the yard filling the bird feeders.

"Mom," said Kelsey, "the yard is always full of finches, starlings, blue jays, and robins. But why don't the hummingbirds come?"

"Some birds are easier to attract than others," replied Mrs. Lawton as she rinsed out the birdbath. "All the birds that have found us know they can get well fed here. The hummingbirds just haven't found us yet."

"But we clean their feeder and put in fresh nectar every week," continued Kelsey. "Don't they know we're waiting for them so we can help take care of them?"

"No, they don't know that yet," said Mrs. Lawton. "It's probably too late to see hummingbirds anymore this season. But next summer, we will fill their feeder and keep watching for them. Maybe someday they will come."

In our Bible reading, Jesus calls Himself the "bread of life." He tells us that people who hunger after God's love and forgiveness will be satisfied as they come to know and believe in Him. Like the robins and finches in Kelsey's backyard, which are attracted easily, many people are led by the Holy Spirit to fill themselves with spiritual food by studying God's Word.

But like the hummingbirds, some people are hard to attract. They don't know that God's spiritual food is offered also to them. They pass right by God's house without stopping to sample the food that God offers inside. God continues to offer the bread of life to these reluctant souls and patiently waits for them to receive His love and forgiveness.

PRAYER

Dear Father, thank You for providing me with food, clothing, family, and everything I need in this life. Thank You most of all for giving me Jesus, the bread of life. Help me to tell those who don't know Jesus about His love for them. In Jesus' name I pray. Amen.

Cynthia Lemke

PENTECOST / TRINITY

Come and See

John 1:35–40

"Go into all the world and proclaim the gospel to the whole creation" (Mark 16:15). There are few Christians—above the age of five or six—who don't know that verse by heart. There are few who don't know what Jesus meant when He spoke these words. He wants all Christians to tell the world how He came to take away our sins.

But some people feel just a little shy about doing this. "I can't do that," they say. "I wouldn't know what to say."

There is a very simple way of introducing people to Jesus. It is simply to say, "Come and see."

One day, two disciples of John the Baptist were following Jesus. They wanted to know more about Him but were too timid to ask.

When Jesus turned around and saw them following, He said, "What are you seeking?"

They replied, "Rabbi [which means Teacher], where are You staying?"

"Come and you will see," He answered. They did as Jesus told them. They learned and believed in Him as their Savior.

Philip used the same words when he invited his friend Nathanael to follow Jesus. Nathanael was hard to convince. "Can anything good come out of Nazareth?" he asked.

Philip said to him, "Come and see" (John 1:46).

This is an invitation that anybody can give. Even if we can't explain everything there is to explain about our faith and our Church, we can invite people to come and hear Jesus' Word. This is the way they can "come and see" for themselves.

The next time you have a chance to speak to somebody about Jesus but feel a little afraid because you don't know what to say, remember what Jesus and Philip said. Invite your friend to "come and see."

PRAYER

Lord Jesus, I know that You want all people to be saved. Help me to invite others to hear Your Word so they may believe and trust in You too. Amen.

Hubert Riedel

PENTECOST / TRINITY

"Father, I Have Sinned"

Luke 15:20–24

"I was wrong" is a hard thing to say to anyone at any time. Kids hate to say it. Grown-ups hate to admit it. Important people try to cover it up. Criminals plead innocent. It's even hard to tell your friend that you were wrong.

When the runaway son realized how wrong he was, he began to appreciate his father's love. He thought about all the wrong things that he had done. He knew he didn't deserve to be treated as a son. He ran home to his father and said the hard words, "Father, I have sinned." Before he could finish speaking, his dad hugged him and forgave him. He ordered a banquet to celebrate the son's homecoming.

As a young monk, Martin Luther confessed his sins. But he was always afraid he had forgotten some. He was troubled because he knew he deserved nothing but God's punishment. He could never do enough penance deeds to be called God's child again.

God the Father's welcoming hug came when Luther read these words: "One is justified by faith [in Jesus]" (Romans 3:28). Because Luther believed in Jesus, he knew he was God's child. He would be welcome in God's heavenly home.

We need to stop every day and tell God we are poor, miserable sinners. Like the runaway, we need to say, "Father, I have sinned." We need to think about the things we have done wrong and tell God we are sorry. We need to remember that we justly deserve punishment, now and forever.

When we confess the ugliness of our sins, we receive the forgiveness of our Savior. Because of Jesus, we will hear God call us "Son" or "Daughter." "Be happy," He'll say. "Your sins are forgiven!" Rejoice in His hug.

PRAYER

Dear Jesus, I am sorry for the sins I did today. Please forgive me. Amen.

Mary Lou Krause

Luther's Coat of Arms

Romans 3:19–28

In Martin Luther's time, many families had a family emblem called a "coat of arms." They marked their belongings with this emblem. This custom began during the Crusades, when knights wore a special design on their armor as they went into battle.

Luther's family had such a coat of arms. It pictured a crossbow with a rose on either side. But after Luther found the truth of the Gospel in the Bible, he prepared a new coat of arms. Through it, he wanted to tell the message of salvation.

In the center, Luther put a black cross. This stands for the fact that Jesus paid for the sins of the whole world by His death. On the cross, Jesus was forsaken in the darkness of hell in our place.

Luther then put a red heart around the black cross. This is a reminder that the blood of Jesus cleanses us from all sin. It also shows that "with the heart one believes and is justified" (Romans 10:10). Believing in Jesus, "we are forgiven, righteous and holy in God's sight for the sake of His Son."

The black cross and red heart appear on a white rose. White is the color of purity. It stands for the pure hearts we have by faith in Jesus and for being sanctified by the Holy Spirit in our Baptism.

Luther placed the rose on a field of blue. Blue is a color of hope. It reminds us of heaven, where Jesus has prepared an eternal home for us.

Finally, Luther encircled the field of blue with a ring of gold. The gold ring shows that our joy in heaven is endless and more precious than all other treasures.

This emblem can be every believer's coat of arms. It is a summary of the Bible's central truth: we are "justified by faith" (Romans 3:28).

PRAYER

Dear Father, thank You for giving Your Son to suffer and die for my sins. Thank You for giving me faith to believe in Jesus, my Savior. In His name. Amen.

Donald Poganski

PENTECOST / TRINITY

Unafraid to Speak

Psalm 119:41–48

"Take it back!" said the emperor to the man standing in front of him. "I can't take it back. I *will* not!" the man fearlessly replied. "What I have spoken and written is the truth. God loves sinners and forgives them, not because of their good deeds but because of His great love for all people."

The day was April 18, 1521. The place was Worms, Germany. The man who refused to take back his beliefs was Martin Luther.

Luther didn't fear to speak of God's love though he was in danger of prison and death. The emperor and Church leaders all were ready to condemn him for false teaching. But Luther knew that Jesus would give him courage to stand his ground. He believed and practiced what the Bible says: "I will also speak of Your testimonies before kings and shall not be put to shame" (Psalm 119:46).

On Reformation Day, we think of Martin Luther's great confession. Through this man and others like him, God preserved for us the Bible's teaching that we are saved by grace, not by works. Jesus has freed us from the slavery of the Law, and we can now "walk at liberty" (v. 45 KJV). We also, like Luther, can be ready to speak out for our Savior whenever God gives us the opportunity.

Salvation unto us has come
By God's free grace and favor;
Good works cannot avert our doom,
They help and save us never.
Faith looks to Jesus Christ alone,
Who did for all the world atone;
He is our one Redeemer. Amen. (*LSB* 555:1)

PRAYER

Dear Lord, give me strength from Your Word and from the example of Luther to stand up for the truth. As You have made me free from the Law, help me spread to others the joy of this freedom. Amen.

Unknown

PENTECOST / TRINITY

Worms Today

Romans 3:20–28

It was Sunday morning. The bells of the ancient, four-towered St. Mary's Cathedral began to clang loudly. A few moments later, the bells of Trinity Lutheran Church across the street added their loud tones. What a glorious moment!

This was Worms, Germany, in the 1970s. Its skyline across the Rhine River was much the same 450 years earlier when Luther approached it in a horse-drawn cart. And the citizens of Worms are proud of him. They have a Luther Street, a Luther Square, a Luther monument, and a Luther museum. They have not forgotten that in their town, Luther made his historic stand.

Luther had been worked into a corner. He had been accused of teaching many things against the Church. He was supposed to apologize and take back much that he had taught and believed. But Luther said that unless he were shown clearly from the Word of God where he was wrong, he could not and he would not take it back. His conscience was bound by the Word of God. His final word was "Here I stand! I cannot do otherwise! God help me! Amen!"

As the bells of Worms ring out today, not everybody remembers what Luther said. To some, he was just another folk hero who had the courage to fight the high powers of his day.

As Christians, we are more interested in what he fought *for*. God says we are saved by His grace through faith. Salvation is a gift of God through Jesus Christ, our Savior. Luther believed this—and he felt everyone should have the chance to know and believe it too.

We thank God for men like Luther. And we thank God for His Word, which shows us Jesus, our Savior.

PRAYER

Lord, I thank You that I have been saved by grace, through the gift of faith You gave me. Keep me strong until You take me to be with You in heaven. In Jesus' name I pray. Amen.

Roy Gesch

PENTECOST / TRINITY
Reformation Day

Are You a Saint?

Hebrews 11:32–40

Yesterday was Halloween. Did you dress up in a costume? Were you dressed as your favorite character or perhaps a kind of food? Or did you dress as something really scary? If you wore a costume, the people who looked at you did not see you as you really are. They saw you as the thing you pretended to be.

The day after Halloween is called All Saints' Day. The celebration of All Saints' Day had its beginning in the year AD 360. Throughout the centuries, this day has been a time to remember Christians who have died. On this day, we also look forward to joining them in heaven.

You may be wondering what Halloween and All Saints' Day have in common. On Halloween, you dress up as something you are not. On All Saints' Day, you celebrate the "costume" you received when you were baptized.

Before you became a child of God at your Baptism, God saw your ugly, scary sin. But when the pastor put water on your head and spoke God's Word of forgiveness, you became clothed with Christ's righteousness, or holiness. You "put on" Jesus' perfect, sinless life.

Because you are covered in this way, God no longer sees the scary sin that is a real part of your life. God sees you as if you had no sin. He does not see your sin because it has been removed by Christ. In sin's place is Christ's righteous clothing.

You can celebrate All Saints' Day because you, too, are a saint. You wear the "costume" of Jesus' perfect life.

Prayer

Dear Jesus, thank You for Your holiness, which removes my ugly sin. I'm grateful to be one of Your saints by the work of the Holy Spirit through Your Word and Baptism. Amen.

Kathy A. Schulz

PENTECOST / TRINITY
All Saints' Day

A Day for Remembering

Revelation 21:22–22:5

Today during the church service, I felt like crying. Pastor read my grandma's name during the prayers. When I heard her name, I felt sad all over again. Why did pastor read Grandma's name? She had died last summer. I asked Dad about it on the way home.

Dad told me that on the Sunday closest to November 2, the Church remembers all the people from the congregation who have died during the past year. November 2 is called Commemoration of the Faithful Departed.

"Why does the Church remind people about something that makes them feel sad?" I asked Dad.

Dad gave me a hug and we sat down together. "You're right," he said, "it does make us feel sad when we remember Grandma and think about all the kind things she did for people."

"I remember how she came to my baseball games," I added. "And it always made me feel good when she wanted to give me a Grandma hug. Today I remembered how much I miss her. If it makes people feel sad, why do we even do that at church?"

Dad didn't say anything for a long time. Finally, he said, "I think it's because God wants us to remember that we are His people. Jesus, His Son, gave His life to save us and then became alive again. When we die, He will take us to heaven to live with Him. Grandma believed that."

Dad continued, "It does make us sad to think of Grandma. But we can be happy too. We know she's with Jesus in heaven and that we will all be together again." Dad and I sat there for a long time. I think we were both remembering—remembering Grandma and remembering God's promise that He will take us to heaven.

PRAYER

O sweet and blessed country, The home of God's elect!
O sweet and blessed country That faithful hearts expect!
In mercy, Jesus, bring us To that eternal rest!
With You and God the Father And Spirit, ever blest. Amen. (LSB 672:4)

Judy Williams

PENTECOST / TRINITY

Team Colors

Galatians 3:26–27

The whistle blew; the season was over. The excited volleyball team left the court amid a swell of hoopla. They now had an 8–0 record; they were undefeated! They had managed to bring home the trophy from the Kitten Classic. They had survived Alicia's knee problems and even beat their rivals, the Rockets. To celebrate, all the girls planned to wear their jerseys to school on Friday. Even though the orange and black were fading, the girls were proud to be seen in their colors.

The official orange-and-black jerseys identified the members of the volleyball team. What identifies members of God's team, or family? Could it be that they have managed to bring home the good-behavior-never-been-in-detention trophy? Have they survived temptation to cheat on every single test in fifth grade? Have they beaten the devil at his game and won eternal life for themselves?

The answer to all of these questions is no. The family of God gets its colors from the victory of Christ. He fought the battle; He won the prize. Jesus came from heaven and lived the perfect life, defeated Satan, and rose in victory. We are identified as God's own people by the powerful but invisible sign of the cross on our forehead and heart. We are identified as God's own people by the fruit of God's Spirit, which He produces in us. We are set for certain defeat if we try to win by ourselves. We are doomed. The victory message comes in the words from Galatians. We, too, share in His glory, for we are all "sons [and daughters] of God, through faith [in Christ Jesus]" (Galatians 3:26). He places on us His victory colors; He hands us the trophy He has won. We are amazed at His love and mercy.

PRAYER

Dear Jesus, we thank You for Your suffering, death, and victory. Help us to share this wonderful victory news with others. Amen.

Gail Pawlitz

PENTECOST / TRINITY

How to Scurry

1 Peter 5:6–11

Squirrels have always fascinated me. They scurry here and there with their double-jointed hind legs, going up one tree and down the next. They glide around the trees and grass with their tails waving and bouncing as they run. They gather nuts and seeds for the coming winter. They don't look worried about anything attacking them; maybe that's because their eyes are positioned so they can see some things behind them!

Children have always fascinated me. They scurry here and there, playing instruments and learning all kinds of new things in Scouts or other clubs. They glide around, waving hellos to their friends. They bounce back after illness or a playground fall. They gather friends to play a game or materials to make a project. They don't look . . .

Wait a minute. They *can* look worried! I have seen it. They can be worried about their grades and their friends and their grandparents and their pets and their moms and their dads and their sins. Thoughts grow into worries, and worries can create anxiety.

God's young and old children don't have to be worried. We have a Savior who cares. In God's Word, Peter tells us, "Casting all your anxieties on Him [God], because He cares for you" (1 Peter 5:7). God is inviting us to pray and bring our concerns to Him. As God's children, forgiven by Jesus' death and resurrection, we are washed clean in our Baptism. In Jesus, we are living freely. Now we can scurry—not worry—around each day, secure in God's love.

PRAYER

Gracious heavenly Father, as we scurry about this day, watch over us. In Jesus' name. Amen.

Dean Rothchild

Dad's Birthday

Ephesians 6:1–4

Jon and Jessica were excited. Tomorrow was their dad's birthday, and they had been saving part of their allowance so they could get him something extra special.

For a long time now, Dad had been looking at a case for his fly rod in one of the sporting goods stores. Mom knew all about the surprise, and she had taken off work a little early to take Jon and Jessica to the store. When they told the salesman about their surprise, he gave them a caddis fly for their dad.

The next day, the two children placed the gifts in Dad's chair. Then they waited, crouched behind the chair. They heard Dad open and close the door, hang up his coat, and walk into the family room. "It looks like someone has been shopping," they could hear him say. "Who did all this for me?"

Jon and Jessica jumped up, shouting, "We did! Did we surprise you? Do you like it?"

Dad hugged his children. "Thank you very much," he said. "I am fortunate that God has given me two loving children."

Children are gifts from God. In our Bible reading, God tells children to obey their parents as they would the Lord. He directs parents to train and instruct their family in God's Word. Parents are to tell their children about the wonderful God who made us; who saves us from our sins through the work of His Son, Jesus; who makes us His own through Baptism; and who helps us live as His people. God is so great, and He is so good to us!

PRAYER

Thank You, God, for children. Thank You, God, for parents and other adults who love and care for us. Help us all to honor You with our lives. In Jesus' name. Amen.

Judy Williams

Our Great High Priest

Hebrews 7:23–28

Have you ever wondered why Jesus is called a High Priest in the Bible? We may not understand what this name means unless we know what a high priest did in Bible times.

The Jewish priests, and especially the high priests, offered sacrifices for the people. Lambs, goats, and oxen were among the animals offered to God day after day and year after year.

Before the priest could begin to offer sacrifices for other people, he had to offer a sacrifice of his own to God. This was to remind him and the people that a priest was a sinful human being and also needed to be forgiven.

According to the Bible, Jesus is a much better High Priest than those of the Old Testament. Jesus also made a sacrifice for sins, but not for any sins of His own. Jesus was sinless. The Bible says, "He has no need, like those high priests, to offer sacrifices daily, first for His own sins and then for those of the people, since He did this once for all when He offered up Himself" (Hebrews 7:27).

The sacrifice Jesus offered was Himself. His one sacrifice makes all others unnecessary. Jesus suffered the torments of hell and thus paid for our sins once and for all. That is why "He is able to save to the uttermost those who draw near to God through Him" (v. 25).

The Old Testament sacrifices were only shadows, or symbols, of the perfect sacrifice of Jesus. They pointed to Jesus and His great sacrifice on the cross. How wonderful it is that we are God's forgiven children because of the work of Jesus, our High Priest!

PRAYER

Lord Jesus, my great High Priest, I am forever grateful to You for sacrificing Your holy life for me. Keep me from thinking that there is any other way to be saved than through faith in You. Amen.

Howard Kramer

Banana Pops

Psalm 119:97–104

Cover the bottom of a 9 ✗ 13-inch baking pan with waxed paper. Melt a 12-ounce package of chocolate chips. While the chips are melting, peel several bananas. Cut each one in half. Insert a craft stick into each banana, and then dip it into the melted chips. Set the chocolate-covered banana on the waxed paper and put the pan in the freezer. While you are waiting for your banana pops to freeze, read the rest of the devotion.

Sometimes meals are a collection of foods that taste good and foods that are good for you. Dessert goes down easily, but that vegetable you don't like sneers at you from the plate. There are many foods that we like that are both tasty and good for us. Bananas are sweet, and they are also good for you. They have potassium, an important mineral in a healthy diet.

Now think about God's Law and Gospel. When we try to measure our spiritual health with only the Law, we find that we are sick with sin and in need of a Savior. God sent Jesus to fulfill that Law and seal God's sweet Gospel promise. But when we read the Law as a way of learning about God, we can learn of His love and wisdom. The Law of God can be like that sweet-yet-good-for-you food. The Law tells us how to live a godly life.

The writer of Psalm 119 knew this. In fact, he meditates on God's Word and finds it has the sweetest wisdom. Verse 103 says that God's Word is both good for us and sweet. God's laws, or expectations, show us the great love that God has for His people.

When your banana pops are ready, why not munch on one while you read your Bible? There you will find a sweet understanding of God.

PRAYER

Dear Lord, thank You that Your words are sweet. Help me to follow Your Law as a guide and to share Your love with others. In Jesus' name I pray. Amen.

Kim D. Marxhausen

Forgiveness and Seasons

1 John 1:5–9

Sean threw a handful of leaves into the air. He knew he was supposed to be putting them into trash bags. But it was more fun to jump in the pile and watch the wind blow them around. Soon it would be winter. That would mean shoveling snow. But there would be skating and sliding down the hill on garbage can lids and sleds. And when winter began to get gloomy, spring would come. It would have sunny days and rainy ones that brought flowers and birds and baseball. And then good old summer. Vacation!

God had a good idea, Sean thought. He had made four different seasons instead of just one. They always came on time. And they were always in the right order, one after the other.

Sean was right. When God created the heavens and the earth, He made the seasons. They do come and go, one after the other. We can count on them. But the seasons are just one of the many promises God has made and kept. The most important promise is repeated throughout the Old Testament. God said He would send someone to save us. And He did. We read about it in the New Testament. John 3:16 tells us who the rescuer is. "God so loved the world, that He gave . . ." (Do you know the rest of that verse?) Yes, He gave His Son, Jesus Christ.

There is another valuable promise in God's Word. He has promised that even though we sin, He will forgive us.

In a way, forgiveness is like the four seasons. We can always count on God's forgiveness. When we confess our sins (and even *before* we confess them), this gift is waiting for us. Just as David wrote in Psalm 51:10, we can say, "Create in me a clean heart, O God, and renew a right spirit within me." And He will do this! He never says, "Oh, no, not that one again; not Jason or Holly or Delores or (*your name*)."

PRAYER

Thank You, dear God, for keeping all Your promises. I praise and thank You for forgiving my sins every day for the sake of Jesus, my Savior. Amen.

Loreene Bell

PENTECOST / TRINITY

Language Keys

Matthew 16:19

The following words contain a heavenly treasure. Do you know what it is? The first version is written in Latin, the second in German.

"Sic enim Deus dilexit mundum, ut Filium suum unigenitum daret, ut omnis, qui credit in eum, non pereat, sed habeat vitam aeternam."

"Also hat Gott die Welt geliebet, dass er seinen eingebornen Sohn gab, auf dass alle, die an ihn glauben, nicht verloren werden, sondern das ewige Leben haben."

A foreign language is like a locked treasure chest. Without the right key, you can't get to the treasure. What good are the words without understanding? Do you have the keys to the above words? Your English key is in John 3:16.

People of Germany in the year 1520 were missing the key to the Bible. Since it was written in Latin, most Germans were unable to unlock God's words to them. Even Martin Luther had never seen a complete Bible. Then, one day, he found one in a university library. Since Luther had the language key of Latin, he was able to unlock the "treasure chest." There he discovered the treasure of eternal life and freedom from his sins. If only everyone in Germany could share this treasure, he thought.

In 1521, at Wartburg Castle, Luther translated the New Testament from Latin into the German language. About twelve years later, he finished translating the Old Testament. Imagine the joy of the German people! Now they, too, could share in God's treasure—the free gift of eternal life.

God uses people like Martin Luther to bring this gift to His children. We are especially thankful for English translations so that we, too, may read God's Word. Praise God for Bible translators today who are still making "keys" in many languages. Through them, the treasure of eternal life, Jesus Christ, may be shared by everyone.

PRAYER

O Lord, thank You for people who translate Your Word into languages we can understand so people can know of Your gift of eternal life through Your Son, Jesus Christ. Amen.

Jewel L. Laabs

PENTECOST / TRINITY

How Luther Found Peace

Ephesians 2:2–10

Martin Luther was born on this day in 1483 in Eisleben, Germany. He had six brothers and sisters.

Martin was brought up to know about God, but he was taught from little on to be afraid of God. God could make lightning strike boys who sinned, and only if they did good and prayed to the saints could they be saved. Luther said later that as a boy, he trembled at the name of Jesus.

One day, Martin stuck himself in the leg with a sword and got sick. This frightened him. He thought of how sinful he was and how terrible it would be to die and be punished by God.

Another time, when he was a law student, he was even more scared when he got caught in a thunderstorm. He was sure God was going to strike him with lightning for being such a sinner. He lay on the ground in terror and cried, "Help me, St. Anne, and I will become a monk!" Luther's father was a miner, and St. Anne was the saint of miners.

Luther entered a school for monks and tried hard to make himself good. He got up to pray every morning at two o'clock. For hours he stretched himself in the form of a cross on the cold floor of his cell. But he still felt sinful. He was sure God was not pleased with him.

One day, while reading the Bible, he found that he couldn't make himself holy by doing good works. He understood also that Jesus died for him and gave him forgiveness of sins and peace. Luther spent his life from then on telling the world of Jesus and His love.

Today we thank God especially that Luther rediscovered for us this truth: "By grace you have been saved through faith. And this is not of your own doing; it is the gift of God, not a result of works" (Ephesians 2:8).

PRAYER

Dear God, thank You for the gift of Jesus, my Savior, and for telling me the way to eternal life through Him. Amen.

Theodore W. Schroeder

PENTECOST / TRINITY

The Peace of Jesus

John 14:27

Do you know what holiday is observed today? In Canada, it is called Remembrance Day. In the United States, this holiday is called Veterans Day.

Today we remember the men and women who have served in the armed forces. Many people visit the graves of family members and friends who died in a war. They put flowers on the graves.

Remembrance Day or Veterans Day is a day to be thankful for peace and friendship all over the world. People first celebrated this day after the end of World War I. It was called Armistice Day. They believed that it was the last war that would ever be fought.

Today we are thankful to God for letting us live at a time of peace in our land. The peace we experience is a treasured thing. We pray that God will give our leaders wisdom to keep this peace. But we know that this peace is on shaky ground. It is built on sinful people like you and me. We are people who feel hateful at times and do hateful things.

It may be hard for us to imagine, but there are wars going on this very minute in other countries. People are shooting at others and hurting or killing them.

Thank the Lord that God gives Christians a peace that doesn't depend on people like us. The peace God gives is built on His perfect Son, Jesus Christ. Jesus' peace calms our troubled hearts and makes us confident. His peace keeps us at one with God through faith, knowing that our salvation is sure. We don't need to be afraid, because we have peace from Jesus. It is a peace that passes understanding.

Jesus came into the world to share His peace with all of us. On this day of remembrance, let's thank God for peace—peace on earth and the peace God gives us.

PRAYER

Heavenly Father, we thank You for sending Your Son to give us peace. Help us carry the peace of Jesus with us wherever we go. Amen.

Allison DeWitz

PENTECOST / TRINITY

He Cares for Me

Matthew 6:25–34

Walking to school on a cool November morning, Larisa decided to take a "long cut" through the park. She noticed the brisk smell of damp leaves as she started down the path. There were only a few ducks left on the pond that was so full in the summer. Larisa noticed how slowly and quietly they swam today. Soon the pond would freeze over, and the ducks all would be gone.

The pretty brown cattails were beginning to come apart and blow their seeds around the park. The leaves were off the trees, and everything seemed so quiet. It was as though everything was going to sleep.

As Larisa continued on the path, she noticed funny burrs sticking to the bottom of her jean cuffs. The leaves crunched beneath her feet in some spots and were damp and squishy in others. As she turned the last corner leaving the park, she heard the beautiful call of the red-winged blackbird.

Sitting at her desk in school, Larisa began picking the burrs off her cuffs. She knew these were the seeds of spring. It was such a beautiful morning. She felt so much a part of God's plan today. Just think—she knew a God who took care of everything. He was preparing His creation for a winter's rest. And He was already planting the seeds for spring.

Larisa knew that this same God was her loving Father. He sent His own Son into the world as a baby born in a stable. Jesus grew up as a young boy just like her little brother, but without sin. He played and grew and began a ministry of love and caring.

That same Jesus was her Savior. He died for her sins because He loved her. He rose victorious over death. He lives now with His Father and the Holy Spirit, who strengthens her faith. As Larisa picked the last burr off her cuff, she thought to herself, Thank You, God, for November!

PRAYER

Heavenly Father, thank You for the changes in nature. Help me see Your loving hand in all of Your creations, especially me. Amen.

Barbara Schram Schoenbeck

PENTECOST / TRINITY

Peter Learned a Lesson

Isaiah 55:8–9

One day after tryouts for the basketball team, Peter was on his way out of the gym. He stopped to admire a huge picture an artist was making on the gymnasium wall.

"Boy, you paint well," said Peter. He was fascinated as the artist stroked and dabbed on the wall with his colors. In a few minutes, there was a sketch of a basketball player racing across the court.

"How did you learn to do that?" Peter asked.

The artist turned around and smiled. "Well, I'll tell you. When I was about your age, painting was the last thing I thought of doing. I wanted to play basketball! When I made the team one year, I was so happy I could have burst. Then, just a few days later, I broke my leg. As I lay in bed recovering, I drew pictures of basketball players. My friends liked my drawings so well, they asked me to draw for them. Then somebody gave me paints, and I took up painting. After my leg got better, I kept right on with it."

The artist added, "You know, Peter, God works in mysterious ways. He blesses us even in our troubles."

Several weeks later, the list was posted for the basketball team. Eagerly Peter glanced down the list, feeling sure his name would be on it. But it just wasn't there. Peter felt terrible as he headed for home. Then he remembered the artist's words about how God works through our troubles. After that, he didn't feel so bad. He silently prayed to God to help him believe that this was happening for his good.

God tells us in His Word, "I know the plans I have for you, . . . plans for welfare and not for evil, to give you a future and a hope" (Jeremiah 29:11). The God who gave Jesus to be our Savior surely loves us enough to direct our lives for our future good.

PRAYER

Heavenly Father, I don't always understand Your ways. But help me bow to Your will and trust You to bless me even through my troubles. I ask it for Jesus' sake. Amen.

Martha Rediehs

PENTECOST / TRINITY

Sleeping in Church

Acts 20:5–12

The apostle Paul was in the city of Troas. He had come there to spend a week with a group of Christians. On Sunday afternoon, Paul met with these believers in a room on the third floor. They ate supper together and also celebrated the Lord's Supper. Paul spoke to the people from early evening until midnight.

A young man named Eutychus (YOO-tih-kuhs) was sitting in an open window. As Paul preached, Eutychus fell asleep and fell from the window to the court below. The people went down and found that he was dead. Paul then put his arms around Eutychus and, with God's power, brought him back to life.

We may not have fallen asleep in church like Eutychus, but our minds sometimes wander during the sermon. Our lips may move when the hymns are sung, but we don't always think of the words and what they mean. When we confess the Apostles' Creed or pray the Lord's Prayer, our minds aren't always on what we say.

Martin Luther says in his Small Catechism: "We should fear and love God so that we do not despise preaching and His Word, but hold it sacred and gladly hear and learn it" (Luther's Small Catechism, explanation of the Third Commandment). When we are inattentive in worship, we do not show the proper respect for God. Then we miss the benefits He has in store for us.

Jesus once said, "Blessed rather are those who hear the word of God and keep it!" (Luke 11:28). On Sundays, we have the opportunity to worship the Lord and hear His Word. He offers us the forgiveness of sins, which Jesus won for us. And He gives us the strength to fight temptation and live a holier life.

PRAYER

O Holy Spirit, help me to be a good listener in church. In Jesus' name I ask it. Amen.

Leonard Aurich

God's Mind and Heart

Isaiah 55:8–9

Why doesn't God stop the kids who tease me at school? Why did He let me trip and lose the relay race for my team? Why did He give me my great friend Heidi and then let her move away?

Why *does* God allow so many bad things to happen to His people? We'd like to climb into God's mind and understand why He does what He does. Our minds, however, are much too small to grasp the ways of God. Our attempts to understand God's mind end in frustration and confusion.

Fortunately, God has much more to offer us than complete understanding of His ways. In today's Bible reading, God reminds us, "As the heavens are higher than the earth, so are My ways higher than your ways and My thoughts than your thoughts" (Isaiah 55:9).

We can be thankful that we don't need to understand God's mind. Romans 5:8 says, "God shows His love for us in that while we were still sinners, Christ died for us." In God, sinners have peace and security. We know that no matter what troubles we experience, we can count on Jesus. Through His Word and Sacraments, we learn that He is always taking care of us, forgiving us for not trusting Him, and helping us to grow. We can count on Him because He says so.

PRAYER

Dear Jesus, I know that Your ways are not my ways. Help me to remember that You always love me and do what's best for me. Amen.

Susan Schulz

A Great Battle Hymn

Psalm 46

Gustavus Adolphus (gus-TAY-vus a-DAWL-fus) was a Swedish king during the Thirty Years' War. He made one of our hymns famous by using it before a battle.

In 1632, the king was fighting against the enemies of God's Word and was preparing for an important battle against General Wallenstein. The two armies faced each other on the morning of November 16. While waiting for a fog to lift, Gustavus himself led his troops in singing:

O little flock, fear not the foe
Who madly seeks your overthrow;
Dread not his rage and pow'r.
And though your courage sometimes faints,
His seeming triumph o'er God's saints
Lasts but a little hour. (*LSB* 666:1)

After the fog lifted, the battle began. For a while, it seemed that the Swedish king's forces would surely lose. Late in the morning, Gustavus was struck by a bullet and fell from his horse. Soon all the soldiers knew he was wounded.

But because their king had encouraged them to trust in God, his troops fought bravely and won the battle. Gustavus died the same day, but his name will always be connected with the hymn "O Little Flock, Fear Not the Foe."

We Christians have a King who leads us in the fight against our enemies—the devil and his army of evil angels. This King is Jesus, who also died in battle. But He came to life again and now fills us with new strength and courage. Believing in Jesus, we have the victory that Jesus won for us.

PRAYER

Dear Lord Jesus, give me courage in times of temptation and danger. Help me trust in You for every blessing, especially for victory over our enemy, the devil. In Your own name I ask this. Amen.

Howard Kramer

PENTECOST / TRINITY

Buried Treasure

Matthew 6:19–21

In the days when pirates roamed the seas, many people looked around for buried treasure—solid-oak chests filled with gold coins and precious jewelry. Long John Silver in *Treasure Island* was such a man. He was determined to find the buried treasure no matter what the cost, even if it meant lying, stealing, or killing his shipmates.

Today we also look for buried treasure, although not pirates' gold. When Christmastime rolls around, we look eagerly for a new bicycle or a Louisville Slugger baseball bat or a Barbie doll. We expect our parents to give us some money every week for ice cream or comic books or football trading cards. We think we've reached our Treasure Island when we walk into toyland at the nearest department store.

Maybe we need to ask ourselves what kind of treasure we really want to find. The Bible tells us not to store up treasures on earth that don't last, but rather to store up treasures in heaven that last forever. Even the best Louisville Slugger may crack on a sharp foul ball. Even the best Barbie doll gets put aside after we're tired of it.

So we ask ourselves: what is the treasure that really counts? What is "treasure in heaven"? The answer comes to us from a well-known hymn: "Jesus, priceless treasure . . . truest friend to me" (*LSB* 743:1). Jesus Christ is our greatest treasure. He suffered and died on the cross so we wouldn't have to die eternally. He paid the price for our sins. Because of Him, we will go to heaven.

Long John Silver was looking for the wrong kind of treasure. We often do that too. But thanks to God, we have been found by Jesus, our Savior. This is our real treasure, which will last forever.

PRAYER

Dear Lord Jesus, my priceless treasure, help me appreciate Your great gift of salvation and life. Give me the wisdom to seek treasures in heaven, treasures that last forever. Amen.

Stephen Carter

PENTECOST / TRINITY

The Symbol of the Cross

1 Corinthians 1:18–21

Kathy's room looked like a junk collection. Shells, stones, stamps, and pinecones were scattered everywhere. On the wall were pennants and travel posters.

But Kathy didn't consider this junk. Each item reminded her of a pleasant experience or of a place where she had been. The stone on her dresser came from Canada. She had picked up the starfish when the family took a trip to California. The flag on the wall was from the New York World's Fair.

Things that remind us of something we can't see or touch are called "symbols." Many churches use symbols to remind worshipers of some spiritual truth. How many symbols do you see in your church?

Almost every Christian church has at least one cross. This symbol helps us think of Jesus and His death. When the cross has the figure of Jesus on it, we call it a "crucifix." The "empty cross" reminds us that Jesus did not stay dead but rose on Easter Sunday.

Heathen people sometimes say we Christians worship the cross, because we put it on our altars and wear it on our lapels or on a chain around our necks. But we don't worship the cross. We use it to remind ourselves of God's love for us and the gift of eternal life through His Son.

This message of the cross is the heart of our Christian faith. It is for this reason that we use the symbol of the cross so much. It is also why St. Paul said in the Bible, "Far be it from me to boast except in the cross of our Lord Jesus Christ" (Galatians 6:14).

PRAYER

Thank You, heavenly Father, for Jesus and His death for my sins. Please help me remember Your love for me each time I see the symbol of the cross. Amen.

Charles Reichert

PENTECOST / TRINITY

Short and Sweet

John 3:16–21

Abraham Lincoln's Gettysburg Address is one of the most famous speeches in American history. It is also one of the shortest.

On that November day in 1863 when Lincoln helped dedicate the military cemetery at the Gettysburg battlefield, the main speaker was a famous orator, Edward Everett. He spoke for nearly two hours. President Lincoln spoke next. His speech was so short that the photographer could not get his camera adjusted in time to take Lincoln's picture.

Later, Mr. Everett wrote President Lincoln a letter. "I should be glad if I could flatter myself that I came as near to the central idea of the occasion in two hours as you did in two minutes," he wrote. It took Lincoln only a few words and a few minutes to say something great and lasting.

Many people have made long speeches and written long books about Jesus. However, the person who used only a few words to get to the center of who Jesus is and what He did is the apostle John. He wrote by inspiration of God: "God so loved the world, that He gave His only Son, that whoever believes in Him should not perish but have eternal life" (John 3:16).

What John says is short and sweet. Christians who have read the Bible from cover to cover return again and again to these words for comfort and strength. They tell us that God loves us so much that He gave His own Son, Jesus, to live, die, and rise again for us. Now we and all who believe in Him will have eternal life.

John's message, which is really God's message, is that simple—and wonderful. Through Jesus, God gives us life with Him forever.

PRAYER

Father in heaven, through Jesus, You promise me a life with You forever. That's a gift bigger than I can imagine right now. Even so, help me find joy in living this life with You right now. Amen.

Richard Hinz

Shock Absorbers

John 16:33

The first gasoline-powered automobile was built in 1885, more than one hundred years ago. Its top speed was only ten miles per hour. You can probably run faster than that.

Today's cars look much different and certainly go faster than those early ones. They also come equipped with all sorts of gadgets to make driving and riding easier.

One great improvement is the addition of shock absorbers. These springlike devices are mounted so the passengers are not bumped and tossed about. The ride is smoother and more pleasant.

God does something for us like shock absorbers do. Along life's road are many bumps. Sometimes there are big hurts and disappointments. Sometimes problems get to us and leave us feeling very low. Every once in a while, we have one of those "Charlie Brown days" when nothing goes right.

God hasn't promised that everything will go right because we are Christians. But He has promised that He will never let anything happen to us that will take away our happiness in Him. He has also promised to make some good come out of even the worst situations. It helps to remember that God understands our problems and is with us in the bad times as well as the good.

The bumps will still be there. That's part of life in this sinful world. But the ride will be easier when we put our trust in God's wonderful promises. Jesus said, "In the world you will have tribulation. But take heart; I have overcome the world" (John 16:33).

PRAYER

Heavenly Father, thank You for helping me through the bad times and sticking by me no matter what happens. Keep my faith strong as I remember Your promises. Amen.

Diane Butikofer

The Message of Fall

2 Peter 3:8–13

Autumn is an exciting time to be outdoors because of so many changes. You notice the leaves changing color from green to red to brown. Seed pods break open and fill the air with fuzzy white parachutes.

It can also be a sad time when you watch the wind whip the leaves off the trees or see a clump of dried-up plants; you remember that before the first frost, beautiful flowers bloomed there.

In ancient times, people wondered about these changes each fall—and were sometimes afraid. They realized the sun was shining for a shorter time each day and wondered if it might not shine at all.

They knew that nothing could live without the sun. Of course, they knew that spring, with its longer days and blossoming plants, had always followed fall and winter. But still they dreaded the autumn when the thought came to them that perhaps this year the sun won't come back.

Of course, now we know why we have seasons. The earth is tilted on its axis. In summer, the northern half of the earth gets more sunlight; in the winter, it gets less. We no longer become frightened when the days grow short.

But a Christian knows that one day the world will end. The Last Day may come at any time. In the Bible, Peter wrote, "But the day of the Lord will come like a thief, and then the heavens will pass away with a roar, and the heavenly bodies will be burned up and dissolved, and the earth and the works that are done on it will be exposed" (2 Peter 3:10).

This sounds terrible, but it isn't—at least not for believers in Jesus. The Bible also says, "But according to His promise we are waiting for new heavens and a new earth in which righteousness dwells" (v. 13). Christians know that when this world does end, Jesus will take them to a better one.

PRAYER

Dear God, help me remember that the end of the world is coming. Thank You for giving me faith to believe in Jesus, my Savior. I ask it in His name. Amen.

Ruth Hummel

What's in a Name?

John 14:1–11

Many years ago, missionaries began translating the Bible into the Chinese language. When they came to the word *God,* there was a great deal of argument. They couldn't decide whether God's name should be written as *Shen* or *Shang Ti.*

This seems to be a minor thing about which to argue. After all, we call God by a number of different names like Savior, Redeemer, Messiah, Bread of Life, and the Good Shepherd. But these words don't tell us everything about God. God Himself tells us who He is. He told us by coming into the world. God is Jesus Christ, who is one with the Father and the Spirit.

Once Jesus' disciples asked Him to show them the Father. Jesus marveled at their question and asked, "Do you not believe that I am in the Father and the Father is in Me?"

What a wonderful God we have! He doesn't only say that He loves us. He *shows* us. Jesus came down to earth to show us what grace is all about. First, He lived the kind of life none of us can lead, a life without sin. Then, He willingly suffered and died, taking our punishment on His own shoulders. After three days, He rose from the dead so that someday we, too, can rise.

The different names for God are a help to us. They tell us about God and the things He does for us. Look, for example, at today's Bible reading. Jesus calls Himself the way (to heaven), the truth (the only one that really matters), and the life (here on earth and forever in heaven).

God backs up words with actions. He not only calls Himself Savior; He *is* our Savior. What's in a name? In the name of Jesus we find forgiveness, true happiness, life, and salvation.

PRAYER

Dear Jesus, thank You for being my Redeemer—for buying me back from sin, death, and the devil—that I may be Your child. Thank You for showing me all of God's love. Amen.

James A. Feldscher

Mmm—Mmm, Good!

Hebrews 2:9–10

On Thanksgiving Day, will you be feasting on what fancy restaurants call *calamari?* I've had some. It has an unusual appearance. Actually, I would have been better off not knowing the more common name—squid. Ick! Keep those tentacles off my Thanksgiving plate!

I have to admit, though, that I didn't choke on this dinnertime delicacy. It didn't taste bad because it didn't really have a taste. If necessary, you can swallow a few tasteless foods. But I prefer not to eat onions or squid, especially together. Please don't put them on my plate.

As a believer in Christ, I know one thing the Lord will never make me taste. I will not have to taste eternal death. Jesus tasted it for me!

On the cross, He took my portion of sin and death and swallowed all that I should have endured. He cleaned my plate of every bit of God's anger. My death was swallowed up in His own. On Good Friday, Jesus put death to death.

Remember the signs and wonders that were God's witness to that great moment of salvation? People came out of tombs after Jesus died. The curtain of the temple was torn from top to bottom. At least five hundred disciples saw the Savior after His resurrection. Death couldn't hold Him. Because of Christ, it won't hold you either.

So the next time you taste something and don't like it, think of the "bad taste" Jesus endured for you. You'll never have to taste death in the same way He did. And that's mmm-mmm, good!

PRAYER

Thank You, Lord, for doing the eternal "taste test" for me. I know that I'll never have to taste eternal death in hell, because You did that for me. I am grateful to You forever. Amen.

Gregory R. Williamson

Always Rejoicing

Psalm 118:1–9

During World War II, the German and Russian armies occupied the country of Estonia. After the war, a group of Estonian Christians were fleeing from their homeland. Their little boat had a rough trip across the Baltic Sea. Some people were lost, but the rest made it to the shores of Finland. Here was freedom.

The Estonians had left behind their homes, their businesses, and many friends and relatives. Wet with the waves of the Baltic Sea, they stood on the Finnish shore. A Christian pastor was among them. "Pastor," they said, "should we not thank God for our deliverance?"

The people gathered around, and the pastor led them in some hymns and prayers. When he came to the sermon, everyone wondered what he would say. Pastors usually spend many hours preparing their sermons. But this pastor had only a few moments to gather his thoughts. He preached on the Bible words "always rejoicing" (2 Corinthians 6:10).

This must have seemed like a strange theme for a sermon under such conditions. But you see, the Estonians had many things to rejoice about. They were alive and in a free land now. God was still with them. Above all, they knew that the Lord Jesus had died for them and redeemed them.

We today have just as much reason to give thanks to God. Not only do we have all we need for our earthly life, but, like the Estonians, we have the things that really matter: spiritual life, freedom from sin and death, and the salvation Jesus won for us by His death on the cross. On this Thanksgiving Day, we, too, can be "always rejoicing."

PRAYER

Dear Savior, how many blessings You have given me—this free land, my home and family, my health and strength! But even if I should lose them all, I still have You, my greatest blessing. Amen.

Donald Ortner

PENTECOST / TRINITY
Thanksgiving Day

Watch Me

Psalm 139

Without even trying, anyone can think of special days: birthdays, the last day of school—for some people the first day of school, Valentine's Day, Christmas, and Thanksgiving Day.

Every week has special days too. Sundays and Mondays are special because they are the first days of the week. Fridays and Saturdays are special because they come at the very end of the week. Wednesday's specialness is because it is the exact middle of every week. That leaves Tuesday and Thursday as unspecial days. They're just ordinary days, days when nothing important seems to be going on, days in between the special days.

But every day can be special, even Tuesdays and Thursdays, if we think about them as days when God is paying attention to us. From the moment we wake up one morning to the time we wake up the next morning, God is paying attention to us. He knows we may not want to get out of bed or get into bed. He is aware of the way we worry because we don't have some homework finished. He is present while we eat our breakfast and listens when our mother talks to us. God watches while we wait for the school bus or for our friend to come. He knows when it's too warm for a big coat and too cool for just a sweater. All through every ordinary day, God is paying attention to us.

What makes ordinary days into special days is not only that God is watching us but also that He is such a special kind of watcher. He is both powerful and loving. He is the God who made the universe, the God who made people. He can calm the wildest storm and forgive the greatest sins. That great and wonderful God pays attention to us as we walk around or sit down or eat breakfast. And all this in love!

Every day and everywhere, God watches us in love. He makes every day special. And He makes us special too.

PRAYER

Holy Father, Creator and Preserver of all things, watch me as I live each day. Help me enjoy Your presence in the world, and let me be glad to be alive. Amen.

James Nelesen

PENTECOST / TRINITY

When Loved Ones Die

1 Thessalonians 4:13–18

Some people don't ever want to talk about death. Sometimes even Christians don't like to talk about the subject. One thing is certain. Everybody must face death sooner or later.

Perhaps a person very dear to you has died. If you haven't lost anyone close to you, maybe you wonder what it would be like. Will you cry? Will you feel as though the person who died is gone forever?

Of course, people feel sad when a loved one dies. We will miss him or her in this life. But even though we Christians are sad, we also have reason to be glad. The grief of a Christian is different from the grief of an unbeliever.

In this last part of the Church Year, God's people think about those who have died and are asleep in Jesus, and they look forward to their own heavenly rest and the joy of eternal life.

The Bible says, "We do not want you to be uninformed, brothers, about those who are asleep [in death], that you may not grieve as others do who have no hope" (1 Thessalonians 4:13). That's the difference. We have hope; unbelievers don't.

We know that all who believe in Jesus will rise again on the Last Day. Then we will live with Jesus forever. As the Bible says, in heaven, "we will always be with the Lord" (v. 17).

So don't be like most people. Don't be afraid to talk about death. Remember what we say on Sunday in the Apostles' Creed: "I believe in . . . the resurrection of the body; and the life everlasting." What a wonderful hope we Christians have—all because of Jesus!

PRAYER

Dear God, help me trust in Jesus more and more so I will be ready to go to heaven whenever God says it's time. Thank You for this wonderful hope I have. Grant that all people may come to faith in Jesus so they may have this hope too. In Jesus' name I pray. Amen.

Paul Single

PENTECOST / TRINITY

Help Me Understand

Acts 8:26–39

Erica's class was reading *The Long Winter* by Laura Ingalls Wilder. For Erica and most of her classmates in Minnesota, the book spoke of familiar things like snow, blizzards, and snowbanks. But to Keiko, whose family had recently come from Hawaii, the story was strange and hard to understand.

Until she arrived in Minnesota, Keiko had never seen snow or experienced a blizzard. Now Keiko was getting worried. By Friday, she had to turn in a report on the book. When Erica asked how it was coming, Keiko admitted that she didn't understand the book at all.

Erica knew that her friend needed help. So she read the whole book aloud to Keiko. Whenever she came to a part Keiko didn't understand, Erica did her best to explain what was happening. It wasn't long before Keiko became interested and could hardly wait to find out what would happen next.

They finished the book on Wednesday, and Keiko wrote her report on Thursday. She smiled at Erica as she walked up and put it on the teacher's desk. After school, Keiko told Erica she could never have done it without help.

In our Bible reading, the man from Ethiopia had much the same problem as Keiko. He couldn't understand what he was reading in the Bible. God sent Philip to explain it to him. Philip used passages from Isaiah to tell how Jesus was the one who suffered innocently and took away the sins of everyone. The Holy Spirit used Philip's explanation to work faith in the Ethiopian, and he wanted to be baptized.

God can use you also to tell others the Good News about Jesus. Many people hear or read the story of what God has done for us, but they don't understand words like *sin, believe, crucifixion,* and *resurrection*. The Holy Spirit will help you explain what these mean. The Holy Spirit can use the words you say to make another person a child of God.

PRAYER

Lord, give me understanding of Your Word, and help me boldly tell others the Good News about Jesus. Amen.

Judy Williams

PENTECOST / TRINITY

The Miracle of Ice

Psalm 147:12–20

About this time of year, something silently happens to lakes and many rivers in the North. They are covered with a sheet of ice—first only a thin crust, then thicker and thicker, until sometimes it is more than 36 inches thick, strong enough to hold big trucks and bulldozers.

Ice is formed when water cools below $32°F$ or $0°C$. While this may seem very natural and ordinary, a miracle really takes place.

As water freezes, it expands (increases in size). This is an exception to the normal law of nature. Usually, cold contracts (shrinks) things and heat expands them.

How wise of the Creator to turn around the natural law in this case! If it were not so, the ice that forms would sink to the bottom of lakes and rivers. Then more ice would collect on top, until the lakes and rivers became solid masses of ice. Then what would happen to the fish and plants in the water?

Next time you see ice on a lake or in your refrigerator, let it remind you of our Creator. How wonderfully, how plainly, the wisdom and care of God appear in the formation of ice!

However, even more personally, ice can remind us that we have a God who is in control of nature for our good. As He has promised, He will keep the powerful forces of nature in His hand so that we need not be afraid.

Water freezes, the winds blow, the sun shines, fires keeps us warm, the seasons change—all according to God's plan and power.

Therefore, as God's children by faith in Jesus, we also know that we can trust His promises to forgive our sins, to hear our prayers, to protect us, to be with us always, and finally, to take us to heaven.

PRAYER

Dear Father in heaven, I am thankful that You hold the whole world in Your hands, even me. Amen.

Gerald A. Homp

Resurrection Plants

John 11:17–27

Have you ever heard of the resurrection plant? It's a brownish, dried-up-looking thing. It looks about as dead as the plants in your garden at this time of year and you might as well throw it away. But just bring it inside and put it into a bowl of water. What happens is just like a miracle. The leaves uncurl, spread out, and turn green. In a short time, the plant looks alive. And it is! No wonder it's called the resurrection plant.

Maybe it would be a good idea if all Christians had a resurrection plant in their homes to remind them of the Last Day. We often forget that every person will be a kind of resurrection plant then. The difference, of course, is that our resurrection will be real.

That's why God doesn't want us to be sad about those who die believing in Jesus. He wants us to think of death as a sleep from which we will rise. Jesus will wake us from this sleep on the Last Day. We know this because Jesus Himself was raised from the dead, and He will raise us also. Then all believers will live with Him in happiness forever.

St. Paul knew some Christians who were sad about their friends and relatives who had died because they thought that only those who were alive when Jesus returned would live with Him in heaven. But through Paul, the Holy Spirit told them something that made them happy again. He said, "For the Lord Himself will descend from heaven with a cry of command, with the voice of an archangel, and with the sound of the trumpet of God. And the dead in Christ will rise first" (1 Thessalonians 4:16).

This is something for us to be happy about too. As resurrection plants come to life when they are put into water, all who die in the Lord will come to life again to be with Jesus forever in heaven. No wonder St. Paul told the Thessalonian Christians, "Therefore encourage one another with these words" (v. 18).

PRAYER

Dear Jesus, thank You for Your promise, "I am the resurrection and the life." Help me to believe it always. Amen.

Ruth Hummel

PENTECOST / TRINITY

St. Andrew's Cross

John 1:35–42

In a stained glass window at his church, Gordon saw an unusual cross. Most of the crosses he had noticed were shaped like this: †. But the one in the window looked like this: ✕. When Gordon asked his pastor about the ✕-shaped cross, he learned that it is called "St. Andrew's cross."

There is a story that Jesus' disciple Andrew became a missionary in Greece. The Lord blessed his work, and many people believed in Jesus. But a Greek official became angry because of Andrew's teaching. He commanded the disciple to lead some people in sacrificing to a false god.

When Andrew would not do this, he was whipped and crucified on a cross that was shaped like an ✕. But even while he was hanging on the cross, Andrew preached to anyone who would listen. He encouraged the people to repent of their sins and trust in Jesus for forgiveness. It is said that Andrew died on November 30 in the year AD 69.

From the Bible, we know that Andrew was a good missionary. Soon after he learned that Jesus was the promised Messiah, he brought his brother, Peter, to the Savior. Later on, Andrew helped Philip introduce some Greeks to Jesus. The story about Andrew's death fits in very well with what the New Testament says about him.

Of course, Andrew's death on a cross cannot help us. He was a sinful human being, as we are. But the death of Jesus on Calvary is enough to save us. The blood of God's Son wipes away all our sins and makes us holy in His sight. While we can be grateful for Andrew's example of witnessing for Christ, we owe our eternal salvation to the cross of Jesus.

PRAYER

Thank You, dear Lord, for dying in my place. Help me to be faithful to You all my life. Amen.

Victor Constien

PENTECOST / TRINITY

St. Andrew, Apostle